Copyright
Law
Deskbook

2012 Cumulative Supplement

With Cumulative Case Digest on CD-ROM

CD-ROM located inside back cover

Intellectual Property Titles from Bloomberg BNA

Anatomy of a Patent Case by American College of Trial Lawyers

Biotechnology and the Federal Circuit by Kenneth J. Burchfiel

Constructing and Deconstructing Patents by Irah H. Donner

Copyright Law Deskbook by Robert W. Clarida

Drafting Patent License Agreements by Brian G. Brunsvold, D. Patrick O'Reilley, and D. Brian Kacedon

Drafting Patents for Litigation and Licensing Bradley C. Wright, *Editor-in-Chief*

Electronic and Software Patents: Law and Practice Steven W. Lundberg, Stephen C. Durant, and Ann M. McCrackin, *Editors-in-Chief* and AIPLA

Harmon on Patents: Black-Letter Law and Commentary by Robert L. Harmon

Intellectual Property Law in Cyberspace by G. Peter Albert, Jr. and AIPLA

Intellectual Property, Software, and Information Licensing: Law and Practice by Xuan-Thao N. Nguyen, Robert W. Gomulkiewicz, and Danielle Conway

Intellectual Property Taxation: Transaction and Litigation Issues by Jeffrey A. Maine and Xuan-Thao N. Nguyen

Intellectual Property Technology Transfer Aline C. Flower, *Editor-in-Chief*

International Patent Litigation: A Country-by-Country Analysis Edited by Michael N. Meller and William O. Hennessey

Patents and the Federal Circuit by Robert L. Harmon, Cynthia A. Homan, and Charles M. McMahon

Patent Law and Practice by Herbert F. Schwartz and Robert J. Goldman

Patent Infringement Remedies by Lawrence M. Sung

Patent Litigation Strategies Handbook Barry L. Grossman and Gary M. Hoffman, *Editors-in-Chief*

Patent Prosecution: Law, Practice, and Procedure by Irah H. Donner

Patent, Trademark, and Copyright Laws Edited by Jeffrey M. Samuels

Pharmaceutical Patent Law by John R. Thomas

Post-Grant Patent Practice by Nancy J. Linck, Bruce H. Stoner, Jr., Lee E. Barrett, and Carol A. Spiegel

Products Comparison Manual for Trademark Users by Francis M. Pinckney and David R. Higgins

Trademark Dilution: Federal, State, and International Law by David S. Welkowitz

Trademark Infringement Remedies Brian E. Banner, *Editor-in-Chief*

Trademark Litigation Practice by David S. Fleming and John T. Gabrielides

Copyright
Law
Deskbook

2012 Cumulative Supplement

With Cumulative Case Digest on CD-ROM

Robert W. Clarida

Reitler, Kailas & Rosenblatt, LLC
New York, NY

Bloomberg
BNA

Arlington, VA

This publication is designed to provide accurate and authoritative information in regard to the subject matter covered. It is sold with the understanding that the author and publisher are not engaged in rendering legal, accounting, or other professional service. If legal advice or other expert assistance is required, the services of a competent professional person should be sought. In view of the dynamic nature of the law, including copyright law, the vitality of any legal decisions relied upon herein should be updated and confirmed before filing any papers relying thereon in a federal or administrative court.

Library of Congress Cataloging-in-Publication Data

Clarida, Robert W.
    Copyright law deskbook / Robert W. Clarida.
        p. cm.
    Includes index.
    ISBN 978-1-57018-691-2
    1.   Copyright--United States.   I. Title

KF2995.C54 2008
346.7304'82--dc22

2008034912

Published by Bloomberg BNA
1801 S. Bell Street, Arlington, VA 22202
bna.com/bnabooks

ISBN: 978-1-61746-042-5
Printed in the United States of America

Preface

Since the publication of *Copyright Law Deskbook* in the fall of 2009, there have been a number of significant developments in the district courts, the circuits, the Supreme Court and even in the state courts that will affect the practice of copyright law for years to come.

This new Supplement analyzes the diverse responses of the lower courts to the Supreme Court's decision in *Muchnick*, which held that registration is not a "jurisdictional" requirement of bringing suit, but merely a "claims processing rule." The courts have not reached consensus as to just what form that "processing" should take. Some have dismissed claims outright where plaintiff had no registration (*Staggs v. West*), while others (*Axxiom Mfg. v. McCoy Investments*) have allowed for amendment. The courts have also split on whether a dismissal for failure to register should be "processed" under Rule 12(b)(6) or Rule 12(b)(1). And dismissal is not the only method of addressing a lack of registration: in *Jagex v. Impulse Software*, the District of Massachusetts found a plaintiff failed to show likely success on the merits and denied a preliminary injunction where no registration was in place, and in *Kruska v. Perverted Justice Foundation* the District of Arizona granted summary judgment to defendant on this basis.

On another jurisdictional issue, the Second Circuit's recent certification of a personal jurisdiction issue to the New York state Court of Appeal in *Penguin v. American Buddha* led to a superficially narrow but potentially far-reaching ruling regarding where plaintiffs can bring suit for on-line infringement. Also from the Second Circuit, the requirement of proving irreparable harm before obtaining an injunction, established last year in *Salinger v. Colting*, has led to a number of competing approaches in the district courts. Many continue to find in plaintiff's favor despite the heightened standard, as in *Harper Collins v. Gawker Media* (S.D.N.Y.) and *Credit Bureau Connection v. Pardini* (E.D. Cal.), with some even still applying the presumption of irreparable harm that Salinger repudiated (*Software Freedom Conservancy v. Best Buy*). No courts so far show an inclination to put plaintiffs to any very stringent burden of showing irreparable harm, however.

The courts have also confronted a number of new factual scenarios involving claims of implied license, such as *Teter v. Glass Onion*, where an implied license was found in the software context, and *Nearstar Inc. v. Waggoner* where the license argument was rejected.

Other topics of particular interest this year include:

Ownership

In *Jules Jordan Video*, the court held that a work created by the principal and sole shareholder of a corporation was not necessarily a work made for hire by the corporation.

Standing

In *Hyperquest v. N'Site Solutions*, the Seventh Circuit joined the Ninth to hold that a party has no standing to bring an infringement claim if it does not possess an exclusive right under section 106.

Copyrightability

The Southern District of New York in *BanxCorp* offered a sustained discussion as to the standards for copyright protection in numerical indices. And in *Telebrands Corp. v. Del Labs*, a photograph demonstrating the way to use a skin-care device was held to be so "utilitarian" that even an exact copy was not infringing.

Contracts and Licenses

The court in *Agence France Presse v. Morel* held that the terms of use for Twitter, which grant broad permission for re-use of posted material, do not create a general license for third parties to exploit such content.

In *MDY v. Blizzard*, the Ninth Circuit explained the significant differences between covenants and conditions in IP agreements, and the consequences that can flow from a licensor's choice of language in its terms of use.

Statute of Limitations

The Second Circuit in *Kwan v. Schlein* ignored a common distinction between ownership claims and infringement claims, and applied the same statute of limitations analysis to both types of action.

Preemption

The courts continue to be divided over whether Lanham Act claims are preempted by the Copyright Act, even though the express terms of Section 301 apply only to state law claims. The Northern District of Illinois held in *Cyber Websmith v. American Dental Association* that a Lanham Act claim for deceptive practices was preempted, while the District of Massachusetts allowed a similar Lanham Act claim to go forward in *Berklee College of Music v. Music Industry Educators*.

These are some of the highlights of this year's supplement. I invite readers with constructive comments and suggestions to communicate them to me by email at rclarida@reitlerlaw.com.

Robert W. Clarida
Reitler Kailas & Rosenblatt, LLC
New York City
September 2012

Summary Table of Contents

Detailed Table of Contents

1

Jurisdiction and Procedure

I. JURISDICTION AND PROCEDURE

A. Subject Matter Jurisdiction

1. *Arising Under Jurisdiction*

[Add the following text at the end of the section.]

In *Schrock v. Learning Curve International, Inc.*,[1] the district court denied the defendant's motion to dismiss for lack of subject matter jurisdiction. The plaintiff, a professional photographer, and the defendant, a producer and distributor of children's toys, entered into an oral agreement to create photographs of the defendant's toys for marketing purposes. The plaintiff provided services to the defendant for four years, producing about 1,800 photographs and issuing about 100 invoices, which the defendant promptly paid. The agreement was never memorialized in writing. The parties' interpretations of the agreement's terms diverged extensively over time, in particular regarding limitations on use of the plaintiff's photographs. The plaintiff filed a complaint alleging that the defendant's use of plaintiff's photographs violated the license terms regarding duration of use and media, and thus should trigger additional fee payments. The defendant disagreed, and moved to dismiss the plaintiff's complaint for lack of subject matter jurisdiction, arguing that the dispute was fundamentally a breach-of-contract case. The district court, applying a "face of the complaint" test adopted in the Fourth and Ninth Circuits, and a "principal and controlling issue" test adopted in the Second Circuit, found that under either test the plaintiff's complaint fell within the court's jurisdiction because the copyright claim was the "heart of this dispute."[2] The plaintiff alleged in the complaint that he was the author of specific photographs, and had entered into an oral licensing agreement with the defendant for use of those photographs; that payment of invoices was not disputed; that the plaintiff registered his copyright in the photographs; and that the Seventh Circuit had previously held that he had a valid copyright arising by operation of law, and that his work, which was the subject of the dispute, qualified for a limited derivative-work copyright.[3] Accordingly, the court held that the plaintiff's complaint properly arose under the copyright laws, and that federal jurisdiction was established.

2.   Foreign Acts

[Add the following text at the end of the section.]

Even when no infringing acts occur in the United States, the claim need not be *jurisdictionally* beyond the reach of U.S. courts. Thus, in *Litecubes, LLC v. Northern Light Products, Inc.*,[4] the Federal Circuit held that U.S. courts had jurisdiction over the subject matter of copyright and patent infringement claims, despite the defendants' contention that jurisdiction was lacking because no infringing acts occurred within the territorial limits of the United States. Territoriality is merely one substantive element of a claim to be proven, the court held, and not a jurisdictional requirement. Following the recent Supreme Court decision

---

[1] 744 F. Supp. 2d 768 (N.D. Ill. 2010).

[2] *Id.* at 773.

[3] *Id.* at 773–74.

[4] 523 F.3d 1353, 86 USPQ2d 1753 (Fed. Cir. 2008).

in *Arbaugh v. Y & H Corp.*,[5] the court applied a "bright-line rule" that where Congress "clearly states that a threshold limitation on a statute's scope shall count as jurisdictional, then courts and litigants will be duly instructed . . . . But when Congress does not . . . , courts should treat the restriction as nonjurisdictional in character."[6] The *Litecubes* court then noted that no absolute rule prohibits the extraterritorial reach of statutes, and the issue "is simply a question of statutory interpretation. . . . Thus, in these respects, a limitation on the extraterritorial scope of a statute is no different than any other element of a claim which must be established before relief can be granted under a particular statute."[7] Under the Copyright Act, the statute does not by its terms require infringing "distribution" to occur in the United States. Though "it has long been established" that acts occurring entirely abroad are not actionable,[8] this limit relates purely to the elements of the claim, and is not a jurisdictional requirement under *Arbaugh*'s "bright-line rule." A contrary pre-*Arbaugh* decision from the Eleventh Circuit was rejected, and the court found jurisdiction was properly asserted below. Moreover, the court found substantial evidence supporting the jury verdict that sales had in fact occurred in the United States, notwithstanding the delivery of infringing merchandise F.O.B. from the Canadian defendant to U.S. customers.

3. *The Role of Registration*

[Add the following text at the end of the section.]

The Supreme Court's March 2, 2010 decision in *Reed Elsevier v. Muchnick*[9] has significant implications both for class actions involving a combination of registered and unregistered works, and for cases in which a sole plaintiff sues on a registered work and obtains a consent judgment covering additional works that were not registered. *Muchnick* effectively reinstates a class-action settlement of claims by freelance journalists for the online use of their articles, but it could have much broader implications as well.

The *Muchnick* decision is the latest (and perhaps nearly the last) chapter in the long-running dispute between freelance journalists and various publishers who used or licensed the writers' articles in electronic form without consent. In 1993, a group of six freelancers led by Jonathan Tasini filed an infringement action challenging the publishers' assertion that the unauthorized electronic uses were privileged as "revisions" of licensed print publications under Section 201(c) of the Copyright Act. The *Tasini* case was ultimately resolved by the Supreme Court,[10] which sided with the freelancers, holding that the particular electronic uses

---

[5]546 U.S. 500 (2006).

[6]*Id.* at 515–16.

[7]*Litecubes*, 523 F.3d at 1363.

[8]*Id.* at 1366.

[9]130 S. Ct. 1237, 176 L. Ed. 2d 1893, 93 USPQ2d 1719, 2010 U.S. LEXIS 2202 (2010).

[10]New York Times Co. v. Tasini, 533 U.S. 483 (2001).

at issue were not "revisions" under 201(c), largely because they did not preserve the full context in which the plaintiffs' articles appeared in print.

Other freelancers, who were not the plaintiffs in the *Tasini* case, filed lawsuits asserting similar claims. The claims included infringement allegations as to both registered and unregistered works. These actions were consolidated into a class-action proceeding after the Supreme Court decided *Tasini*. After years of mediation, a class-action settlement was reached in 2005 and submitted to the Southern District of New York for approval, which was granted.

A group of 10 authors challenged the approval of the class action on various procedural and substantive grounds, and filed an appeal. On appeal, the Second Circuit sua sponte concluded that neither it nor the district court had subject matter jurisdiction to approve the settlement.[11] The court observed that under Section 411(a) of the Copyright Act, no infringement action can be brought with respect to unregistered U.S. works. The full text of Section 411(a) reads as follows:

> Except for an action brought for a violation of the rights of the author under section 106A(a), and subject to the provisions of subsection (b), no civil action for infringement of the copyright in any United States work shall be instituted until preregistration or registration of the copyright claim has been made in accordance with this title. In any case, however, where the deposit, application, and fee required for registration have been delivered to the Copyright Office in proper form and registration has been refused, the applicant is entitled to institute a civil action for infringement if notice thereof, with a copy of the complaint, is served on the Register of Copyrights. The Register may, at his or her option, become a party to the action with respect to the issue of registrability of the copyright claim by entering an appearance within sixty days after such service, but the Register's failure to become a party shall not deprive the court of jurisdiction to determine that issue.[12]

Citing extensive precedent, including its own rulings in *Well-Made Toy Manufacturing Co. v. Goffa International Corp.*[13] and *Morris v. Business Concepts, Inc.*,[14] a majority of the Second Circuit panel held that the Section 411(a) registration requirement is a jurisdictional prerequisite to bringing suit. Accordingly, the court was required to deny approval for the proposed settlement insofar as it purported to govern unregistered works at all. Even though no party took that position before the court, the Second Circuit majority gave itself little choice: If registration is truly jurisdictional under Section 411(a), the parties' failure to raise the issue does not result in a waiver.

Judge John Walker dissented. He disagreed that the registration requirement under Section 411(a) is jurisdictional. Primarily relying on non-copyright precedent regarding subject matter jurisdiction, Judge Walker argued that the registration requirement is not a jurisdictional

---

[11] 206 F.3d 161 (2d Cir. 1999).

[12] 17 U.S.C. §411(a).

[13] 354 F.3d 112, 114–15, 69 USPQ2d 1090, 1091–92 (2d Cir. 2003).

[14] 259 F.3d 65, 72–73, 59 USPQ2d 1581, 1586–87 (2d Cir. 2001).

prerequisite, despite any precedent to the contrary. Instead, it is a "claim processing" rule, the violation of which may cause a party to lose its case but will not deprive the court of adjudicatory authority.

The Supreme Court granted certiorari. Argument was heard on October 7, 2009, and on March 2, 2010, a unanimous 8–0 Court reversed the Second Circuit. (Justice Sonia Sotomayor took no part in the decision, having ruled on the original *Tasini* case when she was on the Southern District of New York in 1997.)

Justice Clarence Thomas authored the Court's opinion, with Justice Ruth Bader Ginsburg filing a concurrence joined by Justices John Paul Stevens and Stephen Breyer. Justice Thomas' opinion offers an analysis similar to that proposed by the Second Circuit dissent. Under *Arbaugh v. Y & H Corp.*,[15] the Supreme Court in 2006 articulated a "general approach" to deciding whether a statutory requirement is jurisdictional, as opposed to being merely an element of the claim or a "claim-processing" rule:

> "If the Legislature clearly states that a threshold limitation on a statute's scope shall count as jurisdictional, then courts and litigants will be duly instructed and will not be left to wrestle with the issue. But when Congress does not rank a statutory limitation on coverage as jurisdictional, courts should treat the restriction as nonjurisdictional in character."[16]

Thus, *Arbaugh* looks primarily to the language of the statute. If the statute states on its face that a requirement is jurisdictional, it is. Otherwise, it is not. *Arbaugh* involved an "employee-numerosity" rule under Title VII for employment discrimination claims: Certain claims can be filed only against employers having "fifteen or more employees." Because that limitation is not expressly said to be jurisdictional, however, and because it is located in a statutory section separate from the jurisdiction-granting provisions, the *Arbaugh* court held that it does not " 'speak in jurisdictional terms or in any way refer to the jurisdiction of the district courts.' "[17] As a result, the defendant in *Arbaugh* was held to have waived the registration defense by failing to raise it until after the trial.

Applying that analysis to Section 411(a) of the Copyright Act, the *Muchnick* Court was confronted with the fact that Section 411(a) does, in its last sentence, refer to the jurisdiction of the court, in a passage dealing with the ability of the Register of Copyrights to intervene. That reference was inapposite, held the Court, because it was limited to the (non-)effect of intervention on a court's ability to determine the registrability issue: "The word 'jurisdiction,' as used here, thus says nothing about whether a federal court has subject-matter jurisdiction to adjudicate claims for infringement of unregistered works."[18] Further, the Court noted that here, as in *Arbaugh*, the Section 411(a) registration requirement is located in

---

[15]546 U.S. 500 (2006).

[16]*Muchnick*, 130 S. Ct. at 1244 (quoting *Arbaugh*, 546 U.S. at 515–16).

[17]*Id.* (quoting *Arbaugh*, 546 U.S. at 515).

[18]*Muchnick*, 130 S. Ct at 1245.

a provision that is separate from those granting subject matter jurisdiction; jurisdiction over copyright claims is granted by 28 U.S.C. §§1331 and 1338, not by Title 17. Neither of those provisions "conditions its jurisdictional grant on whether copyright holders have registered their works before suing for infringement."[19]

Additionally, the Court observed that Section 411(a) expressly permits district courts to hear claims over unregistered works in three situations: where the work is not a "United States work"; where the claim concerns a violation of the artist's rights under Section 106A (the Visual Artists Rights Act); and where registration of the work has been attempted but refused by the Copyright Office. A jurisdictional requirement, the Court observed in a footnote, "can never be forfeited or waived."[20] Thus, "[i]t would be at least unusual to ascribe jurisdictional significance to a condition subject to these sorts of exceptions."[21]

One further argument addressed by the Court was the relevance of extensive precedent in copyright cases describing the registration requirement as jurisdictional. Because none of the parties to the action agreed with the Second Circuit's jurisdictional ruling, the Court appointed an *amicus*, Prof. Deborah Jones Merritt of The Ohio State University Moritz College of Law, to brief and argue the case on behalf of the Second Circuit. Professor Merritt cited *Bowles v. Russell*[22] for the proposition that "where Congress did not explicitly label a statutory condition as jurisdictional, a court nevertheless should treat it as such if that is how the condition consistently has been interpreted and if Congress has not disturbed that interpretation."[23] The Court explained, however, that *Bowles* involved a statutory condition that was "of a type" that the Court had long recognized as jurisdictional, even absent an express statutory label. Neither *Arbaugh* nor the copyright-registration requirement in *Muchnick* was of such a "type," however, so the statutory label was controlling.

Justice Ginsburg's concurrence proposed that *Arbaugh* and *Bowles* could be reconciled more directly. All of the precedent to which the Court deferred in *Bowles* was Supreme Court precedent entitled to *stare decisis*, Justice Ginsburg observed. In the case of Section 411(a), however, although more than 200 decisions refer to the registration requirement as jurisdictional, "not one is from this court, and most are drive-by jurisdictional rulings that should be accorded no precedential effect."[24]

The *Muchnick* decision was certainly welcome news to the many litigants in that class-action proceeding. Its significance to the wider copyright world is less dramatic, but it should not be dismissed too easily.

---

[19] *Id.* at 1246.

[20] *Id.* n.5.

[21] *Id.* at 1246.

[22] 551 U.S. 205 (2007).

[23] *Muchnick*, 130 S. Ct at 1247.

[24] *Id.* at 1251 (Ginsburg, J., concurring) (internal quotation marks omitted).

Most clearly, the *Muchnick* decision will remove a cloud of uncertainty the Second Circuit had raised over the routine practice of including both registered and unregistered works in a settlement agreement. It often happens that a copyright owner will bring an action over the infringement of registered work *A*, and later learn in discovery that the defendant has also infringed unregistered work *B*. Prior to the recent Supreme Court reversal in *Muchnick*, litigants in the Second Circuit could not resolve all their claims and potential claims as to both works, in one so-ordered settlement, even if the adversaries agreed to do so. *Muchnick* makes it safe to go back to business as usual in this respect.

The Court omits needed guidance to the practicing bar, however, as to other registration and jurisdiction issues. Most notably, the various circuits do not agree as to what qualifies as "registration" under Section 411(a). Some circuits permit claims to be filed when a plaintiff has submitted an application to the Copyright Office, while others require that the registration certificate be issued; most circuits have not announced a rule. The Supreme Court was not squarely faced with this issue in *Muchnick* and expressly declined to address it, despite the confusion in the circuits. For practitioners in the majority of circuits with no definitive rule, a little Supreme Court guidance, even of a "drive-by" nature, might have been welcome.

Muchnick could also make life hard for copyright owners who happen to make the mistake of bringing a claim over an unregistered work which is then dismissed with prejudice for failure to meet Section 411(a)'s claim-processing requirement. Here's how: If the registration requirement were jurisdictional, as the Second Circuit had held, a plaintiff who mistakenly sued without a registration would be out of court, but because the court lacked subject matter jurisdiction the result could have no possible res judicata effect. The plaintiff, therefore, presumably could correct the error and file a new action. Under *Muchnick*, however, there is now a risk, however slight, that the same plaintiff could arguably be barred under res judicata; the court would have adjudicatory authority and its decision, under which the plaintiff is held to have no viable claim, could bar a future claim for the same infringement.[25] The plaintiff could avoid that result only by dismissing the case without prejudice, which would require the defendant's, and the court's, consent if an answer had already been filed.

This possible res judicata effect could be particularly unfortunate for plaintiffs who make a good-faith mistake about the application of Section

---

[25]See Black's Law Dictionary (9th ed., p. 1425): "*Res judicata.* . . . a final judgment *rendered by a court of competent jurisdiction* on the merits is conclusive as to the rights of the parties and their privies, and, as to them, constitutes an absolute bar to a subsequent action involving the same claim, demand or cause of action. And to be applicable, requires identity in thing sued for as well as identity of cause of action, of persons and parties to action, and of quality in persons for or against whom claim is made. The sum and substance of the whole rule is that a matter once judicially decided is finally decided. Allen v McCurry, 449 U.S. 90." (Emphasis added.)

411(a) to their particular circumstances. A plaintiff might, for example, believe that his or her work is a non-U.S. work, and thus need not be registered prior to filing suit. If the court later decides to the contrary, *Muchnick* would seem to imply that res judicata could bar a subsequent action even after the chastened plaintiff obtains a registration.

After *Muchnick*, courts quickly began to relax the registration standards some had previously imposed, finding that mere submission of an application was sufficient to satisfy the requirements of Section 411(a). Most notably, the Ninth Circuit, in *Cosmetic Ideas, Inc. v. IAC/InterActiveCorp*,[26] reversed the district court's dismissal of a copyright infringement action for lack of subject matter jurisdiction under Section 411(a), finding that receipt by the Copyright Office of a complete application constitutes "registration" for purpose of Section 411(a). The plaintiff, a jewelry designer, sued the defendant for manufacturing and distributing copies of a necklace that was "virtually identical" to a necklace previously manufactured and sold by the plaintiff.

The plaintiff submitted an application to register copyright in the necklace design on March 6, 2008, and on March 12, 2008 received confirmation of receipt from the Copyright Office. On March 27, 2008, before the registration certificate issued, the plaintiff filed suit, alleging infringement of the plaintiff's copyright in the necklace. The district court dismissed the plaintiff's claim for lack of subject matter jurisdiction under Section 411(a). The Court of Appeals reviewed the issue of statutory interpretation de novo. Applying the Supreme Court's intervening 2010 *Muchnick* decision, the court held that dismissal on subject matter jurisdiction grounds was in error. The court then considered the defendant's second ground for dismissal, failure to state a claim under Federal Rule of Civil Procedure 12(b)(6). Noting the circuit split—with the "application approach" favored by the Fifth and Seventh Circuits and the "registration approach" favored by the Tenth and Eleventh Circuits—and finding ambiguity in the plain language of the statute, the court considered the broader context and purpose of the statute as a whole, and concluded that the "application approach better fulfills Congress's purpose of providing broad copyright protection while maintaining a robust federal register."[27]

The court reasoned that the application approach avoids the unnecessary delay inherent in the registration approach. During such delay infringement could continue; the application approach avoids that problem by permitting an infringement action to proceed immediately. The registration approach, on the other hand, requires the plaintiff to wait for action by the Copyright Office (despite the fact that the plaintiff can bring suit eventually, regardless of the outcome in the Copyright Office). Both approaches equally serve the purpose of a robust register, because both have equal filing requirements. The court

---

[26]606 F.3d 612 (9th Cir. 2010).

[27]*Id.* at 619.

concluded that the registration approach is little more than a formality, and can sometimes result in a plaintiff's losing the ability to sue if the Copyright Office does not act before the statute of limitations lapses, a result at odds with the policy of retroactive dating of the registration back to the filing date.[28] As to the "deference to the Register" argument, the court found that the registration process and litigation can occur simultaneously with little risk of prejudice, particularly considering the slow pace of litigation. The Ninth Circuit therefore held that receipt by the Copyright Office of a complete application satisfies the registration requirement of Section 411(a). In the instant case, since the Copyright Office received the plaintiff's complete application before the plaintiff filed suit, the Court of Appeals vacated the district court's dismissal and remanded for further consideration.

In the same week as the Ninth Circuit's reversal in *Cosmetic Ideas*, a Missouri district court, in *Charles F. Vatterott Construction Co. v. Esteem Custom Homes, LLP*,[29] granted the plaintiff's motion for reconsideration and found that it had subject matter jurisdiction over a copyright infringement claim. The plaintiff had filed an application to register the works at issue prior to filing the action, but the registration had not issued at the time of filing the action. The court previously granted the defendant's motion to dismiss for lack of subject matter jurisdiction. The plaintiff filed motions for reconsideration, and sought leave to amend the complaint to update the status of its copyright registrations. After *Muchnick*, the court reasoned, the registration requirement in Section 411(a) is not jurisdictional, but rather a " 'precondition to filing a claim that does not restrict a federal court's subject-matter jurisdiction.' "[30] The court therefore found that it could no longer "dismiss a copyright infringement claim based on lack of subject matter jurisdiction due to failure to register the copyright at issue."[31] The court did not rule on the issue of whether the copyright registration must have issued before the filing of copyright infringement. Instead, the court found that issue to be whether the plaintiff's registration was sufficient, and noted that the defendant did not raise that issue, and *Muchnick* does not indicate whether such an issue may be raised sua sponte. The court granted the plaintiff leave to amend the complaint to reflect the change in its copyright registration status, and to relate the complaint back to its original date. Since the effective date of the plaintiff's registration was before the original date of the complaint, the issue of whether the registration must have issued before a copyright infringement suit can be filed would become moot after the amendment of the complaint.

---

[28]The court noted that "[o]nly the application approach fully protects litigants from any disadvantage caused by this timelag." *Id.* at 620–21.

[29]713 F. Supp. 2d 844 (E.D. Mo. 2010).

[30]*Id.* at 846 (quoting *Muchnick*, 130 S. Ct. at 1241).

[31]*Id.*

Even after *Muchnick*, the courts have held that a plaintiff must *allege* registration, as in *Staggs v. West*.[32] There, the district court granted the defendant's motion to dismiss plaintiff's copyright infringement claim where the plaintiff failed to allege federal copyright registration for the work at issue, holding that the statutory prerequisite of registration before an infringement action may be filed was not disturbed by the Supreme Court's decision in *Muchnick*. Plaintiff Dayna Staggs sued defendants Island Def Jam Music Group, Universal Music Group, and Vivendi, alleging that the defendants' song "Good Life," recorded by Kanye West, infringed the copyright in Staggs' song "Volume of the Good Life." Although Staggs submitted a certificate of registration for his musical composition, he did not allege or produce a registration for the sound recording. Staggs' claims relating to the musical composition had been dismissed earlier, following a finding by the court of no substantial similarity.[33] Defendants moved to dismiss Staggs' claims on jurisdictional grounds based on Section 411(a), which provides that federal registration is a prerequisite to filing an infringement claim. However, the Supreme Court subsequently held in *Muchnick* that Section 411(a)'s condition does not restrict subject matter jurisdiction.[34] The district court nonetheless found that *Muchnick* did not disturb Section 411(a)'s prerequisite filing requirement, and therefore treated the defendants' motion as a motion to dismiss for failure to state a claim upon which relief can be granted. Since Staggs neither alleged nor produced evidence of registration of his sound recording, the claim was dismissed.[35]

The requirement that registration be alleged is not hard and fast, however, and a plaintiff may be allowed to amend a deficient complaint, as in *Axxiom Mfg., Inc. v. McCoy Investments, Inc.*[36] In that case, plaintiff Axxiom designed, manufactured, and sold abrasive blasting equipment using a sales catalog that was protected by federal copyright. The defendant, doing business as Forecast Sales, manufactured and sold aftermarket abrasive blasting equipment and parts meant as replacements or substitutes for Axxiom products. Axxiom brought an action alleging that Forecast copied and used Axxiom's operation and maintenance manual in Forecast's promotional materials, but failed to allege ownership of a federal copyright registration for the manual. Forecast moved to dismiss for lack of lack of subject matter jurisdiction and failure to state a cause of action. Under *Muchnick*, even if the plaintiff files a claim for copyright infringement without satisfying the Section 411(a) registration requirement, the federal district court has jurisdiction over the claim. The motion to dismiss for lack of subject matter jurisdiction was therefore denied. Noting that *Muchnick* does not address the effect of the plaintiff's

---

[32] 96 USPQ2d 1049 (D. Md. 2010).

[33] *Id.* at 1050.

[34] *Muchnick*, 130 S. Ct. at 1248.

[35] *Staggs*, 96 USPQ2d at 1052.

[36] No. 09-3735, 2010 U.S. Dist. LEXIS 61206 (S.D. Tex. June 21, 2010).

failure to allege registration, the district court granted Axxiom leave to amend the complaint to address the pleading deficiency. Because the Fifth Circuit requires only that the Copyright Office receive the copyright application, deposit, and fee before the plaintiff files the action, the court noted that resolution of the question of compliance with Section 411(a) might require reference to matters outside the pleadings. The court therefore converted Forecast's motion to a motion for summary judgment, and allowed time for the parties to supplement the record.[37]

Litigants have also wrestled with the question of which is the proper subsection of Rule 12 under which to dismiss an improper complaint after *Muchnick*:12(b)(6) or 12(b)(1). In *Estate of Edgerton v. UPI Holdings, Inc.*,[38] an action concerning song mixes selected and arranged by recently-deceased disc jockey Club Queen K-Swift, the plaintiff alleged claims under the Copyright and Lanham Acts, as well as state law claims. The defendants moved to dismiss, alleging, inter alia, lack of subject matter jurisdiction with respect to the copyright claim. Defendants argued first that the works at issue were not protectible, as they failed to satisfy the originality requirement of *Feist*. The court rejected this argument, finding plaintiff's compilations protected, at least with respect to selection and arrangement.[39] Defendants then argued that the plaintiff had failed to allege sufficient facts to establish copying. In rejecting this argument, the court explained that to defeat a motion to dismiss, as opposed to a motion for summary judgment, the plaintiff need not present any evidence and may rely on bare allegations of copying.[40] Finally, defendants argued that jurisdiction was lacking because, while the plaintiff had applied for copyright registration, it had not yet received a certificate of registration. Because the Supreme Court in *Muchnick* had clarified that this prerequisite is not jurisdictional, the court analyzed the issue under Fed. R. Civ. P. 12(b)(6) rather than 12(b)(1). The court noted a lack of governing precedent in the Fourth Circuit, as well as a split between and within circuits, regarding whether filing an application for registration is sufficient to satisfy the registration prerequisite for a claim of copyright infringement. The court engaged in its own close reading of relevant sections of the Copyright Act, finding the question to be a close one, before determining that as the issue was not jurisdictional, it need not be decided, and accordingly denied without prejudice defendant's motion to dismiss the copyright claim.[41]

Also in flux after *Muchnick* is the precise nature of the disadvantage a plaintiff might suffer if it files a claim on an unregistered work. In *Jagex Ltd. v. Impulse Software*,[42] the court actually denied plaintiff's application

---

[37] *Id.* at *13–14.

[38] No. 09-1825, 2010 U.S. Dist. LEXIS 66274 (D. Md. July 1, 2010).

[39] *Id.* at *14–15 n.5.

[40] *Id.* at *15.

[41] *Id.* at *23.

[42] 750 F. Supp. 2d 228 (D. Mass. 2010).

for a preliminary injunction on this basis, finding that there could be no likelihood of success on the merits because the work was unregistered. The plaintiff owned and operated the massive, multiplayer online game "Runescape," which was recognized by the Guinness Book of World Records in 2008 as the world's most popular free online role-playing game. Runescape allowed players to navigate through a fantasy world and interact with one another by participating in challenges. The defendant operated websites offering tools to allow players to cheat at Runescape, by purchasing "bots" that enabled users to advance virtual characters through the game with little human participation, affording an unfair advantage over other (fully human) players. The plaintiff brought the action for, inter alia, copyright infringement, asserting that defendant directly and contributorily infringed its copyrights by selling bots that copied the game and violated Runescape's terms and conditions, and by encouraging others to use those bots. Section 411 of the Copyright Act requires "registration or preregistration of a copyright of a United States work before filing suit." Plaintiff argued that, because the Runescape game software was entirely developed and initially published in the United Kingdom, it was not a "United States work" and therefore registration was not required prior to filing suit. Plaintiff attempted to rely instead on 21 visual arts copyright registrations for various two-dimensional icons appearing in Runescape. The court found that even if the absence of copyright registration for the software did not bar injunctive relief, it made it unlikely that plaintiff would succeed on the merits of the claim. Moreover, even if the 21 registered images were included in the Runescape software, plaintiff failed to explain how bot users infringed those copyrights when they played the game. Thus, the court found, in the absence of a registered copyright in the software, the plaintiff had not demonstrated a likelihood of success on the merits.[43]

Even more drastic was the holding in *Kruska v. Perverted Justice Found., Inc.*,[44] where the court granted defendants' motion for summary judgment based on the pro se plaintiff's failure to register the photographs and written works at issue prior to filing his copyright infringement action. Section 411(a) provides that "no civil action for infringement of the copyright in any United States work shall be instituted until ... registration of the copyright holder's claim has been made...." In *Muchnick* the Supreme Court had held that, while failure to register does not disturb the court's subject matter jurisdiction, registration remains a precondition to filing a copyright infringement claim. In *Kruska*, the court noted that there had been some debate regarding when registration should be deemed to have been made—at the time of receipt of the executed application, or at the time of issuance of the registration certificate. In this case, however, registration had never occurred at all. The plaintiff

---

[43]*Id.* at 236.

[44]No. 08-54, 2010 U.S. Dist. LEXIS 80956 (D. Ariz. Aug. 9, 2010).

would not be able to cure this deficiency, since copyright registration is a "prerequisite to a suit."[45]

And regardless of what constitutes a registration—an issued certificate or a mere application on file—it must unequivocally pertain to the work in suit, as the plaintiff learned to its chagrin in *Kema, Inc. v. Koperwhats.*[46] The plaintiff alleged that defendants "downloaded, sold, licensed, distributed, shared, or otherwise transferred" plaintiff's software without consent. The defendants argued that plaintiff's copyright claim was subject to dismissal because plaintiff's registration certificate did not, in fact, pertain to any work alleged to have been infringed, and consequently the court lacked jurisdiction. Specifically, the registration certificate identified work completed in 2008 and first published on June 16, 2008, and did not identify any preexisting work or works. As alleged by the plaintiff, however, many of the allegedly infringed software versions were published prior to June 16, 2008, including version 3.3, which was published on the defendant's website on February 27, 2006. In light of these allegations, the defendants argued that plaintiff's copyright registration certificate could not pertain to version 3.3. The district court noted that it lacked jurisdiction over a copyright claim where the allegedly infringed work was published before the date of first publication identified in the registration unless such registration identifies the registered work as derivative of, or a compilation containing, the allegedly infringed work. Accordingly, the court granted the defendants' motion to dismiss.[47]

B. Personal Jurisdiction

1. Intentional Acts Directed at the Forum

a. Sales in Forum

[Add the following text at the end of the section.]

In *John Wiley & Sons, Inc. v. Swancoat,*[48] the court denied the defendant's motion to dismiss or transfer venue from New York, where the defendant, through his website, allegedly sold and shipped at least seven electronic copies of the plaintiff's copyrighted work to buyers in New York. The plaintiff, a publishing company with headquarters in New Jersey, brought a copyright infringement action, alleging that the defendant sold electronic copies of the plaintiff's copyrighted books through his website, Gannscience.com. The website allowed customers to purchase copies of texts online, and allowed for the exchange of contact and mailing information between the defendant and its customers. The defendant resided in Michigan when he was served, but claimed

---

[45] *Id.* at *7–8.
[46] 96 USPQ2d 1787 (N.D. Cal. 2010).
[47] *Id.* at 1792–93.
[48] No. 08-5672, 2009 U.S. Dist. LEXIS 71820 (S.D.N.Y. Aug. 14, 2009).

to be a student in Missouri at the time he filed the motion. Pursuant to 28 U.S.C. §1400(a), a plaintiff may bring a copyright action in any district in which the defendant or his agent "resides or may be found." Furthermore, the defendant " ' "may be found" in any district in which he is subject to personal jurisdiction.' "[49] Under the New York long-arm statute, the plaintiff had to show that the defendant transacted business in New York and that there was a substantial relationship between that business and the plaintiff's claim. The court noted that a sufficient connection can be established when the defendant sells a single item into New York through his website. Because the defendant made several sales of books into New York, and the cause of action for copyright infringement directly related to these sales, the plaintiff satisfied the requirements of the long-arm statute. The court also found that jurisdiction comported with the "minimum contacts" and "reasonableness" constitutional due process requirements. Because the defendant sold books to New York, received payment for those books, and exchanged contact and mailing information with New York residents, he could reasonably have been expected to be subject to suit in New York.

b.   *Other Intentional Acts Directed at Forum*

[Add the following text at the end of the section.]

In the Tenth Circuit, it has been held that sending a notice of claimed infringement to eBay is enough to establish personal jurisdiction under the effects test. In *Dudnikov v. Chalk & Vermilion Fine Arts, Inc.*,[50] the plaintiffs were eBay "power sellers" who sold fabrics on the Internet from their home in Colorado. The plaintiffs launched an eBay auction offering fabric with an imprint of cartoon character Betty Boop wearing various gowns, including a design by noted artist and designer Erte. The defendants, who owned the rights to Erte images, filed a notice of claimed infringement ("NOCI") under eBay's "Verified Rights Owner" ("VeRO") program, created to take advantage of the safe harbor provision of DMCA §512.[51] On receipt of the NOCI, eBay cancelled the plaintiffs' auction and notified the plaintiffs. The defendants refused the plaintiffs' request to withdraw the NOCI, and the plaintiffs filed a counter notice with eBay, contesting the defendants' claim. On receipt of the counter notice, eBay notified the defendants that it would reinstate the contested auction in 10 days unless notified of pending litigation to adjudicate the parties' rights. In response, the defendants notified the plaintiffs that they intended to file an action in federal court within 10 days. Before the defendants could sue, the plaintiffs filed a pro se complaint in the District of Colorado seeking declaratory judgment that their sale of Betty Boop fabric did not infringe the defendants' copyrights, and also

---

[49] *Id.* at *2–3 (quoting Lipton v. Nature Co., 781 F. Supp. 1032, 1035 (S.D.N.Y. 1992)).

[50] 514 F.3d 1063, 85 USPQ2d 1705 (10th Cir. 2008).

[51] For further discussion of the DMCA, see the Main Volume, Chapter 1, sec. I.C.3. and Chapter 10, sec. II.

seeking an injunction preventing the defendants from interfering with future sales of the fabric. The defendants moved to dismiss for lack of personal jurisdiction. The district court held that neither specific nor general jurisdiction existed and granted the defendants' motion.

The Tenth Circuit reversed. The court noted that under *Calder v. Jones*,[52] personal jurisdiction requires (a) intentional action, (b) expressly aimed at the forum state, with (c) knowledge that the brunt of the injury would be felt in the forum state. The Tenth Circuit found that the defendants' act of sending the NOCI to eBay constituted "intentional action." The Tenth Circuit also found that the defendants' actions were "aimed at the forum state" because the NOCI was sent to eBay to cancel the plaintiffs' auction, which originated in Colorado, and email threatening a lawsuit was sent to the plaintiffs in Colorado. With regard to the third requirement under *Calder*, the Tenth Circuit assumed that the defendants knew the plaintiffs' business and auction were based in Colorado because the auction site displayed their location. Finally, the Tenth Circuit found no basis in traditional notions of fair play or substantial justice that would preclude suit in Colorado.

Another recent case emphasized that in any application of the effects test, there must be some affirmative evidence that the defendants knew that their acts would harm a plaintiff in the forum state. In *Browne v. McCain*,[53] the court granted defendant Ohio Republican Party's ("ORP's") motion to dismiss for lack of personal jurisdiction. Plaintiff Jackson Browne sued Sen. John McCain, the Republican National Committee, and the Ohio Republican Party for claims arising from the defendants' use of Browne's song and sound recording "Running on Empty" in a campaign commercial for Sen. McCain. The defendants received neither license nor permission to use the song in their commercial, which was posted on YouTube and aired on television and cable networks and on other websites. Browne asserted claims for, *inter alia*, copyright infringement and vicarious infringement. The ORP contended that the court lacked specific jurisdiction over it because ORP lacked sufficient minimum contacts with California. Browne's contention that he was a well-known Southern California resident, alone, was insufficient to establish that the ORP knew its acts would cause Browne harm in California. Moreover, the ORP had presented evidence that its officers did not know that Browne was a California resident.

The effects test was further applied in *Brayton Purcell, LLP v. Recordon & Recordon*,[54] where the Ninth Circuit confirmed that the second part of the *Calder* test is satisfied when the defendant knows that the copyright owner is located in the forum state.

---

[52] 465 U.S. 783 (1984).

[53] 612 F. Supp. 2d 1118 (C.D. Cal. 2009).

[54] 575 F.3d 981 (9th Cir. 2009). *Superseded by, rehearing denied by (as moot)* Brayton Purcell LLP v. Recordon & Recordon, 2010 U.S. App. LEXIS 10928 (9th Cir. Cal., May 28, 2010). The holding of the Ninth Circuit remains valid with regard to the forum issue despite the subsequent case history.

The plaintiff sued the defendant for copyright infringement, alleging that the defendant had "willfully, deliberately and knowingly used Plaintiff's copyrighted work for the purpose of promoting its business and attracting new business in the field of elder abuse law, in competition with" the plaintiff.[55] The court employed the three-prong test from *Schwarzenegger v. Fred Martin Motor Co.*[56] to determine whether Recordon had sufficient minimum contacts to be susceptible to personal jurisdiction:

(1) The non-resident defendant must purposefully direct his activities or consummate some transaction with the forum or resident thereof; or perform some act by which he purposefully avails himself of the privilege of conducting activities in the forum, thereby invoking the benefits and protections of its laws;

(2) the claim must be one which arises out of or relates to the defendant's forum-related activities; and

(3) the exercise of jurisdiction must comport with fair play and substantial justice, *i.e.*, it must be reasonable.[57]

The first prong of the test is satisfied by "either purposeful availment or purposeful direction;"[58] since the purposeful direction test is most often used in tort suits, it was held to be the proper analytical framework for copyright cases. The court evaluated the purposeful direction element using the three-part "effects" test from *Calder v. Jones*,[59] whereby the defendant must have allegedly " '(1) committed an intentional act, (2) expressly aimed at the forum state, (3) causing harm that the defendant knows is likely to be suffered in the forum state.' "[60] The first prong was easily satisfied by the defendant's creation and posting of the elder law section on its website, thereby infringing the plaintiff's copyright. With regard to the second prong, the court found that "[t]aking Brayton Purcell's allegations and statements as true, Recordon individually targeted Brayton Purcell by making commercial use of Brayton Purcell's copyrighted material for the purpose of competing with Brayton Purcell for elder abuse clients" and thus "expressly aimed its conduct at the Forum by individually targeting a known forum resident."[61] The third prong was satisfied in that it was "foreseeable" that the plaintiff "would be harmed by infringement of its copyright, including harm to its business reputation and goodwill, and decreased business and profits. It was also foreseeable that some of this harm would occur in the Forum, where Brayton Purcell was known to reside."[62]

---

[55] *Id.* at 984.

[56] 374 F.3d 797 (9th Cir. 2004).

[57] *Brayton Purcell*, 575 F.3d at 985 (quoting *Schwarzenegger*, 374 F.3d at 802).

[58] *Id.*

[59] 465 U.S. 783 (1984).

[60] *Brayton Purcell*, 575 F.3d at 986 (quoting Yahoo! Inc. v. La Ligue Contre Le Racisme et L'Antisemitisme, 433 F.3d 1199, 1206 (9th Cir. 2006) (en banc)).

[61] *Id.* at 987.

[62] *Id.* at 988.

Where there is no evidence that defendants knew the copyright owner was a forum resident, however, jurisdiction may be found lacking. For example, in *Royalty Network, Inc. v. Dishant.com, LLC,*[63] the district court granted the defendants' motion to dismiss for lack of personal jurisdiction under Federal Rule of Civil Procedure 12(b)(2). The plaintiff, the U.S. music administrator for a foreign recording company, brought copyright infringement claims against the defendants, operators of a website that provided users with unauthorized access to music produced and owned by the plaintiff's principal. The court lacked jurisdiction under N.Y. C.P.L.R. §302(a)(1) (conferring jurisdiction to a non-domiciliary who "transacts any business within the state") because there was "no evidence that any New York resident actually . . . registered with the website or downloaded material from it—or that defendants did anything to indicate their knowing and purposeful transaction with New York visitors."[64] Furthermore, there was no evidence that the defendants sold advertisements to the New York office of any of its advertisers, or even that the defendant knew such advertisers had New York offices and there was no nexus between the registration of defendant's domain name in New York and the instant litigation. Finally, jurisdiction was lacking under N.Y. C.P.L.R. §302(a)(3)(ii) (conferring jurisdiction to a non-domiciliary who commits a "tortious act without state that causes injury within state" where the non-domiciliary "expects or should reasonably expect the act to have consequences in the state and derives substantial revenue from interstate or international commerce") because there was no evidence that defendants knew plaintiff held the copyrights in the music at issue, or that defendants purposefully targeted any state residents.

In *Marvel Worldwide, Inc. v. Kirby,*[65] the Southern District of New York held that the mere sending of a termination notice into the forum state subjects the sender to personal jurisdiction under New York's long-arm statute. The defendants were heirs of Jack Kirby, who "collaborated with other individuals engaged by Marvel to contribute to the creation of many now-treasured comic books, featuring such familiar and enduring characters as the Fantastic Four, the Incredible Hulk and the X-Men."[66] The defendants sent multiple termination notices to Marvel. Marvel sued, seeking a declaration that the Kirby contributions to the works were works made for hire, and that termination notices were invalid. The court noted that on a Rule 12(b)(2) motion, the plaintiff " 'bears the burden of showing that the court has jurisdiction over the defendant.' "[67] In opposing a pre-discovery motion to dismiss, the plaintiff "need only make a *prima facie* showing that the non-domiciliary Defendants are amenable

---

[63]638 F. Supp. 2d 410 (S.D.N.Y. 2009).

[64]*Id.* at 420.

[65]No. 10 Civ. 141, 2010 U.S. Dist. LEXIS 38701 (S.D.N.Y. Apr. 14, 2010).

[66]*Id.* at *2.

[67]*Id.* at *6 (quoting *In re* Magnetic Audiotape Antitrust Litig., 334 F.3d 204, 206 (2d Cir. 2003)).

to personal jurisdiction in New York."[68] The inquiry under N.Y. C.P.L.R. §302(a)(1) involves two elements: "first, did the non-domiciliary defendant 'transact business' in New York; and second, does the plaintiff's claim against the defendant arise out of that activity?"[69] The court found that the defendants, acting collectively, "transacted business" in New York within the meaning of New York's long-arm statute when they "dispatched a multitude [of] self-executing Termination Notices to Marvel entities and licensees in New York in September 2009."[70] "Unlike a cease and desist letter, which merely warns a party that he may be infringing upon another's intellectual property rights, communications like the Termination Notices confer transactional personal jurisdiction over non-domiciliaries because they alter the status quo between the parties, by requiring the recipient to take legal action or lose his intellectual property rights."[71] The court rejected the defendants' argument that because the Copyright Act *required* them to serve termination notices on Marvel in New York, service of the notices did not constitute availment of New York laws. "The relevant question is not whether Defendants' contacts with New York were voluntary, but whether Defendants purposefully projected their interests into the State," and here, the court found, they "plainly did just that."[72] The requirement that the plaintiff's cause of action must arise out of the defendants' contacts with the forum was easily met, the court found. There was unquestionably a substantial relationship between the sending of notices to New York and Marvel's claim that notices were invalid. Moreover, the underlying dispute involved works that were "created in New York while Kirby lived in New York, pursuant to work assignments given by Marvel to Kirby in New York, delivered to editors and publishers in New York, and for which Kirby received payment in New York."[73]

In an even more significant New York decision, the New York Court of Appeals—the state's highest court—interpreted New York's long-arm statute to provide for personal jurisdiction in a case of online piracy. In *Penguin Group (USA) Inc. v. American Buddha*,[74] American Buddha, a not-for-profit corporation based in Arizona, scanned and uploaded electronic copies of four Penguin books to its websites, making the books freely available to anyone anywhere with an Internet connection. Penguin, based in New York, sued in federal district court in Manhattan. The district court granted American Buddha's motion to dismiss on the ground that the court lacked personal jurisdiction over it. The New

---

[68] *Id.* at *7 (citing A.I. Trade Fin., Inc. v. Petra Bank, 989 F.2d 76, 79 (2d Cir. 1993)).

[69] *Id.* at *8.

[70] *Id.* at *10.

[71] *Id.* at *13. The defendants "'knew or reasonably should have known that by sending the [Termination Notices] into New York, [they were] running the risk of suit in New York in connection with that activity.'" *Id.* at *16 (quoting Sluys v. Hand, 831 F. Supp. 321, 325 (S.D.N.Y. 1993)).

[72] *Id.* at *18.

[73] *Id.* at *19.

[74] 16 N.Y.3d 295 (2011).

York long-arm statute, N.Y. C.P.L.R. §302(a)(3)(ii), allows the court to exercise jurisdiction over a nondomiciliary who commits a tortious act outside New York that causes injury within the state, if he expects or should reasonably expect the act to have consequences in the state, and derives substantial revenue from interstate or international commerce. The district court held that "injury" occurred only where the infringing acts were committed, presumably Arizona or Oregon, and not in New York, where Penguin is located. Penguin appealed. The Second Circuit acknowledged a split of authority within New York federal courts on the issue of where "injury" occurs when a copyright is infringed, with some courts finding that injury occurs only where infringing acts are committed, and others finding that a New York copyright holder is injured in New York, where it resides or has its principal place of business. The Second Circuit, faced with conflicting approaches taken by lower courts, found that "deciding which approach better comports with the intent of the New York Legislature is more appropriate for the New York Court of Appeals than it is for us," and certified the question to New York's highest court.[75] The New York Court of Appeals framed the issue as follows:

> In copyright infringement cases involving the uploading of a copyrighted printed literary work onto the Internet, is the situs of injury for purposes of determining long-arm jurisdiction under N.Y. C.P.L.R. §302(a)(3)(ii) the location of the infringing action or the residence or location of the principal place of business of the copyright holder?[76]

The New York Court of Appeals found the situs of injury to be the principal place of business of the copyright holder. Because online infringement is "dispersed throughout the country and perhaps the world," it is "illogical" to extend the traditional tort approach, locating the plaintiff's injury "where its business is lost or threatened" to the context of online infringement, "where the place of uploading is inconsequential and it is difficult, if not impossible, to correlate lost sales to a particular geographic area."[77] The injury inflicted by digital piracy is felt throughout the United States, which necessarily includes New York.[78]

Another recent web jurisdiction decision is *Berklee College of Music, Inc. v. Music Industry Educators, Inc.*[79] The Massachusetts district court in *Berklee* denied defendant's motion to dismiss plaintiff Berklee's copyright action for lack of personal jurisdiction where the wrong arose out of publication of defendant's website, continuously available to Massachusetts residents, that caused tortious injury in Massachusetts. Berklee, a Massachusetts corporation with its principal place of business in Massachusetts, operated websites at www.berklee.edu and www.berkleemusic.com

---

[75]Penguin Group (USA) Inc. v. American Buddha, 609 F.3d 30, 38, 95 USPQ2d 1217 (2d Cir. 2010).

[76]16 N.Y.3d at 301.

[77]16 N.Y.3d at 305.

[78]*Id.* at 306.

[79]733 F. Supp. 2d 204 (D. Mass. 2010).

which offered online music courses and provided information, including course descriptions, to current and potential students. Defendant Music Industry Educators (MIE), a Florida corporation with its principal place of business in Florida, also operated several websites offering online music courses. Berklee brought a copyright infringement action alleging, *inter alia,* that Berklee's copyrighted course descriptions appeared on MIE's websites in connection with courses offered by MIE. Although MIE did not have any other contacts with Massachusetts, MIE's websites were continuously available to Massachusetts residents, and four individuals with Massachusetts addresses submitted emails to MIE through its websites. The court thus found that MIE had sufficient minimum contacts with Massachusetts "'such that maintenance of the suit does not offend "traditional notions of fair play and justice." ' "[80] The court further found that specific jurisdiction existed as to MIE because allegedly infringing material was taken from a website located in Massachusetts; the cause of the action therefore arose out of MIE's forum-based contacts; infringing materials were continuously available to Massachusetts residents; and the actions were almost certain to cause injury in Massachusetts. The court also noted that MIE purposely availed itself of privileges of doing business in Massachusetts by "targeting" Berklee by taking content from its website. Weighing First Circuit factors, the court found that (1) MIE knowingly assumed the risk of being sued in Massachusetts; (2) Massachusetts had an interest in protecting Massachusetts corporations; (3) witnesses and other evidence were located in Massachusetts; (4) ready access to evidence would result in the most effective resolution of the controversy; and (5) requiring alleged infringers to bear the burden of traveling to the forum in which their voluntary actions caused foreseeable injury encourages consideration of that burden before the action.[81] Similarly, because MIE's corporate officer was the "moving, active, conscious force behind the infringement," the court found the exercise of personal jurisdiction over MIE's corporate officer was proper.[82] Thus, MIE's motion to dismiss for lack of jurisdiction was denied.

3.   *Contract Clauses*

[Add the following text at the end of the section.]

Forum selection clauses have also been held effective when presented in the form of a click-on license in the online environment. In *Stockart.com, LLC v. Engle*[83] the magistrate judge recommended a finding of personal jurisdiction over a non-resident defendant based upon (a) defendant's failure to rebut the prima facie validity of a forum selection clause in an

---

[80]733 F. Supp. 2d at 208 (quoting Platten v. HG Berm. Exempted Ltd., 437 F.3d 118, 135 (1st Cir. 2006) (quoting Int'l Shoe Co. v. Washington, 326 U.S. 310, 316, 66 S. Ct. 154, 90 L. Ed. 95 (1945))).

[81]*Id.* at 210–11.

[82]*Id.* at 211.

[83]No.10-cv-00588-MSK-MEH, 2011 U.S. Dist. LEXIS 20470 (D. Colo. Feb. 18, 2011).

"intentional infringer" warning statement on plaintiff's website, which the defendant accepted by clicking "OK," and (b) a sufficient nexus between the defendant and the forum to satisfy due process. The plaintiff was in the business of licensing "rights managed," downloadable, "high end" digital imagery created by various artists, and offered said imagery for sale on its website at www.stockart.com. As a condition of using the website, users acknowledged, each time they performed a search, that "disputes concerning use of any image on this site will be resolved in the courts of Colorado."[84] The defendant, a graphic designer whose last known residence was New Mexico, was in the business of selling corporate identity logos via the Internet. The defendant registered with and engaged in extensive use of the plaintiff's website. The defendant searched plaintiff's database 92 times, each time clicking "OK" to the plaintiff's "intentional infringer" warning, thereby agreeing to the plaintiff's forum selection clause. The plaintiff subsequently learned that the defendant had taken images from its site without authorization, removed copyright management information from the images, and sold the images to third parties, including for use as corporate logos. The plaintiff brought suit, and the defendant defaulted. The magistrate judge found the plaintiff's forum selection clause to be prima facie valid, and saw no reason to find the clause unfair or unreasonable.[85] The judge further found that the defendant's commission of a tort that resulted in severe financial injury to the plaintiff, a Colorado resident, created a sufficient nexus between the defendant and Colorado to satisfy due process.[86] The magistrate judge thus recommended finding that Stockart established personal jurisdiction over the defendant.

C. Standing

1. *Standing for Infringement Claims*

[Add the following text at the end of the section]

In *HyperQuest, Inc. v. N'Site Solutions, Inc.*,[87] the Seventh Circuit affirmed the district court's dismissal of plaintiff HyperQuest's copyright infringement claim on the ground that the license it had received from a third-party software owner did not confer any exclusive rights, and therefore plaintiff lacked standing to bring suit. The third party, Safelite Group, had granted HyperQuest a purportedly "exclusive" license to software that was subject to an existing license to defendant N'Site, where ongoing negotiations between Safelite and N'Site related to modifications of existing license, and where certain rights were retained by Safelite. N'Site used the software in ways that, according to plaintiff, exceeded the scope of N'Site's existing license (which was never

---

[84] *Id.* at *6.

[85] *Id.* at *18.

[86] *Id.* at *19.

[87] 632 F.3d 377 (7th Cir. 2011).

modified). HyperQuest claimed standing as an exclusive licensee and brought suit for copyright infringement. The court held that "the right to exclude, standing alone, is not enough" to confer standing under the Copyright Act for a purportedly exclusive licensee to bring suit.[88] Because the court concluded that the license did not indicate "the kind of clearly delineated exclusivity over at least one strand of the bundle of rights that would permit HyperQuest to sue for infringement," the court dismissed the claim.[89]

The claim to ownership of a right under Section 106 does not have to be particularly compelling at the pleading stage, however. For example, the Ninth Circuit in *United Fabrics Int'l, Inc. v. C&J Wear, Inc.*[90] reversed the district court's sua sponte dismissal of plaintiff United Fabrics' copyright infringement claim. United Fabrics held a copyright registration for a collection of fabric designs and alleged that defendants sold infringing fabric and garments. The district court dismissed United Fabrics' claim after finding that evidence of transfer of the source artwork from the original author to the plaintiff was insufficient to establish the plaintiff's ownership of the underlying design. The Ninth Circuit reversed, holding that the district court failed to give proper weight to the plaintiff's copyright registration and erroneously placed the burden to prove copyright validity on the plaintiff.[91]

Even so-called "beneficial owners" have standing to pursue infringement claims. In *Warner/Chappell Music, Inc. v. Blue Moon Ventures,*[92] plaintiffs sought a preliminary injunction enjoining defendants from exploiting certain musical compositions. The defendants argued that plaintiffs had not met their burden of establishing ownership, and thus lacked standing. One plaintiff based its ownership on an Exclusive Administration Agreement granting it exclusive administrative rights and appointing it as attorney-in-fact, although the agreement was silent on the right to bring suit. The court found the plaintiff to be a beneficial owner, and thus to have standing. The court's analysis did not turn on attorney-in-fact language in the agreement, but instead examined whether the agreement transferred to the plaintiff, exclusively, any of the rights vested in an owner by the Copyright Act. To have standing to bring suit, the court noted, a party must have some exclusive ownership of the right for which he or she wishes to sue. Whether or not such right is exclusive is governed by the substance of what was transferred rather than by what the parties chose to call their agreement. Under the agreement at issue here, the court found, the plaintiff had the right of an exclusive licensee to reproduce the work and distribute copies. The court also reasoned

---

[88]*Id.* at 385.

[89]*Id.* at 384–85.

[90]630 F.3d 1255 (9th Cir. 2011).

[91]*Id.* at 1258.

[92]No. 3:10-1160, 2011 U.S. Dist. LEXIS 14886 (M.D. Tenn. Feb. 14, 2011).

that the fact that the plaintiff had a right to grant nonexclusive licenses weighed in favor of finding plaintiff to be a beneficial owner.[93]

3.   *Standing for Copyright Claims Other Than Infringement*

[Add the following text at the end of the section.]

Beneficial owners of copyright also have standing to bring an infringement claim. A slightly unusual example of asserted beneficial ownership is discussed in *Mason v. Jamie Music Publishing Co.*,[94] where the court granted the plaintiff's motion for declaratory judgment of copyright ownership in her own name and denied the defendant's counterclaim for declaration of copyright ownership. The plaintiff, author of a 1965 song entitled "Yes I'm Ready," intervened in the defendant music publisher's infringement action concerning the composition against third parties and filed a motion seeking a declaratory judgment that she owned copyright in the composition. Simultaneously, the plaintiff was finalizing a purchase agreement with a new music publisher. The defendant argued that the plaintiff did not have standing in the declaratory judgment action because she had assigned her rights in the purchase agreement. The court found that the assignment of copyright by the composer to the publisher in exchange for royalties established an equitable trust relationship, giving the composer standing to sue for infringement; "'[o]therwise the beneficial owner's interest in the copyright could be diluted or lessened by a wrongdoer's infringement.'"[95] The court concluded that the plaintiff had standing because the language of the purchase agreement and evidence of the intent of the parties indicated that the assignment was not complete, so the plaintiff was still the owner of the copyright and, after the assignment was complete, the plaintiff would become the beneficial owner.

D.   Pleadings

[Add the following text at the end of the section.]

Most recently, the courts in copyright cases have been grappling with the impact of the Supreme Court's decision in *Bell Atlantic Corp. v. Twombly*[96] on well-settled law regarding copyright-infringement pleadings. Under the best reading, courts have found that *Twombly* does not change the traditional standards under Rule 8. Thus, for example, in *Elektra Entertainment Group, Inc. v. Barker*,[97] the court denied the defendant's motion to dismiss claims for copyright infringement, finding the plaintiffs' allegations of continuing infringement and inclusion of a list of infringing works sufficient to provide notice to the defendant of the

---

[93]*Id.* at 13–15.

[94]658 F. Supp. 2d 571 (S.D.N.Y. 2009).

[95]*Id.* at 579 (quoting Cortner v. Israel, 732 F.2d 267, 271 (2d Cir. 1984)).

[96]550 U.S. 544 (2007).

[97]551 F. Supp. 2d 234, 87 USPQ2d 1427 (S.D.N.Y. 2008).

claims against her. The plaintiffs, major record labels Elektra Entertainment Group, UMG Recordings, Inc., and Virgin Records America, Inc., own copyrights in many sound recordings. The plaintiffs alleged that the defendant infringed the plaintiffs' exclusive rights to reproduce and distribute copyrighted works by downloading, distributing, and/or making available copies of copyrighted sound recordings using KaZaA, a peer-to-peer online media distribution system.

Without stating specific times and dates, the plaintiffs alleged past and continuing infringement and attached exhibits to the complaint listing the allegedly infringed works and screen-shots of the KaZaA program. The defendant moved to dismiss the complaint, arguing in part that the complaint did not plead copyright infringement with adequate specificity. The court rejected the defendant's arguments, finding that Federal Rule of Civil Procedure 8, which requires only a short and plain statement of the claim, is not meant to impose a great burden on the plaintiff. The court found that the plaintiffs adequately alleged:

(1) which original works were the subject of the claim;
(2) that the plaintiffs owned copyrights in their original works;
(3) that the copyrights had been registered, and
(4) by what acts during what time the defendant infringed the copyrights.

Rejecting the argument that *Twombly* demands a more restrictive interpretation of the pleading standard, the court specifically noted that the allegation of past and continuing infringement satisfies the pleading requirement and sufficiently puts the defendant on notice of when the infringement occurred. The court therefore denied the defendant's motion to dismiss for failure to plead with adequate specificity.

2

Copyrightability

I. Originality of Authorship

C. Limiting Doctrines

1.   *Merger Doctrine/Idea-Expression Dichotomy*

[Add the following text at the end of the section.]

A "star ratings" system for evaluating hospitals and granting awards was held potentially protectable in *Health Grades, Inc. v. Robert Wood Johnson University Hospital, Inc.*,[1] because it arguably resulted from the creative judgments of the rating organization. In response to the defendant's Federal Rule of Civil Procedure 12(b)(6) failure to state a claim motion, the court held that the plaintiff properly alleged that its "1-3-5 Star" rating system and award program for hospitals and healthcare providers were protectable expression. The defendant hospital used the star ratings and awards in press releases to promote the high ratings it had been given by the plaintiff. Noting the absence of 10th Circuit guidance, the court applied *CCC Information Services v. Maclean Hunter Market Reports, Inc.*[2] and *CDN, Inc. v. Kapes*[3] to find that the ratings and awards could be copyrightable because, like the car valuations in *CCC* and the coin prices in *CDN*, the plaintiff's materials "are similarly the product of a creative and original process that is informed by [the plaintiff's] judgment and choices on what data to include and how to weight it."[4] The defendant's arguments under the merger doctrine were rejected because the court found the "idea" at issue to be "that of creating rankings for healthcare providers," which can be expressed many ways.[5] The court also declined to withhold protection under the short phrases doctrine, relying on the dissenting opinion in *Southco v. Kanebridge*[6] to find that the Copyright Office regulation regarding short phrases did not create an "absolute rule" against protecting short phrases if they were otherwise sufficiently creative and independently created.[7]

In *Wilson v. Brennan*,[8] however, the Tenth Circuit upheld a ruling that the plaintiff's selection of roadways and design of bicycle racecourses did not qualify for copyright protection. Plaintiff Wilson, after selecting the racecourses, described and expressed them in writings in the form of maps and profiles. The lower court held that the maps and profiles of selected racecourses qualified for protection. However, the plaintiff

---

[1] 634 F. Supp. 2d 1226 (D. Colo. 2009).

[2] 44 F.3d 61 (2d Cir. 1994).

[3] 197 F.3d 1256 (9th Cir. 1999).

[4] *Health Grades*, 634 F. Supp. 2d at 1235.

[5] *Id.* at 1236–37.

[6] 390 F.3d 276 (3d Cir. 2004). "[I]t does not make sense to state categorically that no combination of numbers or words short enough to be deemed a 'phrase' can possess 'at least some minimal degree of creativity.' " *Id.* at 298 (Roth, J., dissenting).

[7] *Health Grades*, 634 F. Supp. 2d at 1238.

[8] 390 Fed. Appx. 780 (10th Cir. 2010).

also sought to copyright the idea of a particular racecourse. The court noted that copyrights protect "language that an author uses to explain, describe, or express whatever ideas or useful arts [he] may have discovered or created, along with the artistic way in which the author draws or illustrates those ideas or useful arts."[9] However, no author may copyright facts or ideas. On that basis, the court affirmed that racecourse selection and design did not qualify for copyright protection, as a matter of law.[10]

II. Compilations

B. The *Feist* Standard

[Add the following text at the end of the section.]

In *Tristar Products, Inc. v. SAS Group, Inc.*,[11] the District Court of New Jersey denied the defendant's motion to dismiss the plaintiff's copyright infringement claim under Federal Rule of Civil Procedure 12(b)(6), finding that the entirety of plaintiff's work was copyrightable even if individual elements were not. The suit involved a claim of infringement of an infomercial for a vegetable peeler. The court rejected the defendant's argument that the plaintiff's infomercial should be denied copyright protection because the "images and phrases used in the advertisements belong in one of three categories that fall outside of copyright protection: 1) they demonstrate the functional elements of all vegetable peelers; 2) they constitute *scenes à faire* which are indispensable to any promotion of a kitchen utensil; and 3) they are examples of material and themes common to all infomercials."[12] But the plaintiff argued that "while many of the specific images and phrases [in the infomercial] are unoriginal if viewed in isolation, the exact sequence of ideas, images, and themes within the advertisement is original, and it is that which [the defendant] copied."[13] The court's review revealed almost identical sequencing in both infomercials.

2. *Protectable Compilations*

[Add the following new section.]

o. *Real Estate Information [New Topic]*

In *Salestraq America, LLC v. Zyskowski*,[14] the court denied the defendants' motion to dismiss the plaintiff's copyright infringement suit, finding that plaintiff's real estate information could be protectable. The

---

[9]*Id.* at 782–83.

[10]*Id.* at 783.

[11]No. 08-6263, 2009 U.S. Dist. LEXIS 94592 (D.N.J. Sept. 9, 2009).

[12]*Id.* at *15.

[13]*Id.* at *15–16.

[14]635 F. Supp. 2d 1178 (D. Nev. 2009).

plaintiff alleged that content on the defendants' website was similar to the plaintiff's copyrighted compilation of information regarding residential properties in Las Vegas and also included exact reproductions of content created by the plaintiff to inform customers of the properties' key attributes. The defendants moved to dismiss on the basis that (1) the court lacked subject matter jurisdiction to consider the infringement action because the plaintiff registered a 2008 version of the compilation rather than the 2007 version that the defendant allegedly infringed, and (2) the plaintiff failed to set forth a cognizable copyright infringement claim because the compilation was comprised of uncopyrightable facts or ideas as opposed to copyrightable expression. As to the registered version argument, the court ruled that "registration of a factual compilation permits a complainant to assert an infringement claim on an underlying work that is owned by the complainant"[15] and, as such, the plaintiff complied with the registration requirements. As to the failure to state a claim, the court noted that the complaint alleged that, as part of its compilation, the plaintiff authored additional content informing users of key attributes of each model of residential property in the compilation. The court ruled that authoring this content "implies a greater degree of creativity that [*sic*] the alphabetization rejected in *Feist*."[16]

[Add the following new section.]

p.   *Financial data [New Topic]*

In *BanxCorp v. Costco Wholesale Corp.*,[17] the court denied in part the defendant companies' motion to dismiss. Plaintiff BanxCorp published database compilations and market indices for use by the finance industry. The indices were described as systematic compilations to be used as benchmarks for industry. The plaintiff and defendant Costco entered into a license agreement allowing Costco to use the indices. BanxCorp, upon learning that Costco had permitted co-defendant Capital One to access the indices, filed suit for copyright infringement. The defendants argued that they did not infringe any protectible elements of the plaintiff's works, as there was no originality in the portions that were copied. The court observed that, to demonstrate that the final values produced from raw data are protectible by copyright, the plaintiff must demonstrate either that (1) the raw data used to create a final value were protectible; or (2) the method of converting raw data into a final value was an original, but not necessarily novel, process that is neither widely accepted as objective, nor an industry standard; or (3) the final value did not attempt to measure empirical reality. The court held that the indices' raw data were simply facts regarding interest rates, and thus were unprotectible.[18] The final arrangements of values were merely measuring statistics such

---

[15] *Id.* at 1181.

[16] *Id.* at 1183.

[17] 723 F. Supp. 2d 596 (S.D.N.Y. 2010).

[18] *Id.* at 606.

as rates paid by investors, which are objective empirical facts about the banking market, and thus unprotectible. However, the court held that the plaintiff's *method* of converting raw data into final values did involve originality in the complex algorithms the plaintiff used to generate final values. BanxCorp utilized unique ways (out of many possible ways) to select and weigh the factors involved in the calculations. This was sufficiently original to merit protection. The court, accordingly, denied the defendants' motion to dismiss the copyright infringement claim.[19]

III. PICTORIAL, GRAPHIC, AND SCULPTURAL WORKS

C. Limiting Doctrines

1. Useful Articles/Separability

c. More Recent Cases

[Add the following text at the end of the section.]

Huebbe v. Oklahoma Casting Co.[20] applies the *Pivot Point* analysis to lighting fixtures. There, the Oklahoma district court denied the defendants' motion for partial summary judgment, finding that artistic aspects of the plaintiff's sculptural works were conceptually separable from the useful articles—here, lighting fixtures—in which they were incorporated. The plaintiff sculptor sued the defendants, manufacturer of gift items including lighting fixtures, for copyright infringement. The defendants argued that the plaintiff's works, as useful articles, were not copyrightable. Lacking Tenth Circuit precedent, the district court looked to the Seventh Circuit's discussion of "conceptual separability" in *Pivot Point*, under which conceptual separability exists if the design elements reflect artistic judgment independent of utilitarian functionality.[21] Applying *Pivot Point*, the court concluded that facts in evidence supported a finding of conceptual separability, and therefore copyrightability, for the design elements of the plaintiff's lighting fixtures, and therefore denied the defendants' motion for summary judgment.

The copyrightability analysis can also have a bearing on whether a work qualifies for protection under the Visual Artists Rights Act (VARA), as it did in *Cheffins v. Stewart*.[22] There, plaintiff Cheffins received a grant from the Burning Man Festival to create an art piece, "La Contessa," which resembled a Spanish galleon ship on top of a school bus. In return, the plaintiff granted Burning Man a license to use La Contessa at the festival. Afterwards, La Contessa was stored on defendant Stewart's ranch. Stewart eventually requested that Burning Man remove the artwork. When Burning Man did not respond, defendant destroyed the artwork

---

[19]*Id.* at 608–09.

[20]No. 06-306, 2009 U.S. Dist. LEXIS 91824 (W.D. Okla. Sept. 30, 2009).

[21]*Id.* at *16 (citing *Pivot Point*, 372 F.3d at 917).

[22]No. 309-cv-00130-RAM, 2011 U.S. Dist. LEXIS 5947 (D. Nev. Jan. 20, 2011).

by burning it. Plaintiff Cheffins and his collaborator, Jones, sued for violation of their rights under VARA. The defendant filed a motion for summary judgment, claiming that La Contessa was ineligible for VARA protection. Under VARA, the author of a work has a right to prevent the destruction of a work of recognized stature, and can obtain relief for intentional violation of that right. However, VARA only protects "works of visual art," and protection is limited to "a painting, drawing, print or sculpture, existing in a single copy ..." and excludes protection for "applied art" and for any "work made for hire."[23] Defendant Stewart claimed this work was not "sculpture" and fell within both exceptions to VARA. The court held that the work was "sculpture," as that term is read in a broad light to include constructions; it was also clearly outside the "work for hire" exception to VARA, as the grant monies given by Burning Man to Cheffins were not compensation for time, but rather for expenses. Further, those parties' agreement said nothing about "work for hire."[24] With regard to the "applied art" exception, however, the court turned for guidance to the legislative history of the 1976 Copyright Act, which states that "applied art" includes sculptural works intended to be embodied in useful articles. Because La Contessa in its fully built form retained the ability to move (as a bus), and because its primary purpose at the Burning Man Festival was to transport people (albeit at reduced speed), it was still a utilitarian object. Therefore, it fell within the scope of the "applied art" exception, did not constitute a "work of visual art," and did not warrant protection under VARA. The court granted the defendant's motion for summary judgment on the claim.[25]

d.   *Clothing*

[Add the following text at the end of the section.]

The unprotectability of clothing is so firmly established that even when a designer can obtain a registration for such a design, courts will not always take it at face value. For example, in *Johnson v. Levi Strauss*[26] the court granted the defendants' motion to dismiss the plaintiff's claim of copyright and design patent infringement for a "Hip Hop Cell Phone and CD Player Pocket" which the plaintiff alleged was for a cell phone pocket or CD player pocket. Even though the plaintiff had registered the work, the court found that the plaintiff had failed to identify any copyrightable authorship because it could not be inferred from the plaintiff's complaint that the cell phone pocket "contained any original pictorial, graphic, or sculptural work."[27] Further, the plaintiff's copyright claim that the cell phone pocket and CD pocket "contains a closure and is located on the hip for clothing and top thigh area and middle thigh

---

[23]17 U.S.C. §101.

[24]2011 U.S. Dist. LEXIS 5947, at *9–11.

[25]*Id.* at *15.

[26]No. 08-461, 2009 U.S. Dist. LEXIS 80630 (S.D. Ohio Aug. 5, 2009).

[27]*Id.* at *11.

area with two pockets on each side for men and women," without more, described functional, useful articles.[28] The court further noted that there were no ornamental or other design elements that were separable from the functional elements.

f.   Toys

[Add the following text at the end of the section.]

In another recent holding, the Ninth Circuit confirmed that toys are generally not considered useful articles. In *Lanard Toys, Ltd. v. Novelty, Inc.*,[29] the court found no reversible error in a district court's ruling, on a post-judgment motion, that substantial evidence supported the jury's findings of valid copyrights in the plaintiff's flying toys and the packaging for the toys. The defendant contended that the plaintiff's "Drop Copter" toy, and the launcher handle for the "Wild Copter" and "Stunt Plane" toys, were uncopyrightable "useful articles" as a matter of law. The classification of "useful articles," the court stated, requires a fact-intensive, case-by-case determination, which should be submitted to the jury when there is a genuine factual dispute.[30] With respect to "Drop Copter," the court reasoned that although a child can make the helicopter toy fly, such flights simply portray real objects; "the toys are not capable of actually flying, or transporting people or supplies, like real helicopters."[31] Thus, the jury could properly have found the "Drop Copter" to be copyrightable.

With respect to the launcher handle, the plaintiff at trial presented (1) evidence that "Wild Copter" was registered with the Copyright Office within five years from first publication, and was thus entitled to the statutory presumption of copyright validity; and (2) expert testimony that "Wild Copter" could have been designed in "a million" other ways, "so long as the launching mechanism could fit inside."[32] The defendant failed to present "any expert testimony or other relevant evidence to prove that any functional elements of these toys were not subject to copyright protection, or to overcome the statutory presumption of validity of [the plaintiff's] 'Wild Copters' toy."[33]

In *Baby Buddies, Inc. v. Toys "R" Us, Inc.*,[34] the Eleventh Circuit affirmed a grant of summary judgment for defendant Toys "R" Us, holding that there was no substantial similarity between the parties' works. Plaintiff Baby Buddies had registered copyright in its teddy bear pacifier holder. Toys "R" Us carried the plaintiff's pacifier holder in its stores until it created its own version. Baby Buddies then sued for copyright

---

[28]*Id.* at *11–15.

[29]375 Fed. Appx. 705 (9th Cir. 2010).

[30]*Id.* at 710.

[31]*Id.*

[32]*Id.* at 710–11.

[33]*Id.* at 711 (citation omitted).

[34]611 F.3d 1308 (11th Cir. 2010).

infringement. The district court held that various elements of plaintiff's work, including the ribbon, clip, and tether, were functional in nature, and thus could not be protected. After comparing the copyrightable aspects of the plaintiff's pacifier holder to defendant's, the district court found that no issue of material fact remained, and granted summary judgment for Toys "R" Us. Baby Buddies appealed. Because the defendant had access to the plaintiff's work, the Eleventh Circuit considered only substantial similarity. The court evaluated only the nonfunctional aspects of the pacifier holder, which it determined were the teddy bear and the bow, in agreement with the district court's determinations. The court then determined that the plaintiff's bear was smaller, more finely sculpted, and more clearly defined, while the defendant's bear was taller, more bloated, less detailed, and more crudely made; accordingly, "no properly instructed juror could find these bears substantially similar."[35]

3. Depictions of Nature

[Add the following text at the end of the section.]

Applying a similar analysis, the Tenth Circuit held that so-called "wire frame" digital representations of cars were not copyrightable under *Feist.* In *Meshwerks, Inc. v. Toyota Motor Sales U.S.A., Inc.,*[36] the Tenth Circuit affirmed a district court grant of summary judgment that digital models of cars and trucks were not sufficiently original for copyright protection. Toyota's ad agency hired Meshwerks to assist in creating digital models of Toyota vehicles for use in animated television commercials. To digitize, Meshwerks took measurements of the vehicles by covering them with a grid of tape and running an articulated arm linked to a computer over the vehicle to measure all the points of intersection in the grid, generating a digital image resembling a wire-frame model. Meshwerks fine-tuned the computer-generated lines manually to make the result resemble the original vehicle as closely as possible, and recreated details such as wheels, headlights, door handles, and the Toyota emblem by hand to create two-dimensional wire-frame depictions of the vehicles that appeared three-dimensional on screen.

Meshwerks alleged that it contracted for a single use of models, but the defendants reused and redistributed the models in numerous other media. The district court granted summary judgment to the defendants, finding that wire-frame models were mere copies of the original vehicles, not sufficiently original to warrant copyright protection, and that Meshwerks' "intent" was to replicate the vehicles as closely as possible. The court analogized to photography, "applying to digital modeling the same legal principles that have come, in the fullness of time and with an enlightened eye, to apply to photographs and other media."[37] Authors of photographs are entitled to copyright protection only for

---

[35] *Id.* at 1319.

[36] 528 F.3d 1258, 87 USPQ2d 1055 (10th Cir. 2008).

[37] *Id.* at 1270.

the "incremental contribution" represented by their interpretation or expression of the objects depicted.[38]

The plaintiff's models, the court found, "are not so much independent creations as (very good) copies of Toyota's vehicles."[39] The court relied on (1) its objective assessment of particular models and (2) the parties' purpose in creating them. The court found that the models depicted "unadorned Toyota vehicles—the car as car."[40] Meshwerks made no decisions regarding lighting, shading, background, and so forth. When the unadorned, unprotectable images of vehicles are filtered out, no copyrightable matter is left. Meshwerks had nothing to do with the designing of the vehicles, at least six of which were still covered by design patents; on the other hand, the use of the models in advertising, including the addition of backgrounds, lighting, angles, and colors, was done by parties other than Meshwerks.

Under *Feist*, the models were held unoriginal in that they were "copied from other works"; the fact that a work in one medium was copied from a work in another medium does not render it any less a "copy." Somewhat more questionably, the court observed that Meshwerks' intent provided additional support for the court's conclusion; if an artist affirmatively sets out to make a copy of someone else's creation, rather than to create an original work, it is far more likely that that result will be unoriginal. Here the parties intended to have Meshwerks create base-layer digital models to which the original and creative elements seen in the actual finished advertisements would be added by others. "Digital modeling can be, surely is being, and no doubt increasingly will be used to create copyrightable expressions,"[41] the court stated. However, Meshwerks' models "expressed" only the depiction of "vehicles *as* vehicles."[42]

In *Lucky Break Wishbone Corp. v. Sears Roebuck & Co.*,[43] the Ninth Circuit affirmed a district court's finding that a plastic wishbone design met the minimal *Feist* standard of originality. The court cited testimony (1) by the author of the sculptural work that he "manipulated the graphite electrodes by hand to make the wishbone 'all nice and round and smooth,' or as he later explained it, 'more attractive and sleek looking [than an actual wishbone].' He sanded down 'sharp areas,' rounded the head of the wishbone, and 'thinned . . . up' the arms"; and (2) by an ornithological expert that the Lucky Break wishbone "had a number of elements that distinguished it from a natural wishbone and did not serve any functional purpose."[44] "[I]t was undisputed," the court stated, "that these multiple variations were the intentional product of [the author's]

---

[38]See discussion of photographs in this supplement in Chapter 2, sec. IV.C.

[39]*Id.* at 1264.

[40]*Id.* at 1265.

[41]*Id.* at 1269.

[42]*Id.* at 1270 (emphasis in original).

[43]No. 08-35933, 2010 U.S. App. LEXIS 7196 (9th Cir. Apr. 7, 2010).

[44]*Id.* at *3.

creativity and aesthetic design. They went beyond mere copying and did not serve a functional purpose; they were therefore sufficient to constitute original expression."[45] New evidence submitted on reconsideration did not present any issue of material fact and, accordingly, the court affirmed the district court's grant of summary judgment to Lucky Break on the question of originality.

IV. DERIVATIVE WORKS

B. "More Than Merely Trivial" Variation Standard

1. *Specific Applications*

e. *Characters*

[Add the following text at the end of the section.]

In *Halicki Films, LLC v. Sanderson Sales & Marketing*,[46] the Ninth Circuit applied character protection to the appearance of a car in an action film, and vacated the district court's grant of summary judgment dismissing the plaintiffs' copyright claim. In 1974, H.B. "Toby" Halicki directed, produced, acted in, and marketed the original movie, *Gone in 60 Seconds* ("Original GSS"). Original GSS featured "Eleanor," a yellow 1971 Fastback Ford Mustang customized to appear as a Mach 1 Fastback Mustang. After Toby Halicki's death, the plaintiff, Halicki's widow, obtained ownership of the 1971 Ford Mustang used to portray Eleanor and "all right, title and interest, including copyrights, of the film 'Gone in 60 Seconds' which were owned by [Toby Halicki]."[47] The plaintiff then began marketing Original GSS on video, set up a website, sold "Gone in 60 Seconds" baseball caps, licensed the Eleanor name and likeness for a line of toy cars, and exhibited the "Original Eleanor" at car shows.

"Remake Eleanor" was a 1967 Shelby GT-500, Ford Mustang variant developed by defendant Carroll Shelby with Ford Motor Company. Subsequently, defendant Unique Motorcars, Inc. began to manufacture, produce, and sell vehicles resembling the Remake Eleanor character. The plaintiff filed a complaint against the defendants based on their alleged unauthorized creation of "replicas of Eleanor from 'Gone in 60 Seconds,' " stating claims for, inter alia, copyright infringement. The district court granted the defendants' motion for summary judgment, finding, *inter alia*, that Halicki lacked standing to bring a claim for copyright infringement because she had no rights in Remake Eleanor, having transferred those rights pursuant to an agreement. On appeal, the defendants asserted that the Eleanor character did not qualify for copyright protection, relying on Ninth Circuit precedent that a character could be granted copyright protection only if it "constituted the story

---

[45] *Id.*

[46] 547 F.3d 1213, 89 USPQ2d 1001 (9th Cir. 2008).

[47] *Id.* at 1217.

being told."[48] Eleanor, the defendants argued, was not "the story being told" but was "simply a car." The court distinguished literary characters, which "are difficult to delineate and may be based on nothing more than an unprotected idea," from cartoon and comic book characters, which have "physical as well as conceptual qualities, [and are] more likely to contain some unique elements of expression."[49]

The Ninth Circuit has also recognized copyright protection for characters that are especially distinctive, and has found that copyright protection may be afforded to "characters visually depicted in a television series or movie" and to "[c]haracters that have received copyright protection [and] have displayed consistent, widely identifiable traits."[50] The defendants argued that, to the extent Eleanor could be regarded as a character, it was not sufficiently distinctive and therefore not deserving of copyright protection. The court reasoned that the Eleanor character can be seen as more akin to a comic book character than a literary character. Moreover, Eleanor "display[s] consistent, widely identifiable traits" and is "especially distinctive."[51] In both films, thefts of other cars go largely as planned, but whenever the main human character tries to steal Eleanor, circumstances "invariably become complicated."

In Original GSS, the main character says "I'm getting tired of stealing this Eleanor car"; in Remake GSS, the main character also refers to his history with Eleanor. The Ninth Circuit held that such a fact-intensive issue must be remanded to the district court for a finding in first instance as to whether Eleanor is entitled to copyright protection. "On remand the court should examine whether Eleanor's 'physical as well as conceptual qualities [and] . . . unique elements of expression' qualify Eleanor for copyright protection."[52]

C. Permission Requirement

[Add the following text at the end of the section.]

Although permission to make a derivative work is required to avoid infringing the underlying work, no separate permission to *register* the derivative work is needed. This proposition seems self-evident from the face of the statute, but it took a Seventh Circuit reversal to correct an errant district court ruling that had held the opposite. In *Schrock v. Learning Curve International, Inc.,*[53] the Seventh Circuit on November 5, 2009 issued a reversal that may help resolve—or at least defuse—a long-running debate about whether certain types of photographs are

---

[48] *See* Warner Bros. Pictures, Inc. v. Columbia Broad. Sys., Inc., 216 F.2d 945, 950, 104 USPQ 103, 107 (1954).

[49] *Halicki Films,* 547 F.3d at 1224 (citation omitted).

[50] *Id.* (citations omitted).

[51] *Id.* at 1225 (citations omitted).

[52] *Id.* (citation omitted).

[53] 586 F.3d 513, 92 USPQ2d 1694 (7th Cir. 2009). The author drafted an *amicus* brief to the Seventh Circuit urging reversal in *Schrock.*

derivative works. The photography cases have appeared to diverge as to three fundamental questions: (1) Is a photograph of a copyrighted work a derivative work at all? (the "Definition Question"); (2) Must such a derivative work exhibit a higher level of originality in order to qualify for copyright protection? (the "Originality Question"); (3) Must the creator of such a derivative work obtain separate specific permission to *register* his/her copyright, over and above the permission required to *create* the derivative work? (the "Permission Question").

The Seventh Circuit explicitly declined to answer the first of these questions in its *Schrock* reversal, but by clearly answering "no" to the other two, the new ruling greatly reduces the significance of the Definition Question. If a derivative work need not meet a higher originality threshold and need not obtain separate permission to register, it really should not matter very much, in most cases, whether the photo at issue is deemed a derivative work of its copyrighted subject or not. By answering "no" to the Originality Question and the Permission Question, moreover, the Seventh Circuit took a giant step (or two) away from its own previous 1983 decision in *Gracen v. Bradford Exchange*,[54] on which the district court had relied heavily (and erroneously) in *Schrock*. The result could be greater uniformity among the circuits and greater fidelity to the text of the Copyright Act, both of which suffered under at least some applications of *Gracen*.

Between 1999 and 2003, defendant Learning Curve retained the professional photographic services of Daniel Schrock to create "product shot" photos of toys being sold by Learning Curve, notably the popular "Thomas & Friends" toy trains and accessories. The photographs were used in print advertising, product packaging, and on the Internet. Schrock retained copyright in his photographs and licensed Learning Curve to use them for two years. After Learning Curve stopped using Schrock's services, it continued to use the photographs, in at least some cases continuing beyond the expiration of the two-year license.

Schrock sued in 2004, alleging copyright infringement as well as state-law claims. In 2008, the Northern District of Illinois granted summary judgment to Learning Curve, holding that Schrock's photographs were derivative works of the Learning Curve toys, and thus Schrock could not register his copyright in the photos without Learning Curve's permission. The district court held that Shrock, lacking a proper registration, had no cognizable copyright claim, and his federal action was dismissed. He was referred to state court to pursue whatever non-federal remedies might be available to him. Learning Curve had also argued below that Schrock's photos lacked sufficient originality to warrant copyright protection; the court declined to rule on that issue, finding it unnecessary to grant summary judgment in Learning Curve's favor.

---

[54]698 F.2d 300, 217 USPQ 1294 (7th Cir. 1983).

The district court's decision was derived largely from *Gracen v. Bradford Exchange*.[55] *Gracen* concerned an artist who entered a contest to create an image based on the classic MGM film version of *The Wizard of Oz*. The best design would be used as the basis for a collectible plate series to be sold by the defendant, Bradford Exchange. Plaintiff Gracen created the winning submission but then had a disagreement with Bradford and ultimately declined to allow her painting to be used. Bradford had another artist create a similar image, which prompted an infringement suit by Gracen.

Affirming the district court, the Seventh Circuit found in favor of Bradford Exchange. It held that the painting, which depicted a smiling Judy Garland-as-Dorothy walking on a yellow brick road in front of an Edenic landscape and a distant rainbow, lacked sufficient originality to be copyrightable. All of the elements were given by the film, and were not the products of Gracen's imagination; accordingly, "Miss Gracen's painting, whatever its artistic merit, is not an original derivative work within the meaning of the Copyright Act."[56]

Gracen's holding on the Originality Question was accompanied by additional discussion of the Permission Question. Specifically, the *Gracen* appeals court noted that Gracen had been allowed to create her derivative painting under the rules of the contest, but had never been given permission (either by Bradford Exchange or the movie studio) to claim her own copyright in the painting: "Even if [Gracen] was authorized to exhibit her derivative works, she may not have been authorized to copyright them."[57] Expanding upon *Gracen*, the district court in *Schrock* found this lack of "permission to register" a sufficient basis for resolving the case in the defendant's favor.

Schrock appealed. As the Seventh Circuit summarized, he argued that:

> the district judge mistakenly classified his photos as derivative works and misread or misapplied *Gracen*. He contends that his photos are not derivative works, and even if they are, his copyright is valid and enforceable because he had permission from Learning Curve to photograph the underlying copyrighted works and his photos contained sufficient incremental original expression to qualify for copyright. . . . Learning Curve defend[s] the district court's determination that the photos are derivative works and argue[s] that the court properly read *Gracen* to require permission to copyright as well as permission to make the derivative works. Alternatively, [defendants] maintain that Schrock's photographs contain insufficient originality to be copyrightable . . .[58]

The Seventh Circuit's analysis dealt most extensively with the Originality Question: Were Schrock's "product shot" photos original enough to support a separate copyright? The district court had made no finding

---

[55] *Id.*

[56] *Id.* at 305.

[57] *Id.* at 303–04.

[58] *Schrock*, 586 F.3d at 517.

on the issue, but, "to clarify another aspect of *Gracen* that is prone to misapplication,"[59] the Seventh Circuit conducted a thorough review of recent cases addressing originality in the photography context. In the course of this analysis, the court flatly rejected the defendant's *Gracen*-based argument that "as derivative works, [the plaintiff's] photos are subject to a higher standard of originality."[60]

Although *Gracen* itself states that a derivative work must be "substantially different from the underlying work to be copyrightable,"[61] the Seventh Circuit explained in *Schrock* that this language must not be read "out of context" to imply a more demanding test for derivative works than for any other works of authorship. It noted that *Gracen* relied on and applied the Second Circuit's ruling in *L. Batlin & Son v. Snyder*[62] that a derivative work need only contain "more than a merely trivial variation" on a prior work.[63] *Gracen* was in turn applied in the Seventh Circuit by *Bucklew v. Hawkins, Ash, Baptie & Co.*,[64] which articulated the test as whether the derivative work could be "readily distinguished from" prior work.[65] The *Schrock* court summarized:

> We think *Gracen* must be read in light of *L. Batlin*, on which it relied, and *Bucklew*, which followed it. And doing so reveals the following general principles: (1) the originality requirement for derivative works is not more demanding than the originality requirement for other works; and (2) the key inquiry is whether there is sufficient nontrivial expressive variation in the derivative work to make it distinguishable from the underlying work in some meaningful way. This focus on the presence of nontrivial "distinguishable variation" adequately captures the concerns articulated in *Gracen* without unduly narrowing the copyrightability of derivative works.[66]

This articulation of the rule is difficult to fault, but it is equally difficult to resist the conclusion that *Gracen* has effectively been "contextualized" out of existence, at least with respect to the "substantially different" standard for derivative works. It is now clear, even in the Seventh Circuit, that "the originality requirement for derivative works is not more demanding than the originality requirement for other works."[67]

The *Schrock* court then turned to an even more problematic aspect of *Gracen*—the Permission Question—and repudiated it outright:

> The author of a derivative work must have permission to make the work from the owner of the copyright in the underlying work; *Gracen* suggested, however, that the author of a derivative work must *also* have permission to *copyright* it. [Citation omitted.] The district court relied on this language

---

[59] *Id.* at 516.

[60] *Id.* at 520.

[61] *Gracen*, 698 F.2d at 305.

[62] 536 F.2d 486, 189 USPQ 753 (2d Cir. 1976).

[63] *Id.* at 490 (internal quotation marks omitted).

[64] 329 F.3d 923, 66 USPQ2d 1820 (7th Cir. 2003).

[65] *Id.* at 929.

[66] *Schrock*, 586 F.3d at 521.

[67] *Id.*

from *Gracen* to conclude that Schrock has no copyright in his photos because he was not authorized by Learning Curve to copyright them. This was error.

First, *Gracen*'s language presupposing a permission-to-copyright requirement was dicta; the case was actually decided on nonoriginality grounds. [Citation omitted.] More importantly, the dicta was mistaken; there is nothing in the Copyright Act requiring the author of a derivative work to obtain permission to copyright his work from the owner of the copyright in the underlying work. To the contrary, the Act provides that copyright in a derivative work, like copyright in any other work, arises by operation of law once the author's original expression is fixed in a tangible medium.[68]

The court is clearly correct on both points: *Gracen*'s permission requirement was *dicta* and is wrong. *Gracen* itself characterized the point at the time as "an issue of fact that the district judge did not address, and that we therefore may have got wrong."[69] And it is unambiguously wrong by the plain terms of the 1976 Copyright Act: Under the statute, "copyright" is not a verb; once a work is created and fixed there is nothing further to be done. If an "original" derivative work is "fixed," then "copyright protection subsists" in that work under Section 102(a). The statute leaves no doubt that such a work is, from the moment of fixation, the subject of a subsisting copyright, not merely a work with some inchoate potential for copyright. The *Schrock* court therefore correctly emphasized that statutory copyright inheres in a fixed, original work by "operation of law" and not by way of permission from anyone else.[70]

Although the *Schrock* decision does not answer the Definition Question—is a photo of a copyrighted work a derivative work *vel non?*—it admirably dispels two pernicious aspects of *Gracen* as to originality and permission that could have done lasting damage to copyright law had they been allowed to stand. The debate about the Definition Question will no doubt continue, and may in some circumstances even alter the outcome of a case. But for now there would seem to be no legally relevant distinction between derivative works and any other works with respect to originality and registrability, and that should render the Definition Question largely moot for most copyright lawyers, most of the time.

---

[68] *Id.* at 523.

[69] *Gracen*, 698 F.2d at 304.

[70] The *Gracen* court's confusion may have arisen in part from the fact that the plaintiff's painting and drawings in that case were all 1909 Act works, as to which statutory copyright did not attach upon fixation. *See* Gracen v. Bradford Exch., 217 USPQ 936 (N.D. Ill. 1981) (reciting that works were registered in 1976 and 1977). The district court in *Gracen* incorrectly assumed, however, that the 1976 Act applied and the Seventh Circuit did the same on appeal without noting: (a) that the works at issue were created and registered prior to January 1, 1978; and (b) that the district court itself (correctly) applied the 1909 Act in its separate decision regarding statutory damages. Gracen v. Bradford Exch., 217 USPQ 940 (N.D. Ill. 1982). Under the 1909 Act, an author did not enjoy statutory copyright upon fixation, but had to register, or publish with proper notice, in order to obtain statutory copyright. There were thus extra steps Gracen had to take, apart from creating her derivative works, in order to own statutory copyright in them.

3

Ownership

I. Works Made for Hire

A. The 1909 Act and the "Instance and Expense" Test

1. Defining "Instance"

[Add the following text at the end of the section.]

On cross-motions for summary judgment, the district court in *Fifty-Six Hope Road Music Ltd. v. UMG Recordings, Inc.*[1] determined that the defendant record company was the statutory author of pre-January 1, 1978, sound recordings. The question before the court was whether the plaintiff, comprising survivors of reggae artist Bob Marley, or the defendant record company owned renewal rights in the recordings. The sound recordings were created under, and were governed by, the 1909 Copyright Act. Under the 1909 Act "instance and expense" test, the Second Circuit applies an "almost irrebuttable presumption that any person who paid another to create a copyrightable work was the statutory author under the 'work for hire' doctrine." The court found that the Marley recordings, according to the terms of multiple recording contracts, were works for hire that were made at the instance and expense of the defendant. The plaintiffs argued, unpersuasively, that Marley would have recorded his music without the inducement of a recording agreement. The court stated, however, that but for recording contracts between Marley and the defendant, these exact works would not have been created. The plaintiffs also argued that Marley exercised artistic control over his recordings, despite contractual provisions granting such rights to the defendant. The court found Marley's exercise of artistic control to be legally irrelevant to the statutory authorship question, as the defendant had a contractual right to accept, reject, modify, and otherwise control the works. Works were made at the defendant's expense because recording contracts provided that the defendant advanced recording costs to Marley, to be recouped only from royalties for the creation of the works.

---

[1]No. 08-6143, 2010 U.S. Dist. LEXIS 94500 (S.D.N.Y. Sept. 10, 2010).

B.   The 1976 Act

1.   *Type 1 Works*

a.   *Defining "Employee" and "Employer"*

iii.   Post-Reid

(1) Work Made for Hire Found

[Add the following text at the end of the section.]

In a recent software case, the *Reid* analysis was applied to find a work-made-for-hire employment relationship even in the *absence* of W-2 tax treatment. In *JustMed, Inc. v. Byce*,[2] Joel Just and Michael Byce worked on and off for several years creating software for use in a digital audio larynx device to create an artificial voice for laryngectomy patients. Byce, a computer programmer, worked on the project from 1994 until 1999, when his wife died and he stopped work on the project. No work was done on the project between 1999 and 2003. In February 2003, Just formed "JustMed, Inc." and started the project again, giving some shares in the new company to Byce. The only employees of the company were Just, his wife, and another programmer, all of whom were paid in shares of the company. In October 2004, Byce again began working on the project, and was paid in shares. In 2005, the project looked promising and it appeared that the company could be sold. Byce thought he did not have a sufficient number of shares, and took steps to recapture the source code from Just. A dispute ensued and a lawsuit was filed. Byce claimed a copyright interest in the work, and JustMed claimed it was a work made for hire under *CCNV v. Reid*. The court held that Byce was an employee of JustMed, and the code was a work made for hire.

The court focused on several factors: JustMed provided the instrumentalities, including previous code, units, chargers, and so forth; though Byce had worked on his own computer, JustMed offered to provide one; Byce communicated with Just on a regular basis regarding his progress and intended next steps, and Just tested the code; Byce was not hired for a specific period, but to work on the code, with no particular end date; Byce was not the sole JustMed employee to write code for the company; computer programming was part of the regular business of JustMed; and Byce was paid a regular salary, not a lump sum based on the project. Based on such factors, the court found that Byce was an employee and the source code was a work for hire. Significantly, however, Byce had not been issued W-2 forms, and no taxes or Social Security payments were withheld; the court did not remark on the anomaly of finding employee status under such facts.

The Ninth Circuit affirmed the finding that Byce was an employee,[3] noting that "the contemplated duration of the relationship, the tasks Byce

---

[2]84 USPQ2d 1174 (D. Idaho 2007).

[3]JustMed, Inc. v. Byce, 600 F.3d 1118 (9th Cir. 2010).

did for JustMed, the fact that Byce earned a salary from JustMed, and the nature of JustMed's business all support the finding that Byce was an employee."[4] The court explicitly noted that "we draw some guidance in weighing the factors from JustMed's status as a technology start-up company."[5] Byce's strongest argument turned on JustMed's tax treatment of Byce, as well as JustMed's failure to pay benefits and fill out appropriate employment forms. However, the court found that "JustMed's treatment of Byce with regard to taxes, benefits, and employment forms" was "more likely attributable to the start-up nature of the business than to Byce's alleged status as an independent contractor."[6]

b.   Defining "Within the Scope of Employment"

[Add the following text at the end of the section.]

Le v. City of Wilmington[7] offers a very cogent discussion of the "scope of employment" concept in a case involving a city employee who created computer code while employed as an information analyst. The plaintiff decided to attempt to develop a software program that would permit the defendant to electronically track citations the city had issued, rather than continue to rely on paper tickets. The plaintiff believed that if successful he could market the software to other municipalities. The plaintiff, who claimed that his supervisor forbade him from working on the program at work, received the authorization to install the software on the city's computer for testing and comment. After several years of testing and implementation, the city council passed a budget that eliminated the plaintiff's job. Three days later, the plaintiff applied to register copyright with the Copyright Office. Two weeks later, he removed the source code from the city's server. Suspended and threatened with prosecution, the plaintiff restored the source code, and was terminated. He then sued for copyright infringement; the city moved for summary judgment. In finding that the work had been made for hire, the court credited the plaintiff's claims that he worked on the program exclusively on his own time, but cited the rule that if a work was created in the scope of the plaintiff's employment, during his employment, and without a specific written agreement to the contrary, the work belonged to the employer. The court found that creation had been within the scope of employ-ment based on the facts that the work had been made to facilitate the city's business; the plaintiff's supervisor had assigned the plaintiff the task of developing software, based upon the plaintiff's skills discussed at his hiring interview, and the city closely supervised the plaintiff as to the project; the city instructed the plaintiff how the form should appear and gave him modifications; the city gave the plaintiff sample paper tickets containing information that needed to be captured in the electronic

---

[4] *Id.* at 1126.

[5] *Id.*

[6] *Id.* at 1128.

[7] 736 F. Supp. 2d 842 (D. Del. 2010).

version; city personnel gathered data for the program; meetings were held about the project, sometimes weekly; the software was tested and revised with assistance of other city personnel, who provided input to the plaintiff about the data the software would work with; the plaintiff admitted to making "small" changes to software at the suggestion of others and the software continued to be adjusted, even after the copyright was registered; the city's network was used for testing, the results of which were shared with city personnel; the plaintiff knew the city was using the software; the plaintiff acknowledged that he had reused code from files he had created for city programs and that he had created and fixed some of the source code at city premises; and the plaintiff had received an award and other recognition from the city for his service on the project.

i. Job Description

[Add the following text to the end of the section.]

The author's job description within his own company played a critical role in *Jules Jordan Video, Inc. v. 144942 Canada Inc.*[8] The plaintiff Gasper, an adult movie star who performed under the pseudonym "Jules Jordan," was president/sole shareholder of the plaintiff Jules Jordan Video (JJV) and the creator of videos in which he appeared. The plaintiffs sued the defendant video companies, alleging that the defendants copied and sold 13 copyrighted DVDs owned by JJV or Gasper that featured Gasper's performances. A jury in the district court returned a verdict for the plaintiffs on their copyright infringement claim, but the court granted the defendants' motion for judgment as a matter of law, concluding that neither Gasper nor JJV had standing to assert a copyright claim. The district court held that because Gasper was employed by JJV, his motion picture works were works for hire under the Copyright Act. Therefore, Gasper lacked standing since JJV, not Gasper, was the author of the motion picture works. The plaintiff appealed the district court's decision, arguing it was erroneous given that only Gasper or JJV could possibly own the copyrights, and both were the plaintiffs in the district court action. The Ninth Circuit held that the district court erred in holding that Gasper's motion pictures were works for hire. The problem with the district court's analysis, the Ninth Circuit reasoned, was that JJV was a "one-man shop," of which Gasper was "sole officer, director and shareholder," "exercised complete control over it," and "made all decisions concerning JJV and production of the films." Indeed, "[s]ince JJV was Gasper, JJV intended whatever Gasper intended, and if Gasper intended that his creative work be outside the scope of his employment with JJV, there was no one to disagree." The Ninth Circuit stated that "even if the films were works for hire, the district court was correct that Gasper simply made a mistake in listing himself as the author on the copyright registration forms. That mistake does not constitute a basis to invalidate the copyright. Inadvertent mistakes on registration certificates

---

[8]617 F.3d 1146 (9th Cir. 2010).

do not invalidate a copyright and thus do not bar infringement actions, unless ... the alleged infringer has relied to its detriment on the mistake, or the claimant intended to defraud the Copyright Office by making the misstatement."

iii. Serving Employer's Interests

[Add the following text to the end of the section.]

In *TAP Worldwide, LLC v. Becker*[9] the court illustrated that failure to establish any of the three elements of the scope-of-employment analysis will result in the failure of the argument. Defendant individual was hired by the plaintiff manufacturing company to manage export operations. While so employed, the defendant on his own developed a software Internet program to expedite processing. The plaintiff asserted that it, and not the defendant, owned rights to the work. Whether the program was a "work for hire" depended on whether it was created within the scope of employment. The plaintiff did fulfill the third prong of the analysis by showing that the defendant created the work largely for the purpose of serving the employer. However, because the first two prongs were not met, the plaintiff failed to prove ownership via the work-for-hire doctrine and, consequently, failed to prove a likelihood of success on the merits of its copyright infringement claim.

II. Transfer of Ownership

A. Fundamentals

[Add the following text at the end of the section.]

It has been held that a third party can sometimes use Section 204 to challenge the sufficiency of a writing to which it was not a party, but it must have compelling evidence that the parties to the writing dispute ownership, and courts will not make such a finding lightly. In *KB Home v. Antares Homes, Ltd.*,[10] for example, the court granted the plaintiff's motion for summary judgment as to ownership of copyright in architectural floor plans despite such a challenge by the defendants. The plaintiff acquired ownership by written transfer of business assets from a predecessor corporation, Royce. The defendants challenged the sufficiency of the writing under Section 204. The plaintiff argued that the defendants could not challenge the transfer because they were not party to the transaction, but the court refused to bar such a challenge per se. However, the court said it "is mindful that other courts have refused to allow a third-party infringer to raise similar ownership issues where there is no dispute between the copyright owner and the transferee."[11] Furthermore, the court reviewed the defendants' proffered evidence as

---

[9]No. 10-4903, 2010 U.S. Dist. LEXIS 78709 (C.D. Cal. July 12, 2010).

[10]83 USPQ2d 1341 (N.D. Tex. 2007).

[11]*Id.* at 1347.

to defects in the transfer documents and held the evidence insufficient, stating: "As alleged third-party infringers, Defendants have failed to show that the parties to the transfer dispute the ownership of the copyrights. Plaintiff has provided enough evidence for the court to determine under the facts before it, as a matter of law, that plaintiff owns the copyrights."[12]

The Ninth Circuit in *Fleischer Studios, Inc. v. A.V.E.L.A., Inc.*,[13] affirmed the district court's ruling that the plaintiff had failed to establish its ownership of copyrights in the Betty Boop character, and affirmed the district court's dismissal of the plaintiff's copyright infringement claim. The animated character Betty Boop was created by Max Fleischer, who subsequently sold his rights to Paramount Pictures. The plaintiff, a corporation established by descendants of Fleischer, alleged that it had repurchased rights in the Boop character, and brought a copyright infringement claim against the defendants, companies that licensed the Boop character for use on merchandise. The parties conceded the existence of separate copyrights in the Boop character. The plaintiff claimed to have acquired the Boop character copyright through following chain of title: Max Fleischer to Paramount Pictures to UM&M TV Corp. to National Telefilm Associates to Republic Pictures to the plaintiff. The court held that the plaintiff had failed to establish each link necessary for the alleged transfer because the contract between Paramount and UM&M explicitly carved out character copyrights and transferred only copyrights in the works containing such characters. Because the plaintiff had failed to raise its other chain of title theories on appeal, the Ninth Circuit, over a dissent, held that the plaintiff had not established ownership of the Boop character copyright and affirmed the district court's dismissal of the plaintiff's infringement claim.

D. Licensees and Assignments

[Add the following text at the end of the section.]

Although emails may satisfy the Section 204 requirement of a "signed writing,"[14] they must spell out the terms of the parties' agreement in sufficient detail, just as any other writing must. Thus the court in *Weinstein Co. v. Smokewood Entertainment Group, LLC*[15] granted the defendant's motion to dismiss a breach of contract claim based on the plaintiff's alleged acquisition of a license to distribute the defendant's motion picture. The plaintiff claimed that an email exchange following a breakfast meeting between the parties evidenced a binding agreement that was breached by the defendant when it subsequently agreed to license its rights to a

---

[12] *Id.*

[13] 636 F.3d 1115 (9th Cir. 2011).

[14] *See* 17 U.S.C. §204(a) ("A transfer of copyright ownership, other than by operation of law, is not valid unless an instrument of conveyance, or a note or memorandum of the transfer, is in writing and signed by the owner of the rights conveyed or such owner's duly authorized agent.").

[15] 664 F. Supp. 2d 332 (S.D.N.Y. 2009).

third party. The plaintiff alleged that it had obtained an express exclusive license and, alternatively, that it had acquired an implied nonexclusive license. The defendant filed a motion to dismiss, claiming that no license existed because it never communicated any form of agreement to the plaintiff. On the issue of the exclusive license, the court cited the Section 204(a) requirement "through a signed writing that clearly (though perhaps succinctly) evidences the parties' rights and responsibilities" to transfer copyright ownership.[16] Alleged oral communications were held to be invalid for purposes of this express license, and the parties' written emails contained no written agreement spelling out the necessary terms, the court stated. The defendant's emails contained only cautionary language that the defendant had to check on certain terms and would call the plaintiff back later. The court held that "[i]f a copyright owner's intention in writing is unclear—even deliberately so—there is no legally valid transfer," and that "[w]ithout language indicating finality, §204(a) is not satisfied."[17] A nonexclusive implied license must be based in part on the licensee's requesting creation of the work, the court noted. Here, the motion picture at issue had already been made, so the plaintiff could not possibly have been requesting its creation. Moreover, the plaintiff's own allegations in emails purported to show that it had obtained "exclusive worldwide distribution rights," thus controverting the notion that the plaintiff had obtained a nonexclusive implied license.[18] The court accordingly granted the defendant's motion to dismiss.

Courts still frequently apply the principle that contracts transferring rights under copyright should be interpreted to leave rights with the copyright owner unless they are specifically transferred. For example, in *Mason v. Jamie Music Publishing Co.*,[19] the Southern District of New York granted the plaintiff's motion for declaratory judgment of copyright ownership and denied the defendant's counterclaim for declaratory judgment of copyright ownership. The plaintiff, author of a 1962 song entitled "Yes I'm Ready," intervened in the defendant music publisher's infringement action against third parties and filed a motion seeking declaratory judgment that she owned the copyright in the composition.

In 1965, the plaintiff and the defendant had entered into a Songwriter's Agreement whereby the plaintiff assigned to the defendant copyright in subsequent compositions and also copyright in certain prior compositions identified in an exhibit to Songwriter's Agreement. The exhibit was omitted from the Songwriter's Agreement, however, so "Yes I'm Ready" was not named in the agreement.

The defendant argued that the plaintiff nevertheless assigned copyright in the subject composition to the defendant through the Songwriter's Agreement. The court disagreed, holding " 'transfer agreements

---

[16]*Id.* at 348.

[17]*Id.* at 341, 342.

[18]*Id.* at 342.

[19]658 F. Supp. 2d 571 (S.D.N.Y. 2009).

should be construed in favor of copyright transferor because section 204(a) reflects [Congress'] policy judgment that copyright owners should retain all rights unless specifically transferred.' "[20] The Songwriter's Agreement did not specifically identify the subject composition, and the ambiguity created by the omission of the exhibit, purportedly identifying prior compositions assigned to the defendant, had to be construed in favor of the plaintiff. The court found unpersuasive the defendant's argument that extrinsic evidence of royalty payments to the plaintiff for exploitation of the composition was proof of assignment. Such evidence, the court stated, was equally indicative of a mere license. The plaintiff's endorsement of royalty checks that did not reference "copyright" was likewise insufficient to satisfy the signed writing requirement for transfer of ownership. Accordingly, the court concluded that copyright was not assigned to the defendant under the Songwriter's Agreement.

III. Joint Works and Co-Ownership

A. Copyrightable Contribution

[Add the following text at the end of the section.]

Merely receiving credit as the "producer" of a song does not establish joint authorship. In *Sebastian Music Group, Inc. v. Ayala-Rodriguez*[21] the plaintiffs, the music publisher Sebastian and DJ Eliel (an "urban music Disc Jockey, producer and composer") sought a declaration that DJ Eliel was the co-author of two musical works, "Lo que Paso, Paso" and "Cuentame," for which defendant Ramon Luis Ayala-Rodriguez (a/k/a "Daddy Yankee") had filed copyright registrations claiming sole authorship. The plaintiffs moved for summary judgment on the issue of joint authorship. The court found that there were factual issues as to DJ Eliel's participation and whether he made independently copyrightable contributions to the two musical works. The plaintiffs asserted that DJ Eliel composed the music and the melody for the works, and used musical instruments to play music added to Ayala-Rodriguez's lyrics; the defendants argued that music for these works was composed by others, and that DJ Eliel's contribution was limited to musical arrangement.

The court found that the parties' inconsistent sworn statements created factual conflicts. It held that the album's designation of DJ Eliel as "producer" did not prove that DJ Eliel's contribution was independently copyrightable, "as the word 'producer' can refer to varying degrees of involvement, including situations where the producer's role does not include any original creative contribution."[22]

---

[20] *Id.* at 581 (quoting Papa's-June Music, Inc. v. McLean, 921 F. Supp. 1154, 1160 (S.D.N.Y. 1996)).

[21] 594 F. Supp. 2d 176 (D.P.R. 2008).

[22] *Id.* at 180.

A panel of the Seventh Circuit was divided as to whether small changes to the lyrics of a song were independently copyrightable for co-authorship purposes in *Janky v. Lake County Convention & Visitors Bureau.*[23] The circuit court reversed the district court's grant of summary judgment to the plaintiff on that issue. The plaintiff, a member of a doo-wop group called Stormy Weather, wrote a song promoting Lake County, Indiana for the defendant, a local tourism bureau, and registered copyright in the composition. The plaintiff then showed the song to Farag, another member of the group. After discussion with the bureau, Farag suggested certain lyric changes to the plaintiff to focus on Lake County specifically instead of Indiana in general, and to reference "Chicago's neighboring south shore" and Lake County's ethnic diversity.[24] The plaintiff incorporated Farag's suggestions into the song and registered copyright in the revised composition, naming Farag as a co-author. Farag issued a nonexclusive license to the bureau, which used the song in various ways to promote Lake County. Subsequently, the plaintiff filed for correction of the second registration to have Farag's name as co-author removed. The plaintiff then sued the bureau for copyright infringement, and a jury awarded plaintiff $100,000 in damages. At issue on appeal was whether the revised composition was a joint work (as the bureau claimed) or the work of the plaintiff as sole author. The majority found that Farag's contributions were copyrightable—although if they were any less, they might not have been. In a dissenting opinion, Judge Ripple disagreed with the majority's analysis and found that Farag's contributions "do not rise above mere ideas, refinements, and suggestions," and thus are not independently copyrightable.[25]

B.   Intent

2.   *Larson Indicia*

a.   *Control*

[Add the following text at the end of the section.]

A Virginia district court recently adopted the test for joint authorship applied in the Second Circuit and Seventh Circuit, rejecting the current Ninth Circuit standard with its more demanding requirement of control. In *Berman v. Johnson,*[26] the court granted plaintiff Maura Flynn's motion for a declaratory judgment declaring the plaintiff to be joint author of the documentary film *Your Mother Kills Animals* (YMKA), based upon jury findings that "each of the putative authors (1) made independently copyrightable contributions to the work; and (2) fully intended

---

[23]576 F.3d 356 (7th Cir. 2009).

[24]*Id.* at 360.

[25]*Id.* at 365 (Ripple, J., dissenting) (internal quotations and citation omitted).

[26]518 F. Supp. 2d 791, 84 USPQ2d 1599 (E.D. Va. 2007).

to be co-authors."[27] The plaintiff and defendant Curt Johnson initially agreed to co-produce two documentary films, one focusing on smoking issues and one focusing on PETA and animal rights. Evidence indicated that the parties were partners and had viewed the films as a common project. However, following a dispute between the parties regarding the content of the film focusing on animal rights, the defendant ultimately ceased all communication with the plaintiff. The defendant subsequently released the film with a significantly different focus, primarily devoted to a favorable portrayal of the animal rights group "Stop Huntingdon Animal Cruelty."

The plaintiff brought a declaratory action requesting that she be declared a joint author of YMKA. The defendant argued that the plaintiff was not an "author," citing to the Ninth Circuit decision in *Aalmuhammed v. Lee*,[28] which held that joint authorship requires, in part, that the party demonstrate control over creation of the work. The *Berman* court, noting a "circuit split regarding the requirements for joint authorship," rejected the Ninth Circuit approach and adopted the rule of the Second Circuit in *Larson* and the Seventh Circuit in *Erickson v. Trinity Theatre, Inc.*,[29] which requires only that putative authors each make an independently copyrightable contribution and fully intend to be co-authors. The court found the Ninth Circuit rule susceptible to inequitable manipulation, as it would allow the defendant to establish sole ownership by wrongfully preventing the plaintiff from exercising control. Accordingly, the court declared the plaintiff a joint author.

In *Huurman v. Foster*,[30] the district court denied the plaintiff's motion for summary judgment on a request for a declaration that she was the exclusive owner of copyright in an educational motion picture, finding a triable issue as to whether the parties intended to enter into a joint authorship relationship. The defendant invited the plaintiff to participate in production of a Chinese-language educational movie. The movie was filmed over three days at the defendant's home, with subsequent voice recordings and retakes recorded at the plaintiff's home. The defendant and her daughter acted in the movie and recorded the English audio component. The plaintiff filmed and recorded the movie's audio tracks, and edited the film. The court found the record silent as to which party exercised final decision-making authority on filming and editing, though the defendant and her daughter signed a "model release" waiving "any right to impact or approve the finished product." Neither the defendant nor the plaintiff was conclusively credited in the movie. When the work was completed, the plaintiff, without the defendant's knowledge, obtained federal copyright registration as the sole author of "all video footage,

---

[27] *See id.* at 797 (quoting Thomson v. Larson, 147 F.3d 195, 200, 47 USPQ2d 1065 (2d Cir. 1998)).

[28] 202 F.3d 1227, 53 USPQ2d 1661 (9th Cir. 2000).

[29] 13 F.3d 1061, 29 USPQ2d 1347 (7th Cir. 1994).

[30] No. 07-9326, 2010 U.S. Dist. LEXIS 61454 (S.D.N.Y. June 21, 2010).

sound recording and visual design, sounds, artworks and effects." The defendant subsequently demanded the return of the master copy of the movie, and the plaintiff brought the action seeking declaration of her sole ownership of copyright in same. The Second Circuit has held that, absent a written agreement establishing joint authorship, the co-claimant bears the burden of establishing that each co-author made more than a de minimis independent contribution of protected expression to the work, and fully intended to be co-authors. To determine the parties' intent, the court must weigh the facts of each case, including (1) the contributors' decision-making authority; (2) the manner in which the parties bill or credit themselves; and (3) the parties' written agreements with third parties. The presumption of ownership created by the plaintiff's copyright registration certificate listing her as sole owner was overcome by the material factual disputes contained in the record, including inconclusive credits on the movie and the existence of a settlement agreement with a third party relating to the movie signed by both the plaintiff and the defendant. Thus, summary judgment was denied.

C. Joint Authorship Versus Joint Ownership

[Add the following text at the end of the section.]

A recent Tennessee decision deals with the uncommon situation in which a co-author claims to be a beneficial owner of copyright in a work. In *Severe Records, LLC v. Rich*,[31] the court dismissed the plaintiff's claim of copyright infringement against a co-author defendant, finding that the co-author was not a "beneficial owner"—" 'an author who had parted with legal title to the copyright in exchange for percentage royalties based on sales or license fees.' "[32] While the co-author was a beneficial owner with respect to the other defendants in the action, she was not a beneficial owner with respect to the plaintiff. She was instead a full co-owner and "a claim of infringement cannot lie against a co-owner of a copyright or its licensees."[33]

D. Distinguishing Joint Works From Collective Works and Derivative Works

2. *Derivative Works*

[Add the following text at the end of the section.]

Conversely, being the co-author of an underlying work does not necessarily give rise to co-authorship of a later derivative work. In *Richlin v. Metro-Goldwyn-Mayer Pictures, Inc.*,[34] the Ninth Circuit affirmed a

---

[31]93 USPQ2d 1404 (M.D. Tenn. 2009).

[32]*Id.* at 1407 (quoting Fantasy, Inc. v. Fogerty, 654 F. Supp. 1129, 1131 (N.D. Cal. 1987)).

[33]*Id.*

[34]531 F.3d 962, 87 USPQ2d 1088 (9th Cir. 2008).

district court's holding that the plaintiffs had no legitimate interest in the copyrighted motion picture *The Pink Panther*. The plaintiffs, heirs of the late author Maurice Richlin, had sued the defendant motion picture company, claiming, inter alia, that Richlin was a co-author of the film, since he was a co-author of a treatment that was incorporated into the movie. Copyright for the movie was renewed in 1991 by the defendants, whereupon the plaintiffs sued, claiming co-authorship. The district court granted the defendants summary judgment on the issue, and the plaintiffs appealed.

The Ninth Circuit held that while Richlin was a co-author of the treatment, that was not determinative under Section 101 to give him rights as a co-author of the subsequent motion picture: "[T]he Treatment is not the appropriate reference point. The Richlin heirs' claim for declaratory relief and an accounting rests on their argument that, by virtue of his contribution to the Treatment, Richlin is coauthor of the Motion Picture. Thus, the work that must be examined to determine joint authorship is the Motion Picture, not the Treatment. The plain language of §101 does not shed light on whether Richlin was a coauthor of the Motion Picture. Applying the *Aalmuhammed* factors to Richlin's involvement in the Motion Picture, however, confirms that Richlin and [Blake] Edwards were not coauthors of that work."[35] Under the first factor of the Ninth Circuit's joint-authorship standard of *Aalmuhammed v. Lee*,[36] the plaintiff's assignment showed no evidence that Richlin intended to become a co-author of the motion picture. Under the second, more important factor, regarding Richlin's supposed control of the motion picture work, the evidence overwhelmingly favored the defendants, in that Richlin had no supervisory power over the motion picture. With both of these factors favoring the defendants, the third factor, relating to the audience appeal of the work being tied to the plaintiff, became moot.

IV. CONTRACTS AND LICENSES

A.   Exclusive Versus Non-Exclusive Licenses

2.   *Non-Exclusive Licenses*

b.   *Non-Exclusive Implied License Doctrine*

[Add the following text at the end of the section.]

Implied licenses can also be found to arise from the sale of shares in a business entity. In *Estate of Hevia v. Portrio Corp.*,[37] the First Circuit affirmed the dismissal of an infringement action in which the plaintiff estate claimed that the defendant, decedent's business partner, infringed the plaintiff's copyright in an architectural design. The decedent and

---

[35] *Id.* at 968–69.

[36] 202 F.3d at 1234, 53 USPQ2d at 1666 (9th Cir. 2000).

[37] 602 F.3d 34 (1st Cir. 2010).

the defendant had jointly participated in various real estate ventures and formed various companies, including a company that owned rights to a planned residential community in Puerto Rico. Immediately before the decedent's death, the decedent transferred all his rights and shares in the company, including the architectural plans, to a trust for the benefit of his children. The trust subsequently sold all its shares to the defendant corporation. The estate claimed it still owned the architectural plans, and that the defendant had to obtain the estate's permission to use the plans. The estate registered copyright in the plans, and subsequently sued the defendant for infringement based on the defendant's use of the plans to build the residential community without the plaintiff's permission.

The defendant argued that it had obtained an implied nonexclusive license upon its purchase of the plaintiff's shares. The First Circuit held that a key aspect of any implied nonexclusive license is the grantor's intent. To determine intent, the court looked to factors such as "whether the licensee requested the work, whether the creator made and delivered that work, and whether the creator intended that the licensee would copy and make use of the work."[38] Because the decedent and the defendant had worked together in hopes of developing the residential community, and their relationship was partially founded on consummating the project, there was a sufficient showing of intent to grant a license to the defendant company to do whatever it took to finish building the residential community.

In *Credit Bureau Connection, Inc. v. Pardini,*[39] the district court granted a motion for a temporary restraining order, finding that the declaratory plaintiff established a likelihood of success on its copyright infringement claim due to a likely finding of implied license and a likelihood of irreparable injury in the absence of an injunction. The plaintiff Credit Bureau Connection (CBC) and the defendant Data Consultants were each in the business of providing finance and insurance software to car dealerships. At one point, CBC and Data Consultants pooled their assets, and CBC became a joint venture. CBC began to work with Darin Larsen, a computer consultant with Data Consultants. Larsen, on behalf of CBC, developed a web-based software system called eF&I Complete (eF&I), which integrated credit reporting services and financial and insurance systems services, the development of which was paid for entirely by CBC. Both CBC and Data Consultants marketed eF&I under their individual names and for their own account, entering into multiple agreements through which CBC and Data Consultants became jointly obligated to provide and support eF&I software. Thereafter, CBC and Data Consultants agreed to separate due to an unrelated conflict. Despite an agreement that both companies would retain access to eF&I, Data Consultants converted the software by blocking CBC's access to features necessary to demonstrate the software to add new customers and service existing

---

[38] *Id.* at 42.
[39] 726 F. Supp. 2d 1107 (E.D. Cal. 2010).

customers. CBC brought the action seeking a temporary restraining order, inter alia, prohibiting Data Consultants from restricting CBC's access to eF&I. Analyzing the ownership issues, the court ruled that a finder of fact was likely to find an implied license. CBC engaged and worked closely with Data Consultants' programmer to create the software. Data Consultants delivered the software to CBC, intending that CBC copy and distribute the software. CBC thereafter enjoyed unlimited use of, and access to, the software, until the dispute arose. CBC thus established a likelihood of success on its claim that it had an unlimited implied license to use the eF&I software, and also separately established a likelihood of irreparable harm.

As noted above, an implied license is generally revocable at will, unless consideration has been paid. In *Nearstar, Inc. v. Waggoner,*[40] the court observed, though arguably in dicta, that continued at-will employment does not constitute sufficient consideration to support an irrevocable license. The defendant performed all original work on the Dataserver computer program prior to forming the plaintiff company and, upon leaving, asserted a claim of copyright infringement based on the plaintiff's continued use of Dataserver. The plaintiff asserted an implied license to copy, modify, sell, and distribute Dataserver without any restriction or limitation. No permissions granted the plaintiff relating to Dataserver were ever memorialized in writing or verbalized. The court noted that a nonexclusive license may be granted orally, or may be implied from conduct. A nonexclusive license may be irrevocable if supported by consideration. The court held that there was no implied license since there was no evidence that the plaintiff requested creation of Dataserver, and there was no evidence that the defendant created Dataserver for the plaintiff and delivered it to the plaintiff. The court also held that even if there was an implied license, the plaintiff failed to offer sufficient evidence to establish as a matter of law that the defendant received consideration to support an irrevocable license. The court noted that continued at-will employment does not constitute sufficient consideration to support an irrevocable license.

In *Teter v. Glass Onion, Inc.,*[41] the plaintiff individual entered into an oral agreement with the defendant whereby the plaintiff agreed to sell his paintings to the defendant's gallery. The Agreement continued until the plaintiff sent a proposed written agreement to the defendant outlining new terms. The defendant claimed an oral agreement was in place, and refused to agree to the written terms. The plaintiff then demanded that the defendant remove copyrighted images of the plaintiff's art from its website; the defendant claimed it had the right to post "thumbnail" images of artwork to advertise. The plaintiff subsequently initiated suit for, among other claims, copyright infringement. Both parties moved for summary judgment. The court held that the plaintiff clearly held

---

[40]No. 09-218, 2011 U.S. Dist. LEXIS 20736 (E.D. Tex. Mar. 2, 2011).

[41]723 F. Supp. 2d 1138 (W.D. Mo. 2010).

copyright in the paintings, and the defendant clearly reproduced images of the paintings for its website, constituting copying. The defendant pled affirmative defenses, including implied license. Here the court held that an implied license did exist, as the plaintiff never objected to or restricted the use of works sold to the defendant. However, further examination required an evaluation of whether the license included permission for the defendant to make copies for online display, and whether that license was subsequently revoked. On these issues, the court held there were fact issues to be determined, and summary judgment for either party was inappropriate. However, the court granted summary judgment for the plaintiff in connection with all copying performed by the defendant after the plaintiff sent the letter that explicitly revoked permission to use images on the defendant's website.

i.   Issues of Fact

[Add the following text to the end of the section.]

The district court in *Techsavies, LLC v. WDFA Marketing Inc.*,[42] denied the defendant's motion for summary judgment on its copyright infringement claim. The plaintiff and the defendant entered into an oral agreement that the plaintiff was to develop a software program based on the defendant's idea, to be used by the defendant for marketing purposes. The plaintiff developed the software program, but the parties disagreed as to the terms of use of the software and its source code by the defendant. While the defendant conceded that the plaintiff owned copyright in the software, the defendant argued that, as a matter of law, it had an implied license to use the software, including its source code, in accordance with the Ninth Circuit's holding in *Asset Marketing Systems, Inc. v. Gagnon.*[43] The plaintiff disagreed, arguing that under *Asset Marketing* the plaintiff never "delivered" software to the defendant and did not intend for the defendant to have a license to the software and its source code. The court found that because the plaintiff always maintained control of the source code on its computers, the plaintiff had not "delivered" software to the defendant. The court also found that the record supported a finding of the plaintiff's intent to deny licensing of the software's source code, because the plaintiff never permitted the defendant to have any access to the source code; the plaintiff itself modified the source code in response to the defendant's requests but without the defendant's participation; and the defendant hired computer programmers to write a new version of the software so it could have access to the source code. The court concluded that it could not find, as a matter of law, that the plaintiff intended to grant an implied license to the defendant. The court reasoned further that, notwithstanding its findings regarding the existence of an implied license, a genuine dispute remained as to whether the defendant exceeded the license's scope by hiring computer programmers to

---

[42]No. 10-1213, 2011 U.S. Dist. LEXIS 13259 (N.D. Cal. Feb. 10, 2011).

[43]542 F.3d 748 (9th Cir. 2008).

gain full control of the copyrighted source code. Accordingly, the court denied the defendant's summary judgment motion.

B.   General Principles of Construction for Copyright Agreements

1.   *Scope of Licenses*

[Add the following text at the end of the section.]

In *Latimer v. Roaring Toyz, Inc.*,[44] the Eleventh Circuit rejected the defendants' argument that the plaintiff's photographs of customized motorcycles were unauthorized derivative works of artwork painted on the motorcycles; the artist knew that the artwork would be displayed for maximum public exposure, and therefore was held to have granted an implied license for such photographs. In connection with the unveiling of the model ZX-14 sport motorcycle, defendant Kawasaki engaged defendant Roaring Toyz to customize its ZX-14 motorcycles. Roaring Toyz hired independent painter Hathaway to apply custom paint and graphics to motorcycles. The plaintiff photographer Latimer was retained by Kawasaki to photograph the customized motorcycles. Latimer subsequently granted permission to Kawasaki to use his copyrighted photos at a press event but claimed that the authorization was limited to use in a screen presentation. During the press event, Kawasaki distributed press kits with digital images of Latimer's photographs to about 30 members of the media, including a representative of *Cycle World* magazine, owned by defendant Hachette. *Cycle World* subsequently published Latimer's photographs in conjunction with an article. Roaring Toyz also displayed Latimer's photographs on its website.

Latimer brought an action for copyright infringement based upon the uses by Roaring Toyz, Kawasaki, and Hachette. The defendants argued, inter alia, that Latimer's photographs were "unauthorized derivative works based upon protectable preexisting works"—i.e., Hathaway's artwork on motorcycles.[45] The Eleventh Circuit affirmed the rejection of this "unauthorized derivative works" argument, finding that the artist Hathaway knew his work would be publicly displayed and photographed, and therefore had granted an implied license to Kawasaki and Roaring Toyz, and that the license extended to Latimer because his photographs were taken at the direction of Roaring Toyz. In light of its finding that the photographs were authorized, the court declined to decide whether they were derivative works of Hathaway's paintings. The Eleventh Circuit nevertheless reversed the district court's grant of summary judgment to Kawasaki, finding that, while Latimer granted Kawasaki an implied license to use his photographs, Kawasaki may have exceeded the scope of the implied license by including the photos in digital format in the

---

[44]601 F.3d 1224 (11th Cir. 2010).

[45]*Id.* at 1231.

press kits. Finding issues of material fact, the court remanded for further proceedings.

3. *Defects in Formation of the Contract*

[Add the following text at the end of the section.]

In *Fodere v. Lorenzo*,[46] the dispute centered on the meaning of the term "publicidad," which Spanish-speaking negotiators for the parties agreed they both had used to describe permissible uses of certain photographs. The defendant, a supplier of marble and quartz, hired the plaintiff photographer to photograph a kitchen featuring the defendant's stone. The plaintiff claimed that the defendant's use of the photographs in a magazine advertisement was beyond the scope of rights granted. The parties cross-moved for summary judgment, with the defendants claiming a license. The court held in favor of the defendant, and dismissed the action. The court found that the parties had entered into an oral agreement prior to the taking of the photographs, contemplating a nonexclusive license. Whether the copyright owner has granted a nonexclusive license is governed by state contract law, which under governing Florida law can be oral. The oral agreement satisfied the basic requirements of offer, acceptance, and consideration, the sole disputed element being whether there had been sufficient specification of essential terms. The defendant submitted evidence that "publicidad" translates as "advertising," while the plaintiff argued, without evidence outside her own deposition testimony, that the term has a second meaning, "publicity." The court took judicial notice that "publicidad" translates as "advertising." The court dismissed the plaintiff's argument, finding it to be based upon a single ambiguous statement in her deposition, finding such a "mere scintilla" of evidence insufficient to defeat summary judgment. The court also dismissed the plaintiff's arguments based upon invoices she subsequently sent to the defendants, which included a "Rights Licensed" section purporting to limit the scope of the license, noting that a party cannot modify a contract unilaterally.

5. *Tacit or Ambiguous Terms by Type of Work*

[Add the following text at the end of the section.]

Regardless of what type of work is involved, it is vital that a copyright transfer clearly indicate that it pertains to the intangible rights in a work, and not merely to physical copies. Thus the court in *Jedson Engineering, Inc. v. Spirit Construction Services*,[47] rejected the defendants' argument that contractual language granting a third party "title to all drawings" constituted a transfer of the plaintiff's ownership of copyright in the drawings. Instead, the court accepted the plaintiff's argument that contractual language stating that "[a]ll creations, ideas, discoveries, developments

---

[46]Civ. No. 9-23120, 2011 U.S. Dist. LEXIS 10908 (S.D. Fla. Feb. 3, 2011).

[47]720 F. Supp. 2d 904 (S.D. Ohio 2010).

and inventions made in performance of this [contract] shall become the property of [the plaintiff]" granted the plaintiff ownership of such works; and rejected the defendants' argument that the plaintiff had granted an implied nonexclusive license to the defendants, based on the absence of evidence of the plaintiff's intent regarding the defendants' use of the works at issue. The plaintiff created designs and drawings for the defendant Spirit Construction Services in connection with three projects involving the design and construction of tissue manufacturing plants. For the third project, Spirit ultimately worked instead with the defendant Baisch Engineering, and agreed to provide Baisch with access to the plaintiff's drawings from two prior projects and the plaintiff's preliminary drawings for the third project. The plaintiff brought the action for copyright infringement based on this distribution of its drawings by Spirit and use of its drawings by Baisch. The defendants argued, inter alia, that the plaintiff, through subcontracts entered into in connection with the two earlier projects, had transferred copyrights in its drawings for those projects to the third party based on contractual language granting "title to all drawings" to such third party. The court distinguished cases cited by the defendants involving contracts that granted "all right, title and interest" in works and held that the plaintiff here had transferred only ownership of certain copies of its drawings—and not the copyrights embodied therein—to the relevant third party.

a.   New Technologies

[Add the following text at the end of the section.]

In *Agence France Presse v. Morel*,[48] the defendant Morel, a famous photographer in Haiti, posted photographs of the aftermath of the 2010 Haiti earthquake on his Twitter webpage. Third-party Suero copied Morel's pictures and posted them on his Twitter page, claiming title to the pictures. Various news outlets, including the plaintiff, requested to purchase Morel's pictures for publication. However, before Morel responded, the plaintiff downloaded the photos from Suero's Twitter page, and distributed the photos through its agreements with third-party defendant Getty Images and with Turner Broadcasting (TBS). Morel filed a copyright infringement suit, claiming the plaintiff, Getty, and TBS knew Suero had misappropriated the copyrighted pictures from Morel. Further, Morel claimed the plaintiff failed to "kill" or supervise the appropriated images even after a demand from Morel's licensing agent, thus causing further loss of revenue for Morel. The plaintiff and third-party defendants filed a motion to dismiss, claiming an affirmative defense of permission via license through Twitter. They pointed to the Twitter terms of use, which include the statement "This license is you authorizing us to make your Tweets available to the rest of the world and to let others do the same." The court held, however, that those terms purport only to grant a license to use the photos on other Twitter-related

---

[48]769 F. Supp. 2d 295 (S.D.N.Y. 2011).

sites. The plaintiff and third-party defendant TBS were not partners of Twitter, nor did they garner the right to reuse the copyrighted posting in distribution of images to CBS News, CNN, etc. The court held that at this stage, the plaintiff and TBS did not put forth sufficient evidence of a license to support a motion to dismiss.

6. *Software Contracts*

[Add the following new section.]

e.   Open Source Licenses [New Topic]

In *Jacobsen v. Katzer*,[49] the Federal Circuit vacated and remanded the district court's denial of a motion for preliminary injunction. The plaintiff-appellant, owner of copyright in software made publicly available without a fee pursuant to an open source license, sued the defendants-appellees for copyright infringement, claiming that they copied and modified portions of the plaintiff-appellant's copyrighted work without meeting the conditions of the open source license. The district court held that the scope of said open source license was "intentionally broad"[50] and, while violations of conditions of the license might constitute breach of contract, they did not constitute copyright infringement. The issue was whether the allegedly infringing use was outside the scope of the license. If the conduct was outside the scope of the license, then a copyright-infringement claim might lie, and a preliminary injunction might be granted as relief if the standard was met. If the conduct were within the scope of the license, the plaintiff-appellant's only remedy would be monetary damages under contract law, which, the parties agreed, might be impossible to calculate. The Federal Circuit found that the district court erred in treating restrictions in the open source license as "covenants," though labeling them "conditions," which error led the district court to find that the defendants-appellees' conduct was within the scope of the license. Accordingly, the district court denied the motion for preliminary injunction because, it erroneously reasoned, since the defendants-appellees' conduct was within the scope of the license, the plaintiff-appellant could establish neither probability of success on the merits nor serious questions going to the merits of the copyright claim. Reversing, the Federal Circuit found that the license restrictions, drafted with language traditionally used to establish conditions, were indeed conditions, not covenants. Therefore, the defendants-appellees' conduct was outside the scope of the license. Accordingly, the Federal Circuit vacated the district court's decision and remanded for findings on the likelihood of success on the copyright-infringement claim.

---

[49]535 F.3d 1373, 87 USPQ2d 1836 (Fed. Cir. 2008).

[50]*Id.* at 1376.

C. Breach

[Add the following text at the end of the section.]

The Ninth Circuit in *MDY Industries, LLC v. Blizzard Entertainment, Inc.*,[51] emphasized that where a party breaches contractual covenants, not conditions, the claim does not amount to copyright infringement, but merely a contract violation. The plaintiff, designer of a software "bot" that automated play of a game created by the defendant, sought a declaratory judgment that the plaintiff's "Glider" bot did not infringe the defendant's copyright in its game *World of Warcraft*. The district court found the plaintiff liable for vicarious infringement and violation of the DMCA. The Ninth Circuit reviewed the terms of the license pursuant to which the defendant provided *World of Warcraft* to its customers, and held that provisions prohibiting customers' use of bots such as "Glider" were covenants, not conditions, because "for a licensee's violation of a contract to constitute copyright infringement, there must be a nexus between the condition and the licensor's exclusive rights of copyright." Since the defendant's customers who used "Gilder" had violated covenants, not conditions, they were liable only for breach of contract, and there was no primary infringement to support a finding of vicarious infringement by the plaintiff.

[Redesignate Main Volume Section IV.E. as IV.D. as follows.]

D. Compulsory Statutory Licenses [Redesignated]

[Add the following text at the end of the section.]

The Copyright Act also provides for a compulsory license under Section 111 for retransmission of cable television programming. In *WPIX, Inc. v. ivi, Inc.*,[52] the district court granted the plaintiffs' motion for a preliminary injunction after holding that Internet transmission of copyrighted content did not fall within the compulsory license scheme of Section 111. The plaintiffs, producers and owners of copyrighted television programming, sought a preliminary injunction after learning about the defendant, whose business model involved capturing the plaintiffs' over-the-air broadcasts and simultaneously, without the plaintiffs' consent, streaming those broadcast signals via the Internet to subscribers who had downloaded the defendant's "ivi TV player." The defendant argued that it was entitled to a compulsory license under Section 111 for "cable systems." The district court examined the relevant aspects of Section 111 and related Communications Act provisions, and concluded that the Section 111 compulsory license was intended to apply to FCC-regulated entities that distributed content in local markets. The defendant, an entity that distributed nationwide and was not FCC-regulated, did not qualify. The district court also found instructive guidance from the Copyright Office suggesting that a distributor of broadcast programming over the Internet does not qualify for a compulsory license under Section 111.

---

[51]No. 09-15932, 2011 U.S. App. LEXIS 3428 (9th Cir. Feb. 17, 2011).

[52]765 F. Supp. 2d 594 (S.D.N.Y. 2011).

4

Formalities

I. NOTICE AND PUBLICATION

B. Publication

5. *International Publication*

[Add the following text at the end of the section.]

Similarly, in *Société Civile Succession Richard Guino v. Renoir,*[1] the Ninth Circuit affirmed a district court's grant of summary judgment to the plaintiff, a French trust, on a copyright-infringement claim. Pierre-August Renoir and one of his assistants, Richard Guino, created certain sculptures from 1913–1917. The sculptures were published in France around the same time but not published in the United States prior to 1978. Guino was adjudged co-author of the works in 1973 in France. His heirs gained control of all reproduction rights to the works and established a trust to implement those rights. In 1984, the trust obtained U.S. copyright registrations for the works. The plaintiff trust filed a copyright infringement suit against the defendant, who reproduced and sold the sculptures in the United States in 2003. The defendant contended that

---

[1]549 F.3d 1182, 89 USPQ2d 1139 (9th Cir. 2008).

the plaintiff had no copyright interests in the United States. The district court granted the plaintiff summary judgment, holding that the works were protected under Section 303(a) because the sculptures were created prior to 1978, "but not theretofore in public domain or copyrighted." Therefore, the sculptures were protected for 70 years after the death of the last surviving author, Guino, in 1973. The defendant appealed, claiming the works passed into the public domain in the United States once they were published in France. The Ninth Circuit, however, held that since the works were published only in France, publication did not cast the works into the public domain in the United States. Further, since the works did not contain copyright notices when they were exhibited in France, the 1909 Act, which would have restricted protection, did not even apply. Thus, the district court had correctly applied Section 303(a) in granting summary judgment, since the works were created prior to 1978 but they neither entered the U.S. public domain nor were they copyrighted until after 1978.

II. REGISTRATION

B. Errors in Deposit

[Add the following text at the end of the section.]

Of course, a fabricated deposit copy can void the registration altogether, as in *St. Luke's Cataract & Laser Institute, P.A. v. Sanderson.*[2] There, the Eleventh Circuit affirmed a jury verdict for the defendant where the plaintiff's registration submission contained materials not actually present on the work that the plaintiff purported to register. The defendant, a doctor, worked at the plaintiff hospital as an oculoplastic surgery specialist. While at the hospital the defendant worked with the hospital's webmaster to create the LaserSpecialist.com website promoting the defendant's oculoplastic surgery practice. Eventually, the defendant left the hospital and had the domain names "laserspecialist. com" and "lasereyelid.com" transferred to his own control. The defendant also used a previously acquired backup of the LaserSpecialist.com website to create his own website with updated changes to the contact and affiliation information for his solo practice. The hospital registered two old versions of the website with the Copyright Office and sued for copyright infringement. A jury returned a verdict for the defendant on the infringement claim, finding the hospital's registrations invalid. The court of appeals affirmed. Under Section 411(a), a copyright registration can be held invalid if "inaccurate information was included on the application for copyright registration with knowledge that it was inaccurate; and . . . the inaccuracy of the information, if known, would have caused the Register of Copyrights to refuse registration." The jury found the inaccuracies to be material and found scienter on the part of the

---

[2]573 F.3d 1186 (11th Cir. 2009).

plaintiff. The Eleventh Circuit held that there was sufficient evidence to show "intentional, material misrepresentations" in the applications. The court pointed to evidence that showed the deposit copies from a February 2003 application contained information that had not been added to the website until months afterward. The plaintiff's applications also claimed copyright in the entire website, but the plaintiff later admitted that many photos and other materials on the website were not original to the plaintiff.

D. Errors as to Ownership

[Add the following text at the end of the section.]

Registration errors as to work-made-for-hire status are seldom fatal. For example, in *Jules Jordan Video, Inc. v. 144942 Canada Inc.,*[3] plaintiff Gasper, an adult movie star who performed under the pseudonym Jules Jordan, was president and sole shareholder of plaintiff Jules Jordan Video (JJV) and the creator of videos in which he appeared. Plaintiffs sued the defendant video companies, alleging that defendants copied and sold 13 copyrighted DVDs owned by JJV or Gasper that featured Gasper's performances. A jury in the district court returned a verdict for the plaintiffs on their copyright infringement claim, but the court granted the defendants' motion for judgment as a matter of law, concluding that neither Gasper nor JJV had standing to assert a copyright claim. The district court held that because Gasper was employed by JJV, his motion picture works were works for hire under the Copyright Act. Therefore, Gasper lacked standing because JJV, not Gasper, was the author of the motion picture works. Gasper appealed the district court's decision, arguing that it was erroneous given that only Gasper or JJV could possibly own the copyrights, and both were plaintiffs in the district court action. The Ninth Circuit held that the district court erred in holding that Gasper's motion pictures were works for hire. The problem with the district court's analysis, the Ninth Circuit reasoned, was that JJV was a "one-man shop," of which Gasper was "sole officer, director and shareholder," "exercised complete control over it" and "made all decisions concerning JJV and production of the films."[4] Indeed, "[s]ince JJV was Gasper, JJV intended whatever Gasper intended, and if Gasper intended that his creative work be outside the scope of his employment with JJV, there was no one to disagree."[5] The Ninth Circuit further stated that

> even if the films were works for hire, the district court was correct that Gasper simply made a mistake in listing himself as the author on the copyright registration forms. That mistake does not constitute a basis to invalidate the copyright. Inadvertent mistakes on registration certificates do not invalidate a copyright and thus do not bar infringement actions, unless ... the alleged infringer has relied to its detriment on the mistake,

---

[3]617 F.3d 1146 (9th Cir. 2010).

[4]*Id.* at 1156.

[5]*Id.*

or the claimant intended to defraud the Copyright Office by making the misstatement.[6]

Here, "The defendants obviously did not rely on the mistake ... to their detriment. The evidence produced demonstrates that they pirated the DVDs without a care to whether the DVDs were copyrighted and, if so, who owned the copyright. Nor did Gasper or JJV ever intend to defraud the Copyright Office."[7]

G. Collective Works

[Add the following text at the end of the section.]

Under a 2010 New York decision, a registration that does not include the names of all the authors who contributed to a collective work, such as a group of photographs, is not valid as to any author not specifically named. The case was *Muench Photography, Inc. v. Houghton Mifflin Harcourt Publishing Co.*,[8] and the harsh result seems even harsher because the plaintiff had confirmed with the Copyright Office that its method of registration would be effective as to all the photographs in the collection. The plaintiffs' works were registered by the image licensing company Corbis as part of a database of many photos by many different authors. In 1997 and again in 2001, the plaintiffs executed written assignments of their works to Corbis, "[s]olely for the purpose of registering my copyright on my behalf," with the proviso that "Corbis shall promptly reassign in writing to me all of my right, title, and interest" in the works upon completion of the registration process and receipt of the certificate.[9] Corbis registered the works claiming itself "& others" or "and (number) other photographers" as authors, and Corbis itself as the lone claimant. The registrations did not name the plaintiffs. The plaintiffs' association counsel wrote to the Copyright Office in 2002 to confirm that Corbis' registration of the databases would be valid as to the individual photos contained therein, and the Copyright Office responded by letter that it "preferred, but did not require, the registration application to contain the names of all of the photographers on continuation sheets."[10]

The court disagreed, and held that the names of all authors are in fact required in Space 2b of registration form VA or on a continuation sheet for database registration to be effective as to such authors' works. Although the regulations in 37 C.F.R. §202.3 were entitled to full "*Chevron* deference," and while Copyright Office circulars and the *Compendium II* were entitled to lesser deference, the court here accorded no deference to "the Copyright Office's interpretations of the Copyright Act as set forth in [the response letter to the plaintiffs]" because those interpretations

---

[6] *Id.* (internal quotation marks omitted).

[7] *Id.*

[8] 712 F. Supp. 2d 84 (S.D.N.Y. 2010).

[9] *Id.* at 87.

[10] *Id.* at 88.

"conflict with a plain reading" of Section 409.[11] The court also faulted the plaintiffs' reliance on *Bean v. McDougal Littell*.[12] The court found that the *Bean* decision was erroneously based on the Second Circuit ruling in *Morris v. Business Concepts*.[13] *Morris* concerned serial registrations, the court noted, but *Bean*, like the instant case, dealt with databases, which were "subject to separate copyright regulations."[14] Under the database regulations, since Corbis was not the author of each individual work within the database, its name on the application was not sufficient to protect the individual works:

> A plain reading of §409 of the Copyright Act mandates that the copyright registrations at issue here contain the names of all the authors of the work. *See* 17 U.S.C. §409(2). [The plaintiff] believes that such a "hypertechnical reading of the Copyright Act" conflicts with the lenient approach that courts should take with respect to copyright registrations, especially in the post-Berne Convention era. [The plaintiff] though, is not asking the court to interpret the statute broadly; rather, it is asking the court flatly to ignore the requirement that the authors' names be listed on the copyright registration form. [The plaintiff's] request goes a bridge too far.[15]

The court concluded by faulting the Copyright Office, not the plaintiff, for the invalidity of the registration:

> The court does not fault [the plaintiff] for its failed efforts to comply with the registration process. Indeed, from the record presented to the Court, it appears [the plaintiff's] actions were completely appropriate—it sought the approval of the Copyright Office to ensure compliance with the statute. Unfortunately, [the plaintiff] received poor advice and is now deprived, at least at this juncture, of the ability to seek statutory damages with respect to the Images not registered . . . . The fault in this case lies solely with the Copyright Office and its relaxed interpretation of the statute.[16]

The case is on appeal to the Second Circuit as of this writing.

A contrary result had been reached in 2009 in an Ohio court in *Corbis Corp. v. Starr*,[17] where defendant Master Maintenance hired a company called West Central Ohio Internet Link to redesign and host its cleaning company website. The plaintiff found four of its images on Master Maintenance's redesigned website, and brought suit for copyright infringement. Both Master Maintenance and West Central disputed the source of the images, each claiming they were supplied by the other. Neither Master Maintenance nor West Central licensed images from the plaintiff. West Central argued that Corbis' copyright registration for the collection containing the copied images was insufficient to establish ownership of copyright in the individual images at issue. The

---

[11] *Id.* at 91–92.

[12] 669 F. Supp. 2d 1031 (D. Ariz. 2008).

[13] 283 F.3d 502 (2d Cir. 2002).

[14] *Muench Photography*, 712 F. Supp. 2d at 93.

[15] *Id.* at 94.

[16] *Id.* at 95.

[17] No. 07-3741, 2009 U.S. Dist. LEXIS 79626 (N.D. Ohio Sept. 2, 2009).

court disagreed. It held, on motion for summary judgment, that Corbis' ownership of copyright in the collection is sufficient to prove copyright ownership of the individual works in the collection even if they are not specifically listed on the registration certificate.

H. Derivative Works

[Add the following text at the end of the section.]

In *Rich & Rich Partnership v. Poetman Records USA, Inc.*,[18] a Kentucky district court held that an applicant's knowing failure to sufficiently identify a prior work was grounds for invalidating the copyright, but it is unclear whether the decision relies on the very thin copyright protection that might attach to the later (registered) work. The plaintiff created an album, containing a so-called "Chandler remix," which was a mix of former Kentucky governor Chandler's *a cappella* rendition of *My Old Kentucky Home* together with recorded crowd noise from the University of Kentucky's Rupp Arena. Subsequently, the defendants created a different album, containing the same remix. The defendants moved for summary judgment on the plaintiff's claim for copyright infringement, arguing that the plaintiff failed to register "Chandler remix" properly. The court stated that under the Copyright Act, registration for a derivative work must include identification of the preexisting work that it is based on or incorporates, together with a brief statement of the additional material covered by the copyright claim. The court found that although the plaintiff knew that it was taking Chandler's work and putting it on its album, the plaintiff, without identifying Chandler's work, merely mentioned in its registration that it used "some sound recording," and provided a deposit of its album. The court found this statement and deposit of the plaintiff's album insufficient, reasoning that the Copyright Office, without knowing which preexisting work was used in which portion of the plaintiff's work, could never have determined whether the plaintiff's contribution to Chandler's work qualified as a protectable derivative work. Accordingly, the court held that the plaintiff's knowing failure to identify, in copyright registration, which preexisting work was used in which portion of the plaintiff's work, rendered the registration unenforceable.

A similar result was endorsed, at least in *dicta*, in *Express, LLC v. Forever 21, Inc.*,[19] where the district court granted defendants' motions for summary judgment based on the unoriginality of plaintiff's purported works. The plaintiff contended that the defendants infringed copyrights in four plaid designs and a jacket created by an employee of the plaintiff and sold in the plaintiff's stores by manufacturing and selling garments that were substantially similar to the plaintiff's. Based on deposition testimony of the plaintiff's employee that the garments were based on

---

[18]No. 08-436, 2010 U.S. Dist. LEXIS 48949 (E.D. Ky. May 18, 2010).

[19]No. CV 09-4514 ODW (VBKx), 2010 U.S. Dist. LEXIS 91705 (C.D. Cal. Sept. 2, 2010).

pre-existing designs; that he could not remember the changes he made to pre-existing designs in creating the garments; and that, to his knowledge, the plaintiff no longer had possession of the pre-existing designs, the court concluded that the plaintiff could not prove that any of its purported works incorporated sufficient original creativity to qualify for copyright protection.[20] In *dicta*, the court noted that it could also have applied the logic used by previous courts to grant summary judgment based on the plaintiff's failure to disclose in its copyright registrations that its works were derivative works.[21]

In *Salestraq America, LLC v. Zyskowski*,[22] the court denied the defendants' motion to dismiss the plaintiff's copyright infringement suit, finding that the plaintiff's real estate information could be protectable and was properly registered, even though the registration was issued on a derivative work of the compilation the defendant had actually copied. The plaintiff alleged that certain content on the defendants' webpage was similar to the plaintiff's copyrighted compilation of information regarding residential properties in Las Vegas, and also included exact reproductions of content created by the plaintiff to inform customers of the properties' key attributes. The defendants moved to dismiss on the basis that the court lacked subject matter jurisdiction to consider the infringement action because the plaintiff registered a 2008 version of the compilation rather than the 2007 version that the defendant allegedly infringed. The court ruled that registration of a factual compilation derived from an earlier work permits a complainant to assert an infringement claim on an underlying work that is owned by the same party.

Conversely, in *KEMA, Inc. v. Koperwhats*,[23] the court dismissed plaintiff's copyright infringement action for lack of subject matter jurisdiction because the copyrights in the works at issue were not registered at the time the action was filed. Plaintiff Koperwhats alleged that defendants "downloaded, sold, licensed, distributed, shared, or otherwise transferred" the plaintiff's software without consent.[24] Defendants argued that the plaintiff's copyright claim was subject to dismissal because plaintiff's registration certificate did not, in fact, pertain to any work alleged to have been infringed, and that consequently the court lacked jurisdiction. Specifically, the registration certificate identified work completed in 2008 and first published on June 16, 2008, and did not identify any preexisting work or works. However, as alleged by the plaintiff, many of the allegedly infringed software versions were published prior to June 16, 2008, including version 3.3, which was published on the defendants' website on February 27, 2006. In light of these allegations, defendants argued that the plaintiff's copyright registration certificate could not

---

[20] *Id.* at *13.

[21] *Id.* at *20–21.

[22] 635 F. Supp. 2d 1178 (D. Nev. 2009).

[23] 96 USPQ2d 1787 (N.D. Cal. 2010).

[24] *Id.* at 1791.

pertain to version 3.3. The court noted that a district court lacks jurisdiction over a copyright claim where the allegedly infringed work was
published before the date of first publication identified in the registration
unless such registration identifies the registered work as derivative of,
or a compilation containing, the allegedly infringed work. Accordingly,
the court granted the defendants' motion to dismiss.[25]

[Add the following new sections.]

I.   Presumption of Facts Stated in Certificate [New Topic]

In *R.F.M.A.S., Inc. v. So*,[26] the court denied the plaintiff's motion for
reconsideration of an order that found that the plaintiff was entitled to
a rebuttable presumption of ownership of a valid copyright but that it
was not entitled to a presumption of the truth of the facts stated in its
supplementary registration. The plaintiff argued that reconsideration
was warranted because (1) "newly produced evidence" (*i.e.*, affidavits)
demonstrated that the plaintiff obtained its supplementary registration
promptly, but had insufficient notice or opportunity to be heard on the
issue of timing; and (2) the court overlooked controlling law regarding
the statutory presumption of the truth of facts contained in a supplementary registration. The plaintiff argued that the court overlooked the
significance of Section 410(c), which the plaintiff argued provided it with
a presumption of validity of facts stated in supplementary registration.
The court found unpersuasive the plaintiff's argument that changes
made to its certificate of registration "do not affect application of the
statutory presumption, unless there is evidence of substantive fraud on
the Copyright Office."[27] The court reasoned that because the cases cited
by the plaintiff addressed the presumptive validity of the copyright itself,
not the presumptive validity of the accuracy of facts contained in the
certificate, and because the plaintiff's copyright was already found to be
presumptively valid, the cited cases were inapplicable.

A defendant can sometimes rebut the presumption established by
the registration, however, and send the issue of copyright validity to the
jury. Thus in *Looney Ricks Kiss Architects, Inc. v. Bryan*[28] the district court
denied plaintiff architectural company's motion for partial summary judgment on the issue of ownership of copyright in architectural drawings
and works. The plaintiff had obtained copyright registrations relating to
the designs of two apartment complexes in Memphis, and claimed that
defendants infringed its copyrights by constructing similar complexes in
Louisiana. Defendants opposed on the ground that the plaintiff's works
lacked originality. The court turned to 17 U.S.C. §410(c), which provides
that a certificate of registration made before or within five years after
first publication of a work constitutes prima facie evidence of copyright

---

[25]*Id.* at 1793.

[26]640 F. Supp. 2d 506 (S.D.N.Y. 2009).

[27]*Id.* at 513.

[28]No. 07-572, 2010 U.S. Dist. LEXIS 110100 (W.D. La. Oct. 14, 2010).

validity. By obtaining timely certificates of registration, plaintiff had carried its burden, and it was up to defendants to rebut the presumption of ownership by, e.g., presenting facts to demonstrate that plaintiff had copied its works from preexisting sources, which would nullify originality. Defendants argued that the plaintiff had copied the plans from a competing architectural firm, and that plaintiff's project manager had previously been employed by a competing firm and had brought copies of plans with him when he gained employment with the plaintiff. The plaintiff's manager and other project leaders denied this during testimony, claiming no copying occurred. The defendants presented expert testimony by a registered architect who opined that, based on similarities between plaintiff's works and the competing firm's previous work, and knowledge that the plaintiff project manager had access to the previous work in his previous employment, plaintiff's work was derived from the competitor's work and thus lacked originality. Because of competing testimony, the court found there was a genuine issue of fact, and denied the plaintiff's motion for partial summary judgment.[29]

J.   Registration of Non-U.S. Works [New Topic]

In *Moberg v. 33T, LLC*,[30] the court denied the defendant's motion to dismiss a complaint for lack of subject matter jurisdiction, where the plaintiff, a foreign national, created works outside the United States; the works were first posted on a foreign website; and the plaintiff did not have or apply for a U.S. copyright registration. The plaintiff, copyright owner of a series of photographs taken in Sweden, first published the photographs on a German website offering copies of the photos for sale. The defendants, U.S. companies, displayed the plaintiff's photographs on various websites without permission. The defendants filed a motion to dismiss the plaintiff's complaint for lack of subject matter jurisdiction, arguing that the plaintiff's photos were "United States works," "published" simultaneously in the United States and Germany when the plaintiff posted them on the German website, and thus subject to the Section 411 registration requirement. The court disagreed with the argument that the photos were U.S. works. The determination of whether the photographs were U.S. works depended on (1) whether the plaintiff's posting of the photographs on the German website was a "publication"; and (2) whether "publishing" on a website causes photographs to be published in one country, or published simultaneously around the world. The court, noting that the first issue was one of first impression, assumed without deciding that the photographs were "published."

Regarding the second issue, the court ruled that, as a matter of law, the photographs were not simultaneously published in the United States when they were posted on a website in Germany. Ruling otherwise:

---

[29] *Id.* at *24.

[30] 666 F. Supp. 2d 415 (D. Del. 2009).

(1) would be "contrary to the purpose of the Berne Convention. 'The overarching purpose of the Berne Convention is to provide protection to authors whose works will be published in many countries' " and would subject authors "to the very formalities that the Berne Convention eschews";[31]

(2) would "allow American citizens to infringe on foreign copyrighted works without fear of legal retribution,"[32] and

(3) would be contrary to U.S. law, which, in accord with the Berne Convention, "provide[s] for protection of foreign works in the United States without requiring the artists to undertake any formalities in the United States."[33]

Consequently, the court found, the plaintiff's photographs were not "United States works," and the plaintiff's infringement claim could go forward despite the lack of registration.

Perhaps counterintuitively, lack of registration can still be an obstacle as to the availability of injunctive relief for foreign works. In *Jagex Ltd. v. Impulse Software*,[34] the district court denied the plaintiff's motion for preliminary injunction, finding that, in the absence of a registered copyright in its game software, plaintiff had failed to demonstrate a likelihood of success on the merits. Plaintiff Jagex owned and operated a massive, multiplayer online game called Runescape, which was recognized by the Guinness Book of World Records in 2008 as the world's most popular free online role-playing game. Runescape allowed players to navigate through a fantasy world and interact with one another by participating in challenges. Defendants operated websites offering "bots" that enabled users to advance virtual characters through the Runescape with little human participation, thus affording them an unfair advantage over other players. Jagex brought an action for, inter alia, copyright infringement, asserting that defendants directly and contributorily infringed its copyrights by selling bots that copied the game and violated Runescape's terms and conditions, and by encouraging others to use those bots. Section 411 of the Copyright Act requires "registration or preregistration of a copyright of a United States work before filing suit."[35] Jagex argued that, because the Runescape game software was entirely developed and initially published in the United Kingdom, it was not a "United States work" and therefore registration was not required prior to filing suit. Jagex attempted to rely instead on 21 visual arts copyright registrations for various two-dimensional icons appearing in Runescape. The court found that even if the absence of a registered copyright for the software did not bar injunctive relief, it made it unlikely that the plaintiff would succeed on the merits of its claim. Moreover, even if the

---

[31] *Id.* at 422.

[32] *Id.* at 423.

[33] *Id.*

[34] 750 F. Supp. 2d 228 (D. Mass. Aug. 16, 2010).

[35] *Id.* at 236.

21 registered images were included in the Runescape software, Jagex had failed to explain how bot users infringed those copyrights when they played the game. The court thus found that, in the absence of a registered copyright in the software, the plaintiff had not demonstrated a likelihood of success on the merits.[36]

V. RESTORATION OF FOREIGN WORKS

B. Specific Issues

3. *Is Section 104A Constitutional?*

[Add the following text at the end of the section.]

On April 3, 2009, in *Golan v. Holder* ("*Golan II*"),[37] the district court, on remand, held the statute unconstitutional, the first time any copyright provision had ever been struck down on First Amendment grounds. Because the speech restriction at issue under Section 104A was content-neutral, the court reviewed the law under an "intermediate" standard of First Amendment scrutiny[38]—whether "a regulation of speech is substantially broader than necessary to achieve the government's interest."[39]

In making this determination, the district court recognized that Section 104A was designed to implement the important governmental interest of compliance with international treaties and obligations such as the Berne Convention, which prohibits the loss of copyright due to failure to comply with formalities.

The court then considered whether the burden imposed on speech by Section 104A was "substantially broader than necessary" to achieve compliance with Berne. In this respect, the court found Section 104A to be lacking. The court noted only three areas in which the plaintiffs' speech could continue despite Section 104A:

(1) plaintiffs could continue to exploit the restored works unless and until the restored copyright holder filed a notice of intent to enforce the copyright;

(2) they could continue to exploit the restored works for one year after the restoration notice was filed; and

(3) they could continue indefinitely to exploit derivative works prepared before the notice of restoration was filed, provided they paid a reasonable royalty to the holder of the restored copyright.[40]

---

[36]*Id.* at 237.

[37]611 F. Supp. 2d 1165 (D. Colo. 2009), *reversed and remanded*, 609 F.3d 1076 (10th Cir. 2010). The caption changed from *Golan v. Gonzales* to *Golan v. Holder* due to the appointment of the new Attorney General, Eric H. Holder, Jr. In the interim the case had been known as *Golan v. Mukasey*, and it began life as *Golan v. Ashcroft*.

[38]*See* 609 F.3d 1076, 1082 (10th Cir. 2010) for the term "intermediate scrutiny."

[39]*Golan II*, 611 F. Supp. at 1171 (citations and internal quotations omitted).

[40]*Id.* at 1173.

The district court then found that even though the law preserved these categories of the plaintiffs' speech, it still burdened a substantial amount of speech, namely, "any speech that involves copying more than one year after notice has been filed, and any derivative works made after notice is filed and without payment of a royalty."[41] The court concluded that Congress, in enacting Section 104A, could have given reliance parties far more freedom to utilize restored works without causing the United States to violate its obligations under the Berne Convention.

Accordingly, the court found that:

(1) the Congress' "legitimate interest in complying with the terms of the Berne Convention" must be implemented in a manner consistent with U.S. law;

(2) it is a "bedrock principle of [U.S. copyright law] that works in the public domain remain in the public domain";

(3) "[r]emoving works from the public domain violated Plaintiffs' vested First Amendment interests";

(4) the Berne Convention affords member countries discretion to implement its provisions without interfering with plaintiffs' free speech; and

(5) by restricting the right of reliance parties to use works they had exploited while they were in the public domain, Section 104A "is substantially broader than necessary to achieve the Government's interest."[42]

The district court therefore held that Section 104A failed to withstand First Amendment scrutiny.

The government appealed to the Tenth Circuit (*Golan III*).[43] The court applied *de novo* review and agreed with the district court and the parties that "intermediate scrutiny" was appropriate.[44] The appellate court's application of that standard took an interesting departure from the decision below, however.

As noted above, the district court had determined that the speech restrictions imposed by Section 104A were impermissibly broad relative to the government's interest in complying with Berne and other treaty obligations. The Tenth Circuit observed that the government in fact offered three separate interests that were served by Section 104A: not only Berne compliance, but also "obtaining legal protections for American copyright holders' interests abroad" and "remedying past inequities of foreign authors who lost or never obtained copyrights in the United States."[45]

---

[41] *Id.* at 1173.

[42] *Id.* at 1177.

[43] 609 F.3d 1076 (10th Cir. 2010).

[44] *Id.* at 1083.

[45] *Id.*

Among those three interests, the appellate court found that Section 104A was not overbroad in relation to the government's "substantial interest in protecting American copyright holders' interests abroad."[46]

How does enacting a piece of domestic copyright law, benefitting only foreign authors, serve the purpose of protecting U.S. authors abroad? In a word, reciprocity. The court noted that Congress had heard testimony describing the lack of protection for numerous U.S. works abroad, and explained that America's "refusal to restore foreign copyrights was harming American authors' interests abroad: foreign countries were following the United States' example of refusing to restore copyrights in works in the public domain."[47]

The testimony also indicated that America's "trading partners had represented that they would restore American copyrights only if the United States restored foreign copyrights."[48] Thus, the court concluded, "if the United States wanted certain protections for American authors, it had to provide those protections for foreign authors."[49]

The plaintiffs argued that the act's specific reliance-party carve-outs were not necessary to achieve this particular foreign objective, but the court disagreed and found that Congress was very concerned with setting an example for other nations and "squarely faced the need to balance the interests of American copyright holders and American reliance parties," citing Congressional testimony from Sen. DeConcini.[50] Even though some testimony voiced skepticism as to the likelihood of foreign governments' making similar provisions for U.S. works, the court found that it was for Congress to weigh that conflicting evidence. The question presented to the court was not whether Congress was correct about offering limited protection to reliance parties, only whether the conclusion Congress reached was reasonable.

Nor did the court accept the plaintiffs' argument that the government's interest in securing the rights of U.S. authors abroad was "too speculative to satisfy intermediate [First Amendment] scrutiny."[51] Although the courts require "substantial evidence" of a genuine governmental interest, the "evidentiary requirement is not as onerous as plaintiffs would have us impose."[52] Especially in areas involving predictions about the acts of foreign governments, such as the reciprocity question here, "empirical data will rarely be available" and considerable deference is owed to Congress and the executive branch.[53]

---

[46] *Id.*

[47] *Id.* at 1086.

[48] *Id.* at 1087.

[49] *Id.*

[50] *Id.* at 1088. The court also cited Eric Smith, who had testified in support of the law on behalf of a consortium of trade associations representing both copyright owners and reliance parties.

[51] *Id.*

[52] *Id.* at 1089.

[53] *Id.*

The Tenth Circuit next addressed the question of whether Section 104A burdened substantially more speech than was necessary to achieve Congress' objective. The court observed that the statute need not be the least speech-restrictive alternative to advancing the government's interest, but need merely be "congruent to benefits it affords" in order to be "narrowly tailored."[54] Here,

> the United States needed to impose the same burden on American reliance parties that it sought to impose on foreign reliance parties. Thus, the benefit that the government sought to provide to American authors is congruent with the burden that [§104A] imposes on reliance parties. The burdens on speech are therefore directly focused to the harms that the government sought to alleviate.[55]

Significantly, the court recognized in a footnote that the fair use doctrine and idea-expression distinction, which are copyright law's "built-in" First Amendment safeguards, remain operative for restored works as they do for all other copyrighted works. The restoration provision "does not disturb these traditional, built-in protections, and thus, such protected speech remains unburdened."[56]

Near the end of the opinion, the court emphasized directly that the "arguments about what the Berne Convention requires and permits are beside the point":

> [T]he government's interest is not limited to compliance with the Berne Convention. Rather, its interest includes securing protections for American copyright owners in foreign countries, which includes providing copyright protection against foreign reliance parties. Thus, it is immaterial whether, as plaintiffs contend, the government could have complied with the minimal obligations of the Berne Convention and granted stronger protections for American reliance parties. . . . [E]ven assuming for purposes of this appeal that the United States could have provided stronger protections for American reliance parties while complying with the minimum requirements of the Berne Convention, [§104A] does not burden substantially more speech than necessary to further the government's interest.[57]

The court concluded that the plaintiffs' challenge to Section 104A was fundamentally a disagreement over the level of protection that reliance parties should receive, and that Congress properly sought to balance those interests against the interest of U.S. copyright owners abroad. "In so doing, Congress crafted a nuanced statute that offered some protections for both of these competing interests. It is not our role to opine on the best method of striking this balance."[58]

By upholding the constitutionality of Section 104A, the Tenth Circuit avoided a conflict with the result of the District of Columbia Circuit in

---

[54] *Id.* at 1091 (citations and internal quotations omitted).

[55] *Id.*

[56] *Id.* at 1091 n.9.

[57] *Id.* at 1091–92.

[58] *Id.* at 1094.

Luck's Music Library, Inc. v. Gonzales,[59] which sustained the constitutionality of the provision albeit without specifically addressing the First Amendment issues raised in *Golan.*[60] Lacking a split in the circuits, or a conflict with *Eldred v. Ashcroft,*[61] the Supreme Court would seem to have had little reason to grant certiorari, but it did so in March 2011[62] and the case was set down for argument in the 2011–2012 term.

VI. TERMINATION

B. Section 304 and Pre-1978 Grants: Federal Law Governs

1. Section 304 and Derivative Works

[Add the following text at the end of the section.]

More recently, the heirs of the creator of comic-book hero "Superman" succeeded in terminating under Section 304(c), but the extent of that victory remains difficult to quantify. In *Siegel v. Warner Bros. Entertainment, Inc.,*[63] the court granted summary judgment for the heirs, finding that the widow and daughter of one of the creators of the Superman character successfully terminated a 1938 transfer of rights under Section 304(c). Jerome Siegel and Joseph Shuster created the Superman character and assigned all rights in the character to DC Comics in 1938. The original authors sued in New York state court in 1947, seeking to rescind their agreement with DC Comics and recover ownership of Superman. The court found that the 1938 assignment was valid, and that DC Comics was the exclusive owner of all rights in Superman. In 1997, Siegel's widow and daughter served notices of termination under Section 304(c), with an effective date in April 1999. Just prior to the effective date, the parties entered into negotiations, agreeing that the statute of limitations regarding termination notices would be tolled. Negotiations failed, and in 2004 the widow and daughter sued for a declaration that their termination notices were effective. The court explained that "effective date of the termination notices[,] April 16, 1999, mean[t] that, backdating from that date sixty-one years, the termination notices would leave unaffected (or better said, beyond their reach) any statutory copyright that had been secured in the Superman material before April 16, 1938."[64]

The first publication to feature Superman was *Action Comics,* Vol. 1, with a publication date of June 1938. However, DC Comics published promotional material for the first issue of *Action Comics,* including the

---

[59]407 F.3d 1262 (D.C. Cir. 2005).

[60]In *Luck's Music Library,* the plaintiffs' constitutional challenge to §104A was based on the "limited times" provision of the Copyright Clause. They did not make a separate First Amendment-based argument.

[61]537 U.S. 186, 65 USPQ2d 1225 (2003).

[62]131 S. Ct. 1600, 179 L. Ed. 2d 516 (2011).

[63]542 F. Supp. 2d 1098, 86 USPQ2d 1899 (C.D. Cal. 2008).

[64]*Id.* at 1118.

cover image of Superman lifting a car, in other DC publications. The court concluded that the best evidence indicated that the promotional materials were published prior to April 16, 1938, and were the first time Superman "appeared to the public." Thus, the promos were the first time any of the authors' Superman material was protected by statutory copyright. Accordingly, material in promos, including depiction of Superman that later appeared on cover of *Action Comics*, Vol. 1, achieved federal copyright protection before the earliest possible date covered by the termination notice. The court therefore found that the "publication date for at least one of the comics containing the promotional announcements falls outside the reach of the termination notice and, therefore, any copyrightable material contained therein (including that found in the cover to *Action Comics*, Vol. 1, *as depicted* in those announcements) remains for the defendants to exploit."[65] As to "the *scope* of the copyrighted material remaining in defendants' possession by way of the promotional announcements," the court began by "observing what is *not* depicted" in them, *i.e.*, "nothing concerning the Superman storyline . . . , Superman's name, his alter ego, his compatriots, his origins, his mission to serve as a champion of the oppressed, or his heroic abilities in general."[66]

The only remaining copyrightable elements arose from the pictorial illustrations in the promo, which the court found were "fairly limited." Furthermore, while the promo was in black and white, the termination covered the colors of Superman's costume and the *S* crest insignia on Superman's chest, which appeared only as "some vague marking or symbol" in the promo. The defendants, accordingly, "may continue to exploit the image of a person with extraordinary strength who wears a black and white leotard and cape." "[S]till subject to termination (and, of course, what defendants truly seek) is the entire storyline from *Action Comics*, Vol. 1, Superman's distinctive blue leotard (complete with its inverted triangular crest across the chest with a red 'S' on a yellow background), a red cape and boots, and his superhuman ability to leap tall buildings, repel bullets, and run faster than a locomotive, none of which is apparent from the announcement."[67]

2. *Section 304 and New Grants*

[Add the following text at the end of the section.]

Under Sections 304(c) and 304(d), authors or specified statutory heirs (spouse, children and grandchildren) have the opportunity to terminate grants "executed before January 1, 1978," and to take back earlier-granted rights during the extended renewal term. In *Penguin Group (USA), Inc. v. Steinbeck*,[68] a New York district court granted the plaintiff's motion for partial summary judgment, declaring that a notice

---

[65] *Id.* at 1126 (emphasis in original).

[66] *Id.* (emphasis in original).

[67] *Id.*

[68] No. 06-2438, 2009 U.S. Dist. LEXIS 113068 (S.D.N.Y. Dec. 2, 2009).

of termination purporting to terminate pre-1978 copyright grants in John Steinbeck's *The Pearl* was invalid and ineffective. In *Penguin Group (USA), Inc. v. Steinbeck*,[69] the Second Circuit held that a termination notice served by Steinbeck's son and granddaughter with respect to Steinbeck's "early works" was invalid.[70] A 1994 publishing agreement between Steinbeck's widow Elaine and Penguin with respect to Steinbeck's "early works," in which Elaine was the sole copyright owner, had validly terminated by contract all prior grants of rights in the "early works." Thus, there was no longer any pre-1978 grant of rights in the "early works" in existence to be terminated under the Copyright Act. At the same time in 1994, Elaine and Thomas Steinbeck, co-copyright owners of Steinbeck's "later works," entered into a second publishing agreement with Penguin with respect to the "later works" that identically canceled and superseded all previous agreements for the "later works." Steinbeck's son and granddaughter served a notice of termination purporting to terminate pre-1978 grants of rights in the "later work," *The Pearl.* Penguin sought a declaratory judgment that the notice was invalid under Second Circuit precedent. The court agreed. The court applied New York contract law, under which parties to an agreement are free to mutually terminate it, while simultaneously entering into a new agreement dealing with the same subject matter. Both of the 1994 Steinbeck publishing agreements expressly canceled and superseded all previous agreements for Steinbeck works, and made new grants of rights on terms considerably more favorable to the Steinbeck heirs.

---

[69]537 F.3d 193 (2d Cir. 2008), *cert. denied,* 129 S. Ct. 2383, 173 L. Ed. 2d 1326, (2009).

[70]In a separate agreement, Elaine and Thomas Steinbeck, co-copyright owners of Steinbeck's "later works," entered into a second publishing agreement with Penguin with respect to the "later works" that identically canceled and superseded all previous agreements for the "later works." *See id.* at 196 n.1.

5

Infringement

I. ACCESS

A. Standards of Evidence

[Add the following text at the end of the section.]

In *Lessem v. Taylor*,[1] the district court denied the plaintiffs' motion for summary judgment that the defendants' song infringed the plaintiffs' song, and denied the defendants' motion for summary judgment that the two songs share only unprotectable elements. The dispute centered on the use of the lyric phrase "this is how we do," set to the same rhythm, four times, in both the plaintiffs' and the defendants' songs, which also shared the same tempo. The plaintiffs' theory of access involved a third-party producer who worked with the defendants on other songs and to whom the plaintiffs alleged they had given a copy of the plaintiffs' song. The court found genuine issues of material fact as to the connection both between the plaintiffs and the producer and between the producer and the defendants. In essence, the court found that declarations submitted by the producer and the defendants were insufficiently definitive to permit judgment as a matter of law. The producer stated, for example, that he did not recall receiving a copy of the plaintiffs' song, whereas declarants in cases upon which the defendants relied had made stronger statements, to the effect that they had never heard or received a copy of the allegedly infringed work at issue.

---

[1]766 F. Supp. 2d 504 (S.D.N.Y. 2011).

B. Widespread Dissemination

1. *Findings of No Access*

[Add the following text at the end of the section.]

Purely local dissemination, such as in a booth at a county fair, is often insufficient to establish access; a website which is slow to load and does not prominently feature the plaintiff's work may also be held inadequate to establish access. For example, in *Art Attacks Ink, LLC v. MGA Entertainment, Inc.*,[2] the Ninth Circuit affirmed a district court's grant of judgment for the defendant as a matter of law. The plaintiff's copyrighted "Spoiled Brats" T-shirt character featured characteristics similar to the defendants "Bratz" dolls. Although there was no direct evidence of access, the plaintiff presented circumstantial evidence in an attempt to show access by either "(1) establishing a chain of events linking the plaintiff's work and the defendant's access, or (2) showing that the plaintiff's work has been widely disseminated."[3] As to the chain of events argument, the plaintiff argued that the defendant might have attended the county fair at which the "Spoiled Brats" character was displayed. The court held that although there might be some slight chance that the defendant did visit the county fair during the relevant period, that chance did not create more than a "bare possibility" of a chain of events linking the plaintiff's design to the defendant's doll. The plaintiff also argued wide dissemination by (1) the plaintiff's booth itself; (2) the "Spoiled Brats" T-shirts serving as "walking billboards"; and (3) via the Internet. As to the plaintiff's booth, the court ruled that there was no evidence that significant numbers of passersby would notice the plaintiff's booth among many other similar booths at the fair. As to the plaintiff's T-shirts, the court found that the plaintiff could not demonstrate that the "Spoiled Brats" design was widely disseminated to the extent necessary to create more than a "bare possibility" that the defendant had access to it. As to the Internet, wide dissemination was not shown because the plaintiff's website took two full minutes to load; viewers would not see the design without scrolling down the page; and, the webpage did not include "meta tags" that would identify the plaintiff's page to Internet search engines.

C. Third Parties

1. *Findings of No Access*

[Add the following text at the end of the section.]

Where a defendant musician simply uses the same studio facilities and creative team as the plaintiff used, a finding of access is not warranted.

---

[2]581 F.3d 1138 (9th Cir. 2009).

[3]*Id.* at 1143 (citing Three Boys Music Corp. v. Bolton, 212 F.3d 477, 482 (9th Cir. 2000)).

For example, in *Martinez v. McGraw*,[4] the court granted the defendants' motion to dismiss, ruling that the plaintiff failed to plead facts as to access that would entitle him to relief. The plaintiff contended that the defendants were unlawfully exploiting the plaintiff's song "Anytime, Anywhere Amanda" as incorporated into the defendants' song "Everywhere." As to access, the plaintiff alleged, inter alia, that the defendant and a non-defendant third party, Terri Clark, whose song "You're Easy on the Eyes," contained a phrase similar to plaintiff's song entitled "Easy on the Eyes, Hard on the Ticker," recorded its album in the same studio as the plaintiff and used the same songwriters and personnel. The court held that this, without more, "fails to . . . raise even an inference of access" by the defendant.[5] Though "'evidence that a third party with whom both the plaintiff and defendant were concurrently dealing had possession of plaintiff's work [may be] sufficient to establish access by the defendant, access may not be inferred through mere speculation or conjecture.'"[6] The court noted that the plaintiff "does not allege how his song *Anytime, Anywhere Amanda* got into the hands of Ms. Clark's personnel and songwriters or even that his song was played in hearing range of Ms. Clark's personnel and songwriters or that Ms. Clark's personnel and songwriters had any contact with Plaintiff or Plaintiff's Collection."[7]

E. Striking Similarity

[Add the following text at the end of the section.]

A plaintiff cannot easily defeat summary judgment based solely on an expert opinion of striking similarity. In *Vargas v. Pfizer, Inc.*,[8] for example, the Second Circuit affirmed a grant of summary judgment to the defendants, where the plaintiffs' access case relied on the reports and testimony of three experts to establish that the plaintiffs' sound recording "Aparthenonia" and the defendants' recording "Bust Dat Groove" were "strikingly similar." The district court determined "that this evidence was insufficient to create a genuine issue of fact, explaining, inter alia, that the expert reports and testimony were both internally and externally inconsistent."[9] On appeal, the plaintiffs contended that the district court's treatment of the expert evidence was improper at the summary judgment stage. The court of appeals disagreed. The plaintiffs "cannot avoid summary judgment simply by submitting any expert evidence, particularly where that evidence is both internally and externally inconsistent."[10] Furthermore, "'[a] plaintiff has not proved striking similarity sufficient to sustain a finding of copying if the evidence

---

[4]No. 08-738, 2009 U.S. Dist. LEXIS 69862 (M.D. Tenn. Aug. 10, 2009).

[5]*Id.* at *14.

[6]*Id.* at *15 (quoting Jones v. Blige, 558 F.3d 485, 491 (6th Cir. 2009)).

[7]*Id.* at *15.

[8]No. 07-4085, 2009 U.S. App. LEXIS 24263 (2d Cir. Nov. 5, 2009).

[9]*Id.* at *3.

[10]*Id.* at **3–4.

as a whole does not preclude any reasonable possibility of independent creation.' Here, [d]efendants offered ample evidence to establish a reasonable possibility of independent creation. Although [p]laintiffs submitted an affidavit in opposition to that evidence, mere assertions, and equivocal ones at that, are insufficient to satisfy their burden at summary judgment."[11]

Where the plaintiff's design is relatively simple, striking similarity is obviously harder for a plaintiff to establish. In *Tokidoki, LLC v. Fortune Dynamic, Inc.*,[12] for example, the court held that the defendant's heart and crossbones design was an independent creation, not an infringing copy of the plaintiff's design. The plaintiff failed to establish "striking similarity" because "[t]he design, which consists of two relatively commonplace elements—a heart and a crossbones—is sufficiently simple and commonplace that the similarities between Fortune's design and Tokidoki's could easily have been the result of independent creation, coincidence, or some theory other than copying. Tokidoki failed to create a presumption of copying by Fortune."[13] The court held that Fortune "independently created its single heart above crossbones design without knowledge of its prior existence or of Tokidoki's use."[14]

II. COPYING AND SUBSTANTIAL SIMILARITY

A. Evidentiary Issues

[Add the following text at the end of the section.]

The courts generally agree that even where direct copying is conceded, the plaintiff must still show that there is substantial similarity as to copyrightable elements. In *Jedson Engineering, Inc. v. Spirit Construction Services*,[15] the district court denied the plaintiff's motion for summary judgment on the issue of actionable copying and rejected the plaintiff's argument that because the plaintiff provided direct evidence of copying, which the defendants did not dispute, the plaintiff was not required to show substantial similarity. The plaintiff created designs and drawings for the defendant Spirit Construction Services in connection with three projects involving the design and construction of tissue manufacturing plants. For the third project, Spirit ultimately worked instead with the defendant Baisch Engineering, and agreed to provide Baisch with access to the plaintiff's drawings from the prior two projects and the plaintiff's preliminary drawings for the third project. The plaintiff brought the action for copyright infringement based on this distribution of its drawings by Spirit and use of its drawings by Baisch. The defendant Spirit admitted

---

[11]*Id.* at *4 (quoting Gaste v. Kaiserman, 863 F.2d 1061, 1068 (2d Cir. 1988)).

[12]No. 07-1923, 2009 U.S. Dist. LEXIS 65665 (C.D. Cal. July 28, 2009).

[13]*Id.* at **47–48.

[14]*Id.* at *48.

[15]720 F. Supp. 2d 904 (S.D. Ohio 2010).

that it provided the plaintiff's password and CD-ROM containing the plaintiff's drawings to the defendant Baisch. The plaintiff argued that, given this direct evidence of copying, the plaintiff was not required to show substantial similarity between the plaintiff's drawings and Baisch's drawings. Finding an inconsistency in the case law regarding whether a party alleging copyright infringement must prove substantial similarity even when such a party has direct evidence of copying, and noting that no Sixth Circuit decision yet existed on this issue, the court held that "if actual copying is established by means of direct evidence, the plaintiff must then show that the copying amounts to an improper appropriation by demonstrating that substantial similarity to protected material exists between the two works."

The result was similar in *Sater Design Collection, Inc. v. Waccamaw Construction, Inc.*,[16] where the district court denied the plaintiff's motion for summary judgment, finding that, despite direct evidence of "factual" copying of an architectural work, the plaintiff was still required to demonstrate substantial similarity between the works at issue to establish "the actionable" copying. The plaintiff Sater Design Collection, an architectural design firm that created and sold custom and pre-drawn building plans, created and obtained federal copyright protection for its "6804" architectural design. Upon discovering a residence located in Myrtle Beach, South Carolina (Waterton residence) that appeared to be built from its 6804 design, the plaintiff brought an infringement action against the construction company that built the Waterton residence, and subsequently moved for summary judgment. Valid ownership of copyright in the 6804 design was not in dispute, but the defendants denied (1) copying of constituent elements of the 6804 design that were original, and (2) knowledge of the plaintiff's rights in the 6804 design. It was evident that the defendants received the design plan to build the Waterton residence from the owners of the Waterton residence, and that the design plan was a modified version of the plaintiff's 6804 design. The court found, however, that even in the face of direct evidence of "factual" copying it was still necessary to demonstrate "the actionable" copying, i.e., that elements of the 6804 design that were protected expression were copied, and that the works at issue were substantially similar. The court chose not to reach a finding of substantial similarity at this stage due to a lack of detailed analysis as to similarities between the plans, and therefore denied the plaintiff's motion for summary judgment. As to the defendants' knowledge of the plaintiff's rights in the plans, because a builder who uses a set of copyrighted plans to construct a house engages in volitional conduct, and is more than a mere conduit, the builder's claimed lack of knowledge of the plaintiff's rights would not preclude a finding of direct infringement against the builder if other elements of

---

[16]97 USPQ2d 1769 (D.S.C. 2011).

copyright infringement were proven—though it might affect the amount of damages recoverable.

1. More Than de Minimis *Copying*

[Add the following text at the end of the section.]

In another film case, the Southern District of New York held in *Gottlieb Development LLC v. Paramount Pictures Corp.*[17] that the defendant's use of the plaintiff's pinball machine in a movie was so trivial that the copying was not actionable. The plaintiff brought an action alleging copyright infringement based on the brief appearance of the plaintiff's "Silver Slugger" pinball machine in the background of a scene in the defendant's film *What Women Want.* The scene in question lasted only three and one-half minutes, and the copyrighted work appeared in the scene sporadically, for no more than a few seconds each time. More importantly, the copyrighted work was always in the background, never appeared in close-up, was never mentioned and played no role in the plot, and was never fully visible.

The de minimis argument was rejected by the same court in *Dyer v. V.P. Records Retail Outlet, Inc.*[18] There, the court denied a summary judgment motion by the defendants, a record producer and a record store, over their unauthorized use of the plaintiffs' music video featuring the performer Kelly. The defendants produced and aired a television commercial for a record store using, without permission, three clips from the plaintiffs' video, each featuring images of Kelly. The court reasoned that "[w]hile only three shots of Kelly from the Video appear in VP's Commercial, they take up most of the screen when they appear, and Kelly is clearly observable in them. Moreover, . . . the shots each last long enough to show Kelly in motion. . . . The shots of Kelly run consecutively, and together take up almost three seconds of the one-minute video, or approximately five percent of its air time. Further, the three shots constitute all of the visual images in VP's Commercial that promote Kelly and the 'Smile' CD; the remainder of VP's Commercial promotes other artists."[19]

In *Pathfinder Corp. v. Sagamore Training Systems,*[20] the court granted the defendant's motion for summary judgment dismissing a copyright infringement claim concerning the plaintiff's insurance examination course books. Any substantial similarity in the formatting of the books did not extend to original protectable elements. Moreover, while there may have been some slight similarities between two passages in the works, the rest of the contents of the works were wholly different. "When analyzing

---

[17]590 F. Supp. 2d 625, 89 USPQ2d 1862 (S.D.N.Y. 2008).

[18]No. 05-6583, 2008 U.S. Dist. LEXIS 56279 (S.D.N.Y. July 24, 2008).

[19]*Id.* at **11–12.

[20]No. 09-0540, 2010 U.S. Dist. LEXIS 70323 (S.D. Ind. July 13, 2010).

two works to determine whether they are substantially similar, the courts should be careful not to lose sight of the forest for the trees."

3. Other Similarity Issues

[Add the following text to the end of the section.]

In *Watt v. Butler*,[21] the district court granted the defendants' motion for summary judgment in an action for infringement of a musical composition, finding that the plaintiff failed to provide sufficient evidence to overcome evidence of independent creation. In 1995, the rap group Woodlawn Click created a rap song called "Come Up," and subsequently assigned rights in "Come Up" to the plaintiff Watt. Between 1996 and 2005, Watt claimed to have distributed 12,000–15,000 CDs featuring "Come Up" in Atlanta, and the song appeared in the film *Dirty South*, premiering in Atlanta in 2000. Woodlawn Click also performed "Come Up" on multiple occasions in Atlanta, and a video featuring "Come Up" appeared on TV shows aired in Atlanta. In 2004, the defendant rap group D4L wrote and performed the song "Betcha Can't Do It Like Me," with the defendant Teriyakie Smith composing the music. Smith and members of D4L all lived in the Atlanta area. Upon hearing "Betcha" on the radio, Watt brought the action for infringement, alleging that "Betcha" copied a repeating three-note motif or ostinato that served as the underlying rhythmic track to "Come Up." The defendants moved for summary judgment, asserting that "Betcha" was independently created. The court addressed issues of access, substantial similarity, independent creation, and striking similarity. Although access was established, due to the defendants' presence in Atlanta, where "Come Up" was distributed and performed, issues of material fact as to substantial similarity precluded a presumption of infringement. Moreover, the court found that any presumption would be overcome by the defendants' evidence of independent creation, consisting of Smith's testimony that he created the three-note pattern at issue by using music production software and striking adjacent keys on his computer keyboard. Despite expert testimony that "Betcha" was an imitation of "Come Up," the court found that Watt offered no evidence to contradict Smith's testimony. Watt failed to establish complexity or uniqueness, which may have supported a finding of striking similarity sufficient to preclude independent creation. The court thus granted the defendants' motion for summary judgment, finding that simple compositions of short length are susceptible to original creation by more than one composer.

B. Extrinsic/Intrinsic Analysis

1. Motion Pictures and Literary Works

[Add the following text at the end of the section.]

---

[21] 744 F. Supp. 2d 1315 (N.D. Ga. 2010).

When applying the extrinsic/intrinsic analysis, the courts will generally only compare the parties' works one-to-one, and will not compare the plaintiff's work to an entire series of the defendant's works. For example, in *Doody v. Penguin Group (USA), Inc.*,[22] the district court in Hawaii granted the defendant's motion for summary judgment, finding no substantial similarity between the works at issue. The plaintiff had sent the defendant multiple versions of the manuscript for a fictional novel, *Gold of the Khan*. The defendant rejected the manuscripts. The plaintiff contended that protected elements of his manuscript were incorporated into several adventure novels by Clive Cussler and Dirk Cussler, including *Treasure of Khan, Trojan Odyssey, Golden Buddha, The Navigator,* and *Lost City*. The defendant moved for summary judgment dismissing the claim on the ground that the novels were not substantially similar. To determine substantial similarity at the summary judgment stage, the court applied the objective extrinsic test, focusing on " 'articulable similarities between the plot, themes, dialogue, mood, setting, pace, characters, and sequence of events in the two works,' "[23] while ignoring similar but unprotectable elements such as ideas and scenes à faire. The court rejected the plaintiff's contention that substantial similarity should be assessed "not merely between *Gold of the Khan* and each Cussler Book separately, but between *Gold of the Khan* and the Cussler Books collectively."[24] The court stated that "[p]ulling out disparate aspects across multiple works would disembowel this analysis and result in a list of random similarities, which the Ninth Circuit has rejected."[25] Instead, the court compared the plaintiff's work to one specific work, *Treasure of Khan*, that the plaintiff alleged was substantially similar on its own. The court found that any similarities went only to general ideas and scenes à faire, and to unprotectable catch phrases such as "I'll take over from here."[26] Even though the two works shared one word in their respective titles ("Khan"), that was insufficient to warrant a finding of substantial similarity. Accordingly, the court granted the defendant's motion for summary judgment.

Similarly, in *B2B CFO Partners, LLC v. Kaufman*,[27] the court denied the plaintiff's motion for partial summary judgment of copyright infringement. The plaintiff was the largest CFO business in the United States, recruiting experienced CFOs to become partners and then providing them on a part-time basis to other companies. The plaintiff's business manual was distributed to the plaintiff's partners, including the defendant, who was a partner in 2006. After leaving the plaintiff, the defendant formed his own CFO business and created training manuals. The plaintiff sued,

---

[22]673 F. Supp. 2d 1144 (D. Haw. 2009).

[23]*Id.* at 1155 (quoting Kouf v. Walt Disney Pictures & Television, 16 F.3d 1042, 1045 (9th Cir. 1994)).

[24]*Id.*

[25]*Id.* at 1156 (citing Litchfield v. Spielberg, 736 F.2d 1352, 1356 (9th Cir. 1984)).

[26]*Id.* at 1160–61.

[27]No. 09-2158, 2011 U.S. Dist. LEXIS 12738 (D. Ariz. Feb. 8, 2011).

alleging that the defendant's manuals infringed the plaintiff's copyright in the revised manual. With regard to substantial similarity, the court conducted a two-stage inquiry, extrinsic and intrinsic. Because the defendant had a high degree of access to the plaintiff's work, inasmuch as it was given to the defendant by the plaintiff, the court applied a lower standard of proof on similarity, and found that the extrinsic test would be satisfied if both manuals expressed similar ideas and the defendant used the exact same phrases or expression as the plaintiff's manual. The court rejected the defendant's argument under the scenes à faire doctrine, finding that the plaintiff's original decisions on how to arrange and present business practices in its manual did not naturally flow from the business concepts contained in the manual. Regarding the intrinsic test, the court observed that subjective assessment may not properly be made by the court as a matter of law and that it was for the trier of fact to determine whether the intrinsic test was satisfied.

C. Total Concept and Feel Test

[Add the following text at then end of the section.]

In *Allen v. Scholastic, Inc.*,[28] after a "detailed examination" of the plaintiff's book *The Adventures of Willy the Wizard—No. 1 Livid Land* and the defendant's book *Harry Potter and the Goblet of Fire*, the district court granted the defendant's motion to dismiss, finding that no reasonable jury could find substantial similarity between the two books. The plaintiff alleged that the defendant's book unlawfully used protected expression from the plaintiff's book. The defendant filed a motion to dismiss, in which it conceded that the plaintiff had a valid copyright and that actual copying occurred, but argued that no substantial similarity existed between its book and protectable elements of the plaintiff's book. After analyzing "the total concept and feel, theme, characters, plot, sequence, pace and settings of the works," the court agreed with the defendant. Because the books were created for children, the court treated "the total concept and feel of the works" as the most important factor, and found no overlap, given the vast aesthetic and substantive differences, including in length (16 pages in the plaintiff's book versus 734 pages in the defendant's book), structure, mood, details, and characterization (the plaintiff's book progressing as a series of fragmented scenes, each exploring a wizard's exploits, without details or explanation or suspenseful build-up, and having no moral message or intellectual depth, where the wizard contest is merely a background, the defendant's book being a cumulative work with a complex, highly developed storyline, having text rich in imagery, emotion, and suspense, with a highly developed moral core, where the wizard contest serves as packaging for various underlying storylines). The court dismissed the plaintiff's argument that both works evinced the same themes, reasoning that "brief, perfunctory and isolated reference to a subject cannot give a rise to a cognizable

---

[28]739 F. Supp. 2d 642 (S.D.N.Y. 2011).

theme—let alone one specific enough to be infringed," and that the plaintiff's book "provides scant basis upon which to extrapolate any theme." The court also disagreed that the wizards in both books were similar due to being famous male wizards, initiated late into wizarding, who received formal education in wizarding and were chosen to compete in a yearlong tournament, finding such attributes to constitute a general prototype too indistinct for copyright protection. In particular, the court found that the plaintiff's character did not display any creativity, and thus did not constitute protectable expression. Regarding plot and sequence, the court found that although both works told the story of a wizard competition won by the protagonist wizard, the works shared no similarities beyond this abstract level, and instead were overwhelmingly different in plot and sequence. The court further found that the allegedly infringing plot features were not protectable elements, but rather naturally flowed from the work's theme, and that the plaintiff's attempts to portray similarities by selectively extracting various trivialities from each book failed because the works should be compared as a whole, as viewed by an ordinary observer. The court also noted differences in pace (the defendant's book being fast-moving with cliff-hangers in each chapter, the plaintiff's books unrushed with no sense of urgency) and lack of substantial similarities in the settings, where the defendant's work merely mentions the setting in passing, without any creative effort. Accordingly, the court granted the defendant's motion to dismiss.

D. Ordinary Observer Test

[Add the following text at the end of the section.]

Applying the ordinary observer test to architectural works, the Second Circuit held, in *Peter F. Gaito Architecture, LLC v. Simone Development Corp.*,[29] that the parties' respective works lacked substantial similarity as a matter of law. The plaintiff architectural firm and the defendant development company entered into an agreement to submit a joint proposal for the Church Street development project in New Rochelle, New York. Pursuant to their agreement, plaintiff Gaito drafted architectural plans for a residential high-rise tower, retail space at the base of the tower, a pedestrian plaza, a public park, and a parking garage. Defendant Simone was to secure financing for the project. Gaito and Simone subsequently terminated their relationship, and Simone retained the services of architectural firm SLCE to continue work on the project. Gaito brought an action alleging actionable similarity between its design and SLCE's design, attaching the parties' respective designs to its complaint. The defendants moved to dismiss for failure to a state a cause of action, arguing that there was "no substantial similarity between the protectible elements" of the designs.[30] Affirming the ruling below, the Second Circuit ruled that

---

[29]602 F.3d 57 (2d Cir. 2010).

[30]*Id.* at 61.

the district court's consideration of substantial similarity on the motion to dismiss was proper, citing supporting decisions from other circuits. The court held that where the court evaluates the similarity between the parties' works and determines that the works are not substantially similar as a matter of law, it can properly conclude that the complaint does not plausibly give rise to an entitlement to relief. Noting the differences in the parties' respective designs (e.g., Gaito's design consisted of three prominent structures, while SLCE's consisted of only one; Gaito's design included townhouses while SLCE's did not; the designs of the parties' pedestrian plaza and the placement of the park were different), and finding that the "overall visual impressions" of the designs were different, the court concluded that "no average lay observer" would recognize SLCE's design as having been copied from Gaito's design.[31] Further, the only similarities were in unprotectable ideas and concepts common to such developments. Concluding that Gaito failed to allege substantial similarity, the Second Circuit affirmed dismissal of the action.

2.   *Discerning Ordinary Observer Test*

[Add the following text at the end of the section.]

In *Lewinson v. Henry Holt & Co.*,[32] the Southern District of New York granted the defendants' motion for summary judgment, holding no reasonable trier of fact could find substantial similarity between protectable elements of the plaintiff's book, *What Do You Call It?* and the defendants' book, *Can You Say Peace?*. The court applied the "more discerning ordinary observer test," under which unprotectable elements such as ideas, scenes à faire, titles, words, and ordinary phrases, are excluded from comparison of the works. Applying the test, the court considered the issues of " 'total concept and feel, theme, characters, plot, sequence, pace, and setting' " of the works.[33] The court rejected the plaintiff's argument that the titles and main questions of the defendant's work infringed the plaintiff's work. While both works shared the unprotectable idea that children universally desire peace, the plaintiff expressed the idea through the metaphor of a "pacifier"; the defendant did not. The court found de minimis similarities as to scenes, and no similarities between the plaintiff's characters and the defendant's characters. Though both stories were "international" in scope, the similarities in sequence and setting were deemed merely scenes à faire. Of the few similarities in sequence between the two works, none was protectable. The similarity of pace of both works was to be expected in children's stories, and thus not protectable. The works were not substantially similar in total concept and feel; while the plaintiff's work expressed its message through the metaphor of a pacifier, the defendant's work pertained to the United

---

[31] *Id.* at 66–67 (citations and internal quotations omitted).

[32] 659 F. Supp. 2d 547 (S.D.N.Y. 2009).

[33] *Id.* at 565 (quoting Boisson v. Banian, 273 F.3d 262, 273 (2d Cir. 2001)).

Nations' International Day of Peace. Accordingly, the court granted summary judgment to the defendants on the issue of infringement.

E. Scenes à Faire, Stock Themes, and Merger Doctrine

1. *Movies, Stories, and Characters*

a. *No Substantial Similarity*

The court found no substantial similarity between summer camp plays in *Frye v. YMCA Cap Kitaki*.[34] Appellant, freelance author Frye, developed a medieval-themed play, *Kastleland*, for use at YMCA's Camp Kitaki. When Frye ended his association with the YMCA, a dispute arose whether the YMCA could continue to produce *Kastleland*. The dispute was resolved through a settlement agreement and stipulated judgment in federal court whereby the YMCA agreed not to infringe Frye's copyright in *Kastleland*. Several years later, appellee Koos became camp director of Camp Kitaki, writing a medieval-themed play *KnightQuest*. Frye filed a complaint in federal district court in Nebraska, moving to hold the YMCA in contempt for violating the stipulated judgment entered in the earlier dispute. The district court found that Frye failed to prove that *KnightQuest* was substantially similar to any protected expression in *Kastleland*, denied Frye's motion for contempt, and dismissed Frye's lawsuit, finding that the YMCA's play *KnightQuest* did not infringe Frye's copyright in *Kastleland*. The Eighth Circuit affirmed the district court's decision, and noted that its task on appeal was limited to reviewing the district court's finding that *Kastleland* and *KnightQuest* were not substantially similar. The court noted that "*Kastleland* and *KnightQuest* are both interactive plays conducted at the same YMCA summer camp and employing a medieval theme. In each play, campers are invited to join the characters on a quest and are guided through multiple challenges where they can acquire certain skills necessary to defeat the play's antagonists." However, "YMCA's employment of that general idea cannot form the basis for a copyright infringement claim.... Most of those similarities are ... required or at least standard to the plays' shared hero-on-a-quest plot, medieval theme, and summer campfire setting.... After filtering out these ideas and *scenes à faire*, we agree that any remaining similarities between the two plays are insubstantial."

Likewise, in *Davis v. ABC*,[35] the district court granted the defendants' motion to dismiss a claim that the defendants' television series *Eli Stone* infringed the plaintiff's copyrights in two action-mystery books about a fictional Native American warrior in the 1950s named Ely Stone. The only similarities between the works were unprotectable stock items and scenes à faire. The works were completely different in overall feel and expressive elements such as themes, characters, plots, sequences, pace,

---

[34]617 F.3d 1005 (8th Cir. 2010).

[35]No. 10-167, 2010 U.S. Dist. LEXIS 76145 (W.D. Mich. July 28, 2010).

and settings. The mere fact that both characters had visions and were reluctant heroes was insufficient to survive a motion to dismiss.

2.   *Visual Works*

a.   *No Substantial Similarity*

[Add the following text at the end of the section.]

The district court in *Telebrands Corp. v. Del Laboratories Inc.*,[36] granted the defendant's motion to dismiss a copyright infringement claim, finding that no ordinary observer could find the defendant's package to be substantially similar to the plaintiff's copyrighted work. The plaintiff marketed a product "PED EGG," a foot file designed to remove calluses and dead skin from the user's feet. The defendant marketed a similar product known as "Pedi-Perfect." The plaintiff sued the defendant on grounds including infringement of the plaintiff's copyright in two-sided product packaging. The defendant, conceding the plaintiff owned a valid copyright and actual copying occurred, moved to dismiss based on the absence of substantial similarity. The court found that many common features identified by the plaintiff were not protectable because they were unoriginal, including a clear blister pack, a color scheme that included blue and yellow on a white background, a silhouette of a foot, and a metal cartridge displayed through the blister pack, and a ubiquitous feature of foot file packages. The court further found significant differences between possibly protectable elements of the defendant's and the plaintiff's packages, including different pictures one and three in a series of three pictures on the reverse side of each package. The court reasoned that the second picture, showing the foot file in a person's hand, though the same in both packages, served a utilitarian purpose, as it instructed the user on how to hold the foot file, and thus it was not original. The court also highlighted that the "total concept and overall feel" of the works was different because the plaintiff's package contained only one foot file, but the defendant's package contained two additional foot care products, which were prominently displayed on top of the pack. Further, the defendant's package had a markedly different color scheme than the plaintiff's, notwithstanding the presence of shared colors. Thus, the court granted the defendant's motion to dismiss.

The same basic analysis has been applied to restaurant floor plans as well, in *Miller's Ale House, Inc. v Boynton Carolina Ale House, LLC.*[37] There, the court granted the defendant's motion for summary judgment, finding that no reasonable jury could find the plaintiff's and the defendant's floor plans substantially similar. The plaintiff operated a chain of restaurants having multiple features, including a centrally located bar with seating on both sides, dock wood on the walls, an open kitchen, and high-top tables on the right side of the restaurant, common to every restaurant location.

---

[36]No. 09-1001, 2010 U.S. Dist. LEXIS 62401 (S.D.N.Y. June 15, 2010).

[37]745 F. Supp. 2d 1359 (S.D. Fla. 2010).

The plaintiff registered copyright in the common floor plan used in its restaurants. The defendant opened a restaurant with a floor plan featuring a centrally located bar area, open kitchen, dock wood on the interior walls, and high-top seating on the right side. The plaintiff sued, asserting multiple claims including copyright infringement as to the floor plan. The defendant moved for summary judgment on the copyright claim, arguing lack of substantial similarity. The court, observing that architectural works are accorded only "thin" protection for their overall arrangement of common elements, found numerous differences between the interior and exterior arrangements of the plaintiff's and the defendant's floor plans, including the locations of the central bars in relation to restaurants' entryways (the plaintiff's being on the right, the defendant's slightly to the left), interior seating (the plaintiff having several columns of booth seating to the left of the entryway, the defendant having a single column of tables between booths), bathroom entrances (the defendant separating its bathroom entrances from the dining area, the plaintiff not), pool table and video game arrangements (the plaintiff having a column of pool tables between its tables, the defendant separating its pool tables from diners and lining its video games along the wall), and outdoor areas (the defendant having separate outside corner bar and seating, the plaintiff having no outdoor seating). The court concluded that the plaintiff could not have copyright in the idea of a centrally located bar, booth seating on the side of a restaurant, or a restroom located in the rear, and thus as a matter of law the plaintiff could not show substantial similarity or prove its copyright infringement claim.

3. *Toys*

[Add the following text at the end of the section.]

In *Mattel, Inc. v. MGA Entertainment, Inc.*[38] the Ninth Circuit took a very skeptical view of claimed infringing similarities between the popular Bratz dolls and Mattel's classic Barbie line. While still employed at Mattel, Bryant pitched the idea for the Bratz line of dolls to MGA Entertainment (one of Mattel's competitors) and began working with MGA to develop the Bratz dolls. Mattel filed various lawsuits against MGA. In one, the jury found that Bryant thought of the "Bratz" and "Jade" names while employed by Mattel and issued a general verdict finding MGA liable for infringing Mattel's copyrights in Bryant's preliminary Bratz works. The district court granted equitable relief based on the jury's findings. With respect to the copyright claim, the district court issued an injunction prohibiting MGA from producing or marketing virtually every Bratz female fashion doll, as well as any future dolls substantially similar to Mattel's copyrighted Bratz works. The Ninth Circuit evaluated the district court's copyright rulings, noting that "[a]ssuming that Mattel owns Bryant's preliminary drawings and sculpt, its copyrights in the works would cover only its particular expression of the bratty-doll

---

[38]96 USPQ2d 1012 (9th Cir. 2010).

idea, not the idea itself." The Ninth Circuit noted that the district court conducted an extrinsic analysis, determining that certain elements of Bryant's sketches and sculpt were nonprotectable, based on which the district court concluded that "substantial similarity" was the appropriate test for infringement. The Ninth Circuit reviewed the district court's finding de novo. The Ninth Circuit held that the district court erred in affording broad protection against works substantially similar to Bryant's doll sculpt, because due to the narrow range of expression of an "attractive, young, female fashion doll with exaggerated proportions," Bryant's preliminary sculpt was entitled only to thin copyright protection, against virtually identical copying. The Ninth Circuit also held that, although the district court did not err in affording Bryant's doll sketches broad copyright protection against substantially similar works (due to the "wide range of expression" for "complete young, hip female fashion dolls with exaggerated features"), the district court *did* err in failing to filter out all unprotectable elements of Bryant's sketches, noting that "Mattel can't claim a monopoly over fashion dolls with a bratty look or attitude, or dolls sporting trendy clothing—these are all unprotectable ideas." The Ninth Circuit stated that "[a]lthough substantial similarity was the appropriate standard, a finding of substantial similarity between two works can't be based on similarities in unprotectable elements" and noted that "we fail to see how the district court could have found the vast majority of Bratz dolls substantially similar—even though their fashions and hair styles are nothing like anything Bryant drew—unless it was relying on similarities in ideas." The Ninth Circuit vacated the equitable relief granted by the district court.

4. *Music*

[Add the following text at the end of the section.]

In cases alleging similarities in pop song lyrics, the scope of the plaintiff's copyright can be extremely narrow—and the chances of a successful infringement claim exceedingly small—once the common, clichéd elements are filtered out. In *Steele v. Turner Broadcasting System, Inc.*,[39] for example, the court granted the defendants' motion for summary judgment, finding that the plaintiff's song about the Boston Red Sox entitled "Man I Really Love This Team" was not infringed by the defendant Bon Jovi's song "I Love This Town" used as the soundtrack for an allegedly infringing television promotion aired during the 2007 Major League Baseball post-season. The court evaluated the similarity between the music and lyrics of both songs. Experts on both sides found no substantial similarity in the musical elements of the songs, and the court agreed, finding that no reasonable jury could find substantial similarity between the protectable musical elements. The court dissected the lyrics of the plaintiff's song to exclude those phrases such as "come on," "here we go," and "I love this" as too trite, common or clichéd to

---

[39]646 F. Supp. 2d 185 (D. Mass. 2009).

be copyrightable. The court also noted that the common rhyming of "round" and "town" is found in the children's song "The Wheels on the Bus"; a common rhyme scheme and structure do not constitute protectable original expression. The court also considered whether there was any substantial similarity between the defendant's advertisement, including the video elements, and the plaintiff's song. The plaintiff argued that scenes in the promotion coincided with certain lyrics in the plaintiff's song, alleging that the defendants employed "temp tracking"—using the plaintiff's song as a template for the promotion and then substituting the Bon Jovi song. The plaintiff noted four scenes in which the defendants' video coincided with the plaintiff's lyrics. The court found that certain such scenes were "classic scene[s] à faire"; additionally, while the defendant's video showed fans cheering more than a dozen times, just one of these instances happened to coincide with the plaintiff's lyrics "get up off your seats." The court concluded that no reasonable jury could find substantial similarity between the defendant's advertisement and copyrightable elements of the plaintiff's work.

Similarly in *Lessem v. Taylor*,[40] the district court denied the plaintiffs' motion for summary judgment that the defendants' song infringed the plaintiffs' song, and denied the defendants' motion for summary judgment that the two songs share only unprotectable elements. The dispute centered on the use of the lyric phrase "this is how we do," set to the same rhythm, four times, in both the plaintiffs' and the defendants' songs, which also shared the same tempo.

A somewhat less obvious result was reached by the Northern District of Illinois in *Peters v. West*,[41] where the court granted a motion to dismiss an infringement claim alleging copying of portions of the plaintiff's song "Stronger." The plaintiff claimed that the defendants' song infringed the plaintiff's song because the songs had the identical title, "Stronger"; because both songs had lyrics that included the name of the English model Kate Moss; and because the songs had similar refrains or "hooks." As to the title, the court noted that titles by themselves are not subject to copyright protection. Therefore, the plaintiff's complaint did not plausibly allege that the title of the plaintiff's song was a protectable element of the work. As to the reference in the lyrics to Kate Moss, the court noted that individual names and addresses are in the public domain and are not copyrightable; therefore, the complaint did not plausibly allege that the reference to Kate Moss in the defendant's song was a protectable element. As to the phrase "that which does not kill me makes me stronger" in each song's lyrics, because this maxim was copied from a common source that enjoyed a robust existence in the public domain, it was unprotectable. As to the line "can't wait much longer" in each song's lyrics, common phrases and expressions are not protected by copyright. As to the word "wronger" in each song's lyrics,

---

[40] 766 F. Supp. 2d 504 (S.D.N.Y. 2011).
[41] 776 F. Supp. 2d 742 (N.D. Ill. 2011).

the court noted that while this word may not be common, it is not unique to the plaintiff and is instead part of a common rhyme scheme—and rhyme schemes are not protected by copyright. Accordingly, there was no similarity as to protectable elements.

F.   Literary Works (Other Than Software)

1.   *Abstraction-Filtration-Comparison Test*

[Add the following text at the end of the section.]

The abstraction-filtration-comparison method was recently applied to an insurance brochure in *MDM Group Associates, Inc. v. ResortQuest International, Inc.,*[42] where a Colorado district court granted the defendant's motion for summary judgment. The plaintiff designed a rental unit damage waiver brochure for use by the defendant in the rental of vacation properties to clients. The parties terminated the license agreement, but the defendant continued to use the brochure, and later created its own damage waiver brochure. The plaintiff filed suit for infringement, alleging that the defendant's brochure was derived from the plaintiff's in violation of the plaintiff's adaptation right. The defendant moved for summary judgment based on lack of substantial similarity. The court utilized the action-filtration-comparison test to separate out the uncopyrightable elements of the brochures, holding certain aspects not copyrightable because they were generic functional descriptions. Other aspects, such as the damage waiver provision, were not copyrightable because "there are a limited number of ways to convey the basic operation of the damage waiver."[43] The court found significant differences in the copyrightable aspects of the parties' works, including that the defendant's simple layout contrasted with the more complex "legalistic phrasing, formal headings, and defined terms" found in the plaintiff's.[44] The court held, therefore, that there was no substantial similarity from the perspective of the ordinary observer.

A similar result was reached in *Allen v. Scholastic, Inc.,*[45] after a "detailed examination" of the plaintiff's book *The Adventures of Willy the Wizard—No. 1 Livid Land* and the defendant's book *Harry Potter and the Goblet of Fire.* The plaintiff alleged that the defendant's book unlawfully used protected expression from the plaintiff's book. The defendant filed a motion to dismiss, in which it conceded that the plaintiff had a valid copyright and that actual copying occurred, but argued that no substantial similarity existed between its book and protectable elements of the plaintiff's book. After analyzing "the total concept and feel, theme, characters, plot, sequence, pace and settings of the works," the court agreed with the defendant.

---

[42]No. 06-1518, 2009 U.S. Dist. LEXIS 82318 (D. Colo. Sept. 9, 2009).

[43]*Id.* at *42.

[44]*Id.* at *44.

[45]739 F. Supp. 2d 642 (S.D.N.Y. 2011).

3. Words and Phrases

[Add the following text at the end of the section.]

As noted in Section 5.II.E.4., *supra, Peters v. West*[46] resulted in a finding of no infringement in a claim alleging copying of portions of the plaintiff's song "Stronger" by a Kanye West tune of the same title. The court perhaps went a bit overboard, however, to the extent that it implied that plaintiff's "hook" was not even copyrightable. Both songs had lyrics that included the name of the English model Kate Moss, and similar refrains or "hooks." As to the title, the court noted that titles by themselves are not subject to copyright protection. Therefore, the plaintiff's complaint did not plausibly allege that the title of the plaintiff's song was a protectable element of the work. As to the reference in the lyrics to Kate Moss, the court noted that individual names and addresses are in the public domain and are not copyrightable; therefore, the complaint did not plausibly allege that the reference to Kate Moss in the defendant's song was a protectable element. As to the phrase "that which does not kill me makes me stronger" in each song's lyrics, because this maxim was copied from a common source that enjoyed a robust existence in the public domain, it was unprotectable. As to the line "can't wait much longer" in each song's lyrics, common phrases and expressions are not protected by copyright. As to the word "wronger" in each song's lyrics, the court noted that while this word may not be common, it is not unique to the plaintiff and is instead part of a common rhyme scheme—and rhyme schemes are not protected by copyright. Accordingly, there was no similarity as to protectable elements.

G. Unique Issues Due to Nature of Medium

3. Three-Dimensional Works

[Add the following text at the end of the section.]

Merely using a drawing to make a useful article is not infringement, however, in the view of the Northern District of Ohio. In *Niemi v. NHK Spring Co.*,[47] that court granted the defendants' motion for partial summary judgment on a claim involving alleged infringement of drawings for machine parts. The plaintiff created a new process and machine for the development, design, and manufacture of stabilizer bars. The plaintiff entered into an agreement with the defendants, manufacturers of stabilizer bars, whereby the plaintiff created drawings incorporating its process for the defendants. The plaintiff sued the defendants for copyright infringement, alleging that the defendants shared the plaintiff's copyrighted drawings with third parties, which in turn built stabilizer-bar-producing machines based on the drawings. The defendants moved for partial summary judgment dismissing the copyright claim. The court

---

[46]776 F. Supp. 2d 742 (N.D. Ill. 2011).

[47]84 USPQ2d 1766 (N.D. Ohio 2007).

distinguished the plaintiff's drawings from drawings depicting architectural works, as to which the construction of a building depicted in such drawings can infringe copyright; the plaintiff's drawings here fell into the category of "pictorial, graphic, and sculptural works under Section 101" and the use of such works to produce the article depicted in the drawing is not infringement.[48]

I.   Substantial Similarity and the Jury

[Add the following text at the end of the section.]

A remarkable application by the jury of the "fragmented literal similarity" doctrine in the context of a musical composition claim was affirmed in 2009 by the Sixth Circuit in *Bridgeport Music, Inc. v. UMG Recordings, Inc.*[49] In 1998, the defendants released a song entitled "D.O.G. In Me" which incorporated elements of the George Clinton funk classic "Atomic Dog." The defendants copied three elements from "Atomic Dog": use of the word "dog" as musical punctuation, rhythmic panting, and a "bow wow" refrain ("bow-wow-wow, yippee-yo-yippee-yay"). The jury was instructed that substantial similarity could be found based on fragmented literal similarity. Although no prior reported Sixth Circuit opinion explicitly adopted the fragmented literal similarity doctrine, district courts in the Sixth Circuit had previously applied the fragmented literal similarity test. Because the evidence offered at trial supported the conclusion that copied elements were of substantial qualitative importance to the original, the Sixth Circuit held that it was not error to apply the fragmented literal similarity doctrine. As an aside, the finding of infringement makes much more sense on the face of the decision than it does upon actually hearing the songs at issue; the "dog" and rhythmic panting elements are negligible portions of both works, and the "bow wow" refrain only shows up faintly as part of the fade-out in the last few seconds of the defendant's record. Still, a jury found infringement and the Sixth Circuit was predictably reluctant to disturb the jury verdict.

III. Computer Works

D.   Section 117

1.   *Adaptation Exception*

[Add the following text at the end of the section.]

It is clear that licensees are not "owners" for purposes of Section 117. For example, in *MDY Industries, LLC v. Blizzard Entertainment, Inc.*,[50] the court granted summary judgment in favor of the defendants, creators and operators of the online role-playing game *World of Warcraft* (WoW).

---

[48]*Id.* at 1768.

[49]585 F.3d 267 (6th Cir. 2009).

[50]89 USPQ2d 1015 (D. Ariz. 2008).

The court found that the plaintiff, creator of the WoWGlider (Glider) software program, was liable for contributory and vicarious copyright infringement, because Glider created infringing copies of the plaintiff's copyrighted software in game owners' computer RAM, in violation of the defendants' terms of use and End User License Agreement (EULA). The court held that over-the-counter purchasers of WoW were "licensees" rather than "owners," and were thus bound by the terms of the EULA. The court determined that the EULA granted a nonexclusive limited license rather than ownership of copies of the game, because the EULA expressly granted a "limited license," and because several provisions contained express restrictions on the users' transfer and use of the game. Therefore, the court reasoned, use of the defendants' software with Glider fell outside the scope of permitted uses under the license and constituted copyright infringement because the Glider software loaded a copy of WoW into the user's computer RAM memory, which was not allowed under the EULA. The court followed Ninth Circuit precedent in determining that copying software to RAM, outside the scope of a license, constitutes copyright infringement. The plaintiff argued that loading software to RAM was protected by Section 117, which permits owners to copy a program to RAM if the copy is created as an essential step in using the program. However, the court reiterated, under Ninth Circuit precedent, that users of Glider were licensees and not owners, and therefore they were not entitled to the Section 117 defense.

V. Secondary Liability

C. Inducement

[Add the following new section.]

6. *Applying Grokster [New Topic]*

Since *Grokster,* courts have applied the Supreme Court's reasoning to find inducement in other cases related to peer-to-peer file sharing. In *Arista Records, LLC v. Lime Group, LLC,*[51] the court granted summary judgment on secondary liability against providers of the LimeWire P2P file-sharing system on grounds of inducement. Under the Supreme Court *Grokster* decision of 2005, and the subsequent remand decision, inducement requires a showing that the defendant "(1) engaged in purposeful conduct that encouraged copyright infringement, with (2) the intent to encourage such infringement."[52] Although much of the decision dealt with evidentiary disputes, the court's liability analysis cited extensive conduct by the defendants that satisfied the *Grokster* inducement standard which the court noted was "a form of the long-established cause of action for

---

[51]715 F. Supp. 2d 481 (S.D.N.Y. 2010).

[52]*Id.* at 508 (citing MGM Studios, Inc. v. Grokster, Ltd., 545 U.S. 913, 937 (2005)).

contributory copyright infringement."[53] Specifically, the court observed that the defendants were aware of "substantial infringement by users," made affirmative efforts to "attract infringing users" and to "enable and assist users to commit infringement," relied heavily on infringing use for success of their business, and failed to "mitigate infringing activities."[54]

According to a statistical study by the plaintiff's expert, nearly all the files shared by users were copyrighted and unauthorized. Internal emails and public marketing materials showed the defendants' awareness, and the defendants even maintained a news-clipping file labeled "Knowledge of Infringement." The defendants actively sought to capture former users of the Napster service when the latter was enjoined, such as by buying Google AdWords like "replacement napster" and "mp3 free download" and other phrases containing the words "napster," "kazaa," and "morpheus" and by running banner ads touting the defendants' superiority to other (illegal) services. The defendants' web interface allowed users to easily locate infringing content, such as by genre categories like "Top 40." Furthermore, the defendants themselves tested their system by searching for unauthorized content and offered technical assistance to users seeking infringing material. The defendants' business grew more than threefold from 2004 to 2006, growth that "depended greatly on LimeWire users' ability to commit infringement."[55] The defendants failed to mitigate harm by implementing available filtering technology. The defendants "in fact employ active filtering technology, but only to prevent LimeWire users from sharing digital recordings purchased from the LimeWire online store."[56] Citing *Grokster* and *Aimster*, the court stated that "[f]ailure to utilize existing technology to create meaningful barriers against infringement is a strong indicator of intent to foster infringement."[57] Accordingly, the plaintiffs' motion for summary judgment was granted as to inducement, though the court declined to rule on contributory infringement under the traditional "material contribution" rubric because a genuine fact issue existed as to the applicability of the "substantial noninfringing use" defense under the facts at issue.

The *Grokster* inducement standard was also applied in *Arista Records, LLC v. Usenet.com, Inc.*,[58] where the court held an on-line service liable for inducement of infringement by its users and also liable for direct,

---

[53]*Id.* at 508 n.23 (citing *Grokster*, 545 U.S. at 930).

[54]*Id.* at 509.

[55]*Id.* at 512.

[56]*Id.* at 514.

[57]*Id.* at 514–15 ("See *Grokster*, 545 U.S. at 939; *Grokster Remand*, 454 F. Supp. 2d at 989 ('[A]lthough [defendant] is not required to prevent all the harm that is facilitated by the technology, it must at least make a good faith attempt to mitigate the massive infringement facilitated by its technology.'); *cf. Aimster*, 334 F.3d at 653 (in claim of contributory copyright infringement, if the infringing uses are 'substantial,' to avoid liability, the defendant 'must show that it would have been disproportionately costly for him to eliminate or at least reduce substantially the infringing uses'").

[58]633 F. Supp. 2d 124 (S.D.N.Y. 2009).

contributory, and vicarious infringement. The service was not peer-to-peer but instead held infringing content on its own servers that had been uploaded by subscribers. As to inducement, the court found that under *Grokster* the defendant was liable because it knowingly took affirmative steps to foster infringement by its users: it promoted itself as an alternative to Napster after the latter was enjoined, it assisted users in committing infringement, it chose not to use available filtering tools to mitigate infringement, and it built its business in reliance on high-volume infringing use. Thus, infringing intent was so clearly established that no jury trial was necessary. As to traditional contributory infringement, the court declined to apply the "substantial noninfringing use" defense because the defendant maintained an "ongoing relationship" with users and did not merely provide technology in a one-time transaction. The court did not resolve whether the "substantial noninfringing use" defense applies to vicarious infringement, but held that the defense was not established on these facts anyway, so the argument was moot. Regardless, "because the undisputed facts illustrate that [d]efendants garnered a direct financial benefit from copyright infringement and failed to exercise their right and ability to control or limit infringement on their servers," the plaintiff's claim for vicarious infringement was granted.[59]

VIII. CRIMINAL INFRINGEMENT

A. Section 506

[Add the following text at the end of the section.]

In a recent Eleventh Circuit decision, *United States v. Dadamuratov*,[60] the court affirmed a criminal conviction for willful copyright infringement of DVDs. Section 506 makes it a criminal offense to "(1) willfully (2) infringe a copyright, if (3) 'the infringement was committed—(A) for purposes of commercial advantage or private financial gain; (B) by the reproduction or distribution . . . during any 180-day period, of 1 or more copies . . . of 1 or more copyrighted works, which have a total retail value of more than $1,000; or (C) by the distribution of a work being prepared for commercial distribution . . . , if such person knew or should have known that the work was intended for commercial distribution.'"[61] The court held that the government presented sufficient evidence to prove each element of offense. In a police interview in an unrelated battery matter, the defendant-appellant admitted that he was the owner of the Moscow Grocery and was "running the show," and that he rented American movies dubbed in Russian which had been downloaded from the Internet onto DVDs by someone for him. Officers seized electronic equipment at the Moscow Grocery, "including

---

[59]*Id.* at 158.

[60]No. 08-15900, 2009 U.S. App. LEXIS 16871 (11th Cir. July 28, 2009).

[61]*Id.* at **10–11 (quoting 17 U.S.C. §506(a)).

multiple computers, hard drives, and machines to record from a VHS tape or DVD onto a DVD; hundreds of VHS tapes and DVDs; and stacks of blank, recordable DVDs and DVD covers."[62] An employee testified that the defendant-appellant gave her new movies to catalog with other rentals. In addition, the defendant-appellant admitted that he personally rented four movies, one of which was still playing in theaters when it was rented, to one person. Evidence was presented that the movies rented were not authorized—"some of the DVDs (1) were on recordable DVD discs with no art work, (2) had movies on each side of a recordable DVD, (3) lacked FBI warnings, movie previews, and credits, (4) appeared to be filmed by an individual with a video camera in a movie theater, and (5) were screening versions from the Motion Picture Association that contained a warning that they should not be viewed by the public."[63] Finding that a reasonable jury could conclude that the government proved each element of the crime and making all reasonable inferences in favor of the jury verdict, the court affirmed the conviction for willful copyright infringement.

[Add the following new section.]

IX. Distribution and Making Available [New Topic]

Recent cases have focused on an issue that continues to plague the entertainment industry as that industry tries to police the infringement of sound recordings and motion pictures on the Internet—whether it is sufficient for a copyright owner to allege that users of peer-to-peer (P2P) file-sharing networks violate the owner's distribution rights under 17 U.S.C. §106 whenever a digital recording or video is placed in a "share" folder that other P2P users can access. If such an allegation is sufficient to support an infringement claim, the plaintiff owner has an easier evidentiary burden because it need only establish that a particular copyrighted work was in a particular defendant's "share" folder—the plaintiff owner does not need to go the extra step of establishing that anyone actually downloaded the file from the defendant's folder. While early P2P decisions were generally in favor of recognizing the so-called making-available right as a species of distribution under Section 106(3), more recent decisions have weighed in with their own contrary spins on the issue.

The Copyright Act gives the owner of copyright various exclusive rights in the work, including the right "to distribute copies . . . of the copyrighted work to the public by sale or other transfer of ownership, or by rental, lease, or lending."[64] The Act does not define the word "distribute" but the statute does not by its terms require that distribution

---

[62] *Id.* at *13.

[63] *Id.* at *14.

[64] 17 U.S.C. §106(3).

must involve or result in a physical copy literally moving from one place to another.

The courts did not require actual movement of copies in the non-Internet context, as is evident in *Hotaling v. Church of Jesus Christ of Latter-Day Saints.*[65] In *Hotaling*, the Fourth Circuit reversed a lower court to hold that a copyright owner's distribution right was violated when a library placed an unauthorized copy of a book on the shelf. Whether or not any patron ever checked out the book, the court reasoned, the library had made it available to the public, which was enough to violate the distribution right: "When a public library adds a work to its collection, lists the work in its index or catalog system, and *makes the work available* to the borrowing or browsing public, it has completed all the steps necessary for distribution to the public."[66]

In the Internet context, the copies at issue are digital files stored on the hard drive of a user's computer. A P2P transaction between two users does not relocate a physical copy of a recording from one user's possession to another's, but, just as with the library book in *Hotaling*, that should not preclude a finding that distribution has occurred, as the Ninth Circuit recognized in *A&M Records, Inc. v. Napster, Inc.*[67] The Ninth Circuit subsequently distinguished *Hotaling* on its facts in *Perfect 10, Inc. v. Amazon.com, Inc.*,[68] but reiterated that no physical copy ever need change hands in order for distribution to occur: "The Supreme Court has indicated that in the electronic context, copies may be distributed electronically."[69]

Since *Napster*, the majority of P2P cases have involved claims of direct infringement against individual users, and in the earliest of the P2P decisions, starting in 2006, the courts found violations of the distribution right where individuals made files available to other P2P users.[70] That year, the District of Maine so held in *Universal City Studios Productions v. Bigwood*[71] (citing the *Hotaling* and the Ninth Circuit's *Napster* decisions). Also in 2006, in the District of Oregon's decision in *Elektra Entertainment Group, Inc., v. Perez*,[72] Judge Ann Aiken used similar reasoning to deny

---

[65]118 F.3d 199, 43 USPQ2d 1299 (4th Cir. 1997).

[66]*Id.* at 203 (emphasis added).

[67]239 F.3d 1004, 1014, 57 USPQ2d 1729, 1734 (9th Cir. 2001) ("Napster users who upload file names to the search index for others to copy violate plaintiffs' distribution rights").

[68]487 F.3d 701, 719 (9th Cir. 2007) ("This 'deemed distribution' rule does not apply to [defendant] Google. Unlike the participants in the *Napster* system or the library in *Hotaling*, Google does not own a collection of Perfect 10's full-size images and does not communicate these images to the computers of people using Google's search engine.").

[69]*Id.* at 718 (citing New York Times Co. v. Tasini, 533 U.S. 483, 498 (2001)).

[70]A very early case supporting the making-available argument is *Playboy Enters. Inc. v. Frena*, 839 F. Supp. 1552, 29 USPQ2d 1827 (M.D. Fla. 1993), a case involving the relatively primitive bulletin board technology of the early 1990s.

[71]441 F. Supp. 2d 185, 82 USPQ2d 1354 (D. Me. 2006).

[72]No. 05-931, 2006 U.S. Dist. LEXIS 78229 (D. Or. Oct. 25, 2006).

a motion to dismiss a P2P complaint. Also in 2006, the Western District of Texas, in *Warner Bros. Records, Inc. v. Payne*,[73] cited *Hotaling* to hold squarely that "[l]isting unauthorized copies of sound recordings using an online file-sharing system constitutes an offer to distribute those works, thereby violating a copyright owner's exclusive right of distribution."[74]

In October 2007, in *Virgin Records America v. Thomas*,[75] a jury in Minnesota found defendant Jammie Thomas liable for infringement and awarded statutory damages of $222,000 based on the online sharing of 24 tracks. Jury charge No. 15, strenuously contested by the defendant, read as follows: "The act of making copyrighted sound recordings available for electronic distribution on a peer-to-peer network, without license from the copyright owners, violates the copyright owners' exclusive right of distribution, regardless of whether actual distribution has been shown."[76] The court later ordered a new trial on the grounds that it had erred in giving that instruction. See the discussion *infra*, this section.

After *Thomas*, the courts became increasingly reluctant to accept making-available liability for individual file-sharers. In February 2008, the District of Connecticut, in *Atlantic Recording Corp. v. Brennan*,[77] refused to enter a default judgment against a nonappearing defendant, again in a case involving the sharing of music files. The court declined to award judgment for the plaintiff in part because it perceived possible meritorious defenses to the allegation of making available, which the court found "problematic . . . without actual distribution of copies."[78]

Subsequent to *Brennan*, the Southern District of New York in *Elektra Entertainment Group, Inc. v. Barker*,[79] struck a compromise between full recognition of the making-available right and outright hostility to it. Like *Brennan*, above, the *Barker* case arose in the context of a motion to dismiss a complaint against a user of Kazaa P2P software, who was found to have 611 music files in a share folder. In an extensive discussion of the issue, Judge Kenneth M. Karas considered the sufficiency of the plaintiffs' allegation that the defendant had used "an online media distribution system . . . to make the [recordings at issue] available for distribution to others."[80] He found the allegation insufficient to state a cause of action, but suggested amended language that could make it viable.

The court began by noting that the Copyright Act does not define the term "distribute." Congress did define the term "publication," however, and in doing so it used language almost identical to that used in

---

[73]No. W-06-CA-051, 2006 U.S. Dist. LEXIS 65765 (W.D. Tex. July 17, 2006).

[74]*Id.* at *8.

[75]No. 06-1497 (D. Minn. Oct. 5, 2007), *vacated sub nom.* Capitol Records, Inc. v. Thomas, 579 F. Supp. 2d 1210, 92 USPQ2d 1414 (D. Minn. 2008).

[76]*See Capitol Records v. Thomas*, 579 F. Supp. at 1213.

[77]534 F. Supp. 2d 278 (D. Conn. 2008).

[78]*Id.* at 282 (citation omitted).

[79]551 F. Supp. 2d 234, 87 USPQ2d 1427 (S.D.N.Y. 2008).

[80]*Id.* at 236.

establishing the distribution right in Section 106(3). Moreover, the court noted that the legislative history of the Act spoke frequently of creating a right of "publication" under Section 106, although the statutory language that was eventually chosen spoke of a right "to distribute." Judge Karas thus concluded that "the House and Senate of the Ninety-Fourth Congress considered the terms 'distribute' and 'publication' to be synonymous."[81]

Therefore, the court followed a number of earlier decisions in adopting the statutory definition of "publication" to define the scope of the Section 106(3) distribution right. Under that definition, distribution can be shown by " '[t]he offer[] to distribute copies or phonorecords to a group of persons for purposes of further distribution, public performance, or public display.' "[82] This definition, however, was not to be confused with the "contourless 'make available' right proposed by Plaintiff."[83] Specifically, the court declined to follow *Hotaling*, stating "respectfully" that the Fourth Circuit's rule in that case, "even if sound public policy, is not grounded in the statute."[84] Merely alleging, as the plaintiffs did, that the defendant had made the plaintiffs' works *available* would therefore not be sufficient to state a cause of action.

Instead, the *Barker* court applied the full publication-based definition to hold that a making-available allegation must include claims that the defendant "made an offer to distribute, and that the offer to distribute was for the purpose of further distribution, public performance, or public display."[85] The plaintiffs' initial allegation, that the defendant made the works available "for distribution to others," apparently satisfied the "offer to distribute" element, but the court observed in a footnote that "[w]hether use of a peer-to-peer file sharing program such as Kazaa necessarily entails 'further distribution,' however, is still an open question."[86] The plaintiffs were given leave to amend their complaint to add an allegation of "making available . . . for the purpose of further distribution" which would conform to the court's newly articulated standard.

Another, more restrictive approach was taken by the District of Arizona in *Atlantic Recording Corp. v. Howell*,[87] which flatly rejected the argument that the terms "distribution" and "publication" were synonymous under the Copyright Act. Instead, the court in *Howell* concluded that Congress' choice to use both terms within the Copyright Act demonstrated an intent that the terms have different meanings: "It is untenable that the definition of a different word in a different section of the statute was meant to expand the meaning of 'distribution' and liability under

---

[81] *Id.* at 241.

[82] *Id.* at 242 (quoting 17 U.S.C. §101). *But see Atlantic Recording Corp. v. Howell, infra.*

[83] *Id.* at 243.

[84] *Id.*

[85] *Id.* at 244.

[86] *Id.* n.8.

[87] 554 F. Supp. 2d 976, 86 USPQ2d 1796 (D. Ariz. 2008).

§106(3) to include offers to distribute."[88] Under *Howell*'s interpretation, the language of the Copyright Act's definition of "publication" clearly includes "distribution" as *part* of its definition—so all distributions are publications, but not all publications are distributions.

The most recent departure from the prior judicial consensus about the making-available right came in September 2008 from the District of Minnesota in a post-verdict decision in the Jammie Thomas case discussed above, *Capitol Records, Inc. v. Thomas.*[89] After the defendant filed a motion for a new trial as to the constitutionality of the amount of statutory damages, the court sua sponte asked for briefing on the making-available question, specifically whether its jury instruction No. 15 (quoted above) was a "manifest error of law" in light of controlling Eighth Circuit precedent in *National Car Rental Systems, Inc. v. Computer Associates International, Inc.*[90]

After briefing by the parties and numerous *amici*, the court issued a lengthy discussion of the making-available question. First, the court found that the "plain meaning" of the term "distribution" in Section 106(3) did not encompass the act of making a copyrighted work available to others. The language of the statute does not itself contain the words "make available" or "offer" but merely speaks of sale, transfer, rental, lease or lending. Dictionaries and treatises were cited in support of such a restrictive reading, while the contrary opinion of the Register of Copyrights was dismissed as "not binding."

The court noted that although "making available" and "offering" are specifically recognized as forms of distribution in other sections of the Copyright Act, such as Section 901(a)(4) ("stating, in the context of copyright protection of semiconductor chip products, that 'to "distribute" means to sell, or to lease, bail, or otherwise transfer, *or to offer to* sell, lease, bail, or otherwise transfer' "[91]) and Section 506(a)(1)(C) ("imposing criminal penalties for 'the *distribution* of a work being prepared for commercial distribution, by *making it available* on a computer network accessible to members of the public' "[92]), in other sections of the Act, Congress has explicitly confined the term "distribution" to a physical transfer of copyrighted material—for example, Section 115(c)(2) ("in the section of the Act providing compulsory licenses for nondramatic musical works, Congress provides: 'For this purpose, and other than as provided [in Section 115(c)(3)], a phonorecord is considered "distributed" if the person exercising the compulsory license has voluntarily and permanently parted with its possession' "[93]).

---

[88] *Id.* at 985.

[89] 579 F. Supp. 2d 1210, 92 USPQ2d 1414 (D. Minn. 2008). In subsequent legislation, the case name is updated as *Capitol Records, Inc. v. Thomas-Rasset.*

[90] 991 F.2d 426, 26 USPQ2d 1370 (8th Cir. 1993).

[91] *Thomas*, 579 F. Supp. at 1217 (quoting 17 U.S.C. §901(a)(4)) (emphasis added).

[92] *Id.* (quoting 17 U.S.C. §506(a)(1)(C)) (emphasis added).

[93] *Id.* (quoting 17 U.S.C. §115(c)(2)).

The court's discussion of these other sections perhaps raises as many questions as it answers. For example, if a criminal defendant can go to jail under Section 506(a)(1)(C) for making something available on-line—as music pirate Kevin Cogill recently found out[94]—how can that same conduct fail to be sufficient "distribution" for a civil claim? Since when is the standard for imposing criminal liability *lower* than that for a corresponding civil offense? As for compulsory license payments under Section 115(c)(2), the language requiring actual distribution is necessary in light of the narrow purpose of the provision—to calculate how much a licensee should pay to the copyright owner for the sale of copies made under compulsory license. Hence the provision's opening words, "For this purpose." If royalties were deemed payable simply because a work had been offered for sale, and not as a result of an actual sale, copyright owners would be getting a much richer deal from compulsory licenses than from market transactions, to such a degree that there might be little chance of economic viability for the sellers of recordings made under compulsory license.

Further, and leaving aside the peculiarities of Section 115(c)(2), the court's generally restrictive reading of the term "distribute" might preclude any compulsory license *at all* for songs whose authors had chosen to make them available by streaming rather than downloading, because compulsory licenses are only available (under Section 115(a)(1)) once recordings of a song have been "distributed to the public." This would undermine the fundamental purpose of the compulsory license by allowing composers to lock up certain works beyond the reach of the statute.

The *Thomas* court next took issue with the *Barker* decision (discussed above) and its holding that distribution and publication are statutorily synonymous. Rejecting the legislative history on which *Barker* had relied, the *Thomas* court instead followed the Arizona court's decision in *Howell* (discussed above) to conclude that "all distributions to the public are publications, but not all publications are distributions to the public."[95] The court then held that the Copyright Act does not give rise to a freestanding right to "authorize" distribution, notwithstanding the language in Section 106 that the copyright owner has the " 'exclusive right[ ] *to do* and *to authorize*' " distribution.[96]

---

[94]Cogill "agreed to plead guilty to criminal copyright infringement in connection with his unauthorized posting of nine as-yet unreleased tracks from a forthcoming album by the rock band Guns N' Roses. Cogill's blog . . . posted the tracks in June, and reportedly removed them when Cogill received correspondence from the copyright owners shortly thereafter. Nonetheless, Cogill was arrested at his home and questioned by F.B.I. personnel before negotiating the plea, which could result in a maximum prison term of one year for misdemeanor copyright infringement. This is significantly less than the five-year maximum sentence he could have faced under the original felony charge." Robert Clarida, "Man Pleads Guilty to Illegally Making Music Files Available," posted Nov. 17, 2008 at www.askbeforeyouact.com.

[95]*Thomas*, 579 F. Supp. 2d at 1220.

[96]*Id.* (quoting 17 U.S.C. §106) (emphasis added by court).

The court further addressed the argument that the statute should be interpreted in such a way as to avoid placing the United States in violation of its international treaty obligations. The issue arose here because the World Intellectual Property Organization (WIPO) Copyright Treaty and WIPO Performances and Phonograms Treaty clearly recognize a making-available right, and the United States in ratifying and adopting these treaties took the position that domestic law was in compliance with these obligations. Be that as it may, the *Thomas* court concluded that there simply was no "reasonable construction" of the Copyright Act that comported with the treaty requirements, thus the court had no power to construe the statute in that manner.

Perhaps most crucially, the *Thomas* court dismissed the Fourth Circuit's *Hotaling* decision (discussed above), lamenting that it "did not analyze any case law . . . [n]or did it conduct any analysis of §106(3)" but rather "was guided by equitable concerns."[97] Even as it did so, however, *Thomas* sought to mitigate the practical hardships that its ruling would impose on copyright owners:

> Nonetheless, it is appropriate to note that this court's rejection of *Hotaling* in favor of the plain meaning of §106(3) does not leave copyright holders without redress. The specter of impossible-to-meet evidentiary standards raised by amici is overstated. A person who makes an unauthorized copy or phonorecord of a copyrighted work for the purposes of uploading it onto a peer-to-peer network, absent a defense such as fair use, violates the reproduction right. 17 U.S.C. §106(1). That person might also be liable for indirect infringement to the extent that her conduct caused others to engage in unauthorized reproduction, adaptation, public distribution, public performance, or public display of another's copyrighted work.[98]

In the last section of its decision, the court in *Thomas* issued an unusually lengthy and heartfelt plea to Congress to revisit the statutory language. The passage begins by saying: "The court would be remiss if it did not take this opportunity to implore Congress to amend the Copyright Act to address liability and damages in peer-to-peer network cases such as the one currently before this court."[99] After delivering its entire decision on the subject of liability, however, the court's suggestions to Congress deal entirely with the scope of statutory damage awards in P2P cases, emphasizing that the defendant was a single mother, not a "global financial firm," and that she sought no commercial gain from her actions, but only "access to free music . . . . Her alleged acts were illegal, but common."[100] With this conclusion, the court in *Thomas* finally reaches the statutory damage issue that prompted the post-verdict motions in the first place. In doing so, however, *Thomas* opens itself up to the very criticism it leveled at *Hotaling, i.e.*, that it "did not analyze any case law . . . [n]or did it conduct any analysis" but rather "was guided

---

[97] *Id.* at 1224.

[98] *Id.* at 1225.

[99] *Id.* at 1227.

[100] *Id.* at 1227–28.

by equitable concerns." It leaves the distinct impression that the court may have chosen to reinterpret its previous reading of Section 106(3) rather than to squarely address the severity of the damage award, even as it acknowledged that Thomas' acts were "illegal."

The plaintiffs' motion to certify the matter for interlocutory appeal was denied on December 22, 2008, and a new trial was granted. The jury in the second trial returned an even larger verdict, $1.92 million, which Judge Davis remitted to $54,000 on equitable grounds. The plaintiffs rejected the reduced damage award and opted for a third trial, which was held in October and November 2010. The third jury returned a verdict of $1.5 million, which was challenged as unconstitutionally high in a post-trial motion.[101]

The Southern District of Indiana in *Timpco, LLC v Implementation Services, LLC,*[102] used the "making available" doctrine outside the Internet context to find that the defendant "distributed" and "displayed" copies of the plaintiff's literary work *The Carrot Story* without the plaintiff's permission. The plaintiff and the defendant entered into a written asset purchase agreement (APA), according to which the plaintiff purchased certain of the defendant's assets and intellectual property, including copyright to *The Carrot Story.* The plaintiff alleged that the defendant infringed the plaintiff's copyright when the defendant (1) distributed two or three copies of the story to clients for sales presentations and (2) included a copy of the story in package information for a trade show. The defendant conceded that the plaintiff owned a valid copyright in *The Carrot Story.* The defendant argued, however, that there was no evidence that it actually distributed copies of *The Carrot Story* to third parties. The court disagreed, reasoning that the plaintiff was not required to show actual distribution; rather, showing that the defendant made copyrighted material available to the public was sufficient to establish copyright infringement. Accordingly, the court found the defendant's acts, of including *The Carrot Story* in packets of information for use at a trade show and for its clients and/or prospective clients, to be acts of distribution. Further, the court, reasoning that the Copyright Act gives the exclusive right to display copyrighted work publicly, found that the defendant also infringed the plaintiff's copyright by displaying *The Carrot Story* on a table at the trade show.

---

[101]That motion was granted in July 2011, and a final judgment was entered for three times the maximum statutory damages. Case 0:06-cv-01497-MJD-LIB, Docket No. 457, *filed* July 22, 2011 (D. Minn.).

[102]No. 08-1481, 2010 U.S. Dist. LEXIS 103668 (S.D. Ind. Sept. 29, 2010).

6

Fair Use

I. TYPES OF DEFENSES

A. Fair Use

1. *Statute*

b. *General Principles*

iv. Burdens and Presumptions

[Add the following text at the end of the section.]

Because fair use is an affirmative defense, it can be waived if not properly raised by the defendant; the court is not at liberty to raise the defense sua sponte. In *Latimer v. Roaring Toyz, Inc.*,[1] for example, the Eleventh Circuit reversed a grant of summary judgment to defendant Hachette, finding that the district court erred in raising the fair use affirmative defense sua sponte. In connection with the unveiling of the model ZX-14 sport motorcycle, defendant Kawasaki engaged defendant Roaring Toyz to customize its ZX-14 motorcycles. Roaring Toyz hired independent painter Hathaway to apply custom paint and graphics to the

---

[1]601 F.3d 1224 (11th Cir. 2010).

motorcycles. The plaintiff photographer Latimer was retained by Kawasaki to photograph the customized motorcycles. Latimer subsequently granted permission to Kawasaki to use his copyrighted photos at a press event in Las Vegas, but claimed that his authorization was limited to use in a screen presentation, not physical copies. During the press event, Kawasaki distributed press kits with digital images of Latimer's photographs to about 30 members of the media, including a representative of *Cycle World* magazine, owned by defendant Hachette. *Cycle World* subsequently published Latimer's photographs in conjunction with an article in the June 2006 issue of *Cycle World*. Roaring Toyz also displayed Latimer's photographs on its website. Latimer brought an action for copyright infringement. Hachette did not assert fair use in its pleading, but the district court raised the defense sua sponte and allowed the parties to brief same. Latimer argued that fair use was an affirmative defense that Hachette waived since Hachette had not asserted the defense it in its pleadings. The district court ultimately granted summary judgment to Hachette based upon a finding of fair use. The circuit court, on appeal, found that the district court erred by raising fair use sua sponte, holding that fair use is an affirmative defense and as such it must generally be asserted in a party's pleadings. However, the court of appeals remanded to the district court, noting that "there are exceptions to this rule and the district court is free on remand to entertain a motion to amend by Hachette to assert the affirmative defense of fair use."[2]

2. The Four Factors

a. First Factor: Purpose and Character of Use

ii. Educational Use

[Add the following text at the end of the section.]

In the context of student course-pack photocopies, it has been held that copy shops are liable even where customers, and not copy-shop employees, actually push the button to activate the copier. In *Blackwell Publishing, Inc. v. Excel Research Group, LLC,*[3] the defendant copy service provider Excel maintained master copies of portions of the plaintiff's copyrighted course materials that had been selected and gathered by professors. A student needing materials came to Excel's premises and filled out a form stating the class in which the student was enrolled. Excel lent a master copy of the materials to the student for a fee, and the student copied the materials at Excel's facilities. Excel staffers were on hand to assist, but the student was the one who made the copy. Excel did not pay copyright fees to the publishers. The plaintiffs alleged that Excel violated their exclusive rights to reproduce and distribute their works by offering such services to students at the University of Michigan.

---

[2]*Id.* at 1240.

[3]661 F. Supp. 2d 786 (E.D. Mich. 2009).

Excel argued that its use constituted fair use. The court disagreed. First, the purpose and character of the use was for-profit and commercial, and Excel could not "stand in the shoes" of its customers who were making nonprofit, noncommercial use.[4] Second, the nature of the copyrighted work—the material offered for copying—"is certainly creative, which militates against a finding of fair use."[5] Third, "the amount of the use in relation to the copyrighted work as a whole—also favors the publishers"; the fact that professors chose the copied materials as required reading was evidence of their qualitative value.[6] Fourth, Excel was able to charge less than its competition for the materials and it did not pay publishers; "[b]y not paying a fee where others do, it adversely impacts the marketplace."[7] The court rejected the argument that Excel was not reproducing the plaintiffs' works itself—"[t]he fact that the *students* push a button on a copier in the manner described is of no significance."[8]

3.   *Transformative Use—The "Fifth Factor"*

b.   *Specific Examples of Transformative Use*

   i.   Parody

   (1) Parody or Not?

[Add the following text at the end of the section.]

On July 1, 2009, Judge Deborah A. Batts of the Southern District of New York issued a widely reported decision, *Salinger v. Colting*,[9] granting a preliminary injunction to famed author J.D. Salinger in connection with a new book, *60 Years Later: Coming Through the Rye* (*60 Years*), that claims to be a parody of Salinger's 1951 classic *The Catcher in the Rye*. In the new book, Salinger's alienated teenage protagonist, Holden Caulfield, is portrayed as an even more alienated 76-year-old, "Mr. C." The decision has sparked controversy among bloggers and commentators, some of whom describe it as a censorious departure from settled copyright law,[10] but the decision relies almost entirely on defendant-friendly precedent

---

[4] *Id.* at 793.

[5] *Id.*

[6] *Id.*

[7] *Id.* at 793–94.

[8] *Id.* at 794 (emphasis added).

[9] 641 F. Supp. 2d 250, 91 USPQ2d 1319 (S.D.N.Y. 2009).

[10] One comment on the *New York Times* website coverage of the decision, for example, muses that "apparently, there is the actual copyright law passed by Congress and then there's the special secret exception that applies to J.D [*sic*] Salinger," while another notes that "for your information, the Supreme Court has roundly rejected prior restraint." http://citytroom.blogs.nytimes.com/2009/07/01/judge-rules-for-salinger-in-copyright-suit/. More thoughtfully, Rebecca Tushnet critiques the court's application of the law in a July 2, 2009 posting on *Rebecca Tushnet's 43(B)log* at http://Tushnet.blogspot.com/2009/07/if-book-meets-book-coming-through-rye.html.

such as the Supreme Court's *Campbell v. Acuff-Rose Music, Inc.*[11] and the Eleventh Circuit's *SunTrust Bank v. Houghton-Mifflin Co.*,[12] in which the courts have famously permitted arguably comparable uses. As these cases demonstrate, the law does not impose any blanket prohibition on unauthorized retellings of copyrighted works, but neither does it give parodists carte blanche to reuse existing material in any way they choose. Under the Supreme Court's ruling in *Campbell*, the test in each case is whether the parodic character of the defendant's work "may reasonably be perceived,"[13] and the court in *Salinger* simply concluded after a review of both works that Colting's *60 Years* did not have any "reasonably perceived parodic character."[14] That, in a nutshell, is what the case is about—not whether the defendant's work is or is not a parody, but whether it may reasonably be perceived as such.

J.D. Salinger's *The Catcher in the Rye* (*Catcher*) is a classic coming-of-age novel told through the eyes of its protagonist, Holden Caulfield, a troubled adolescent who finds himself adrift in New York City for several emotionally harrowing days following his expulsion from prep school. It has had an enormous impact on postwar American culture, having been included on many lists of the greatest novels of the twentieth century. It has been cited as an inspiration by former president George H.W. Bush, and reportedly played a major contributing role in Mark David Chapman's 1980 shooting of John Lennon. (At the time of Lennon's shooting, coincidentally, it was reportedly both the most-often censored novel, and the second most-often taught novel, in United States high schools.) Salinger, who died in January 2010, consistently refused to create sequels or permit film adaptations of the novel.

The defendants' novel, *60 Years*, is told through the eyes of "Mr. C," a 76-year-old who, like Holden Caulfield, is a frequent liar, constantly complains, is out of shape, has trouble maneuvering in the dark, combs his hair to one side with his hand, wears a red hunting cap, is obsessed with whether birds migrate for the winter, and likes the feeling of time standing still in museums. Like Caulfield, moreover, Mr. C has a younger sister named Phoebe who is his only real friend, an older brother named D.B. who wrote a story about a goldfish, a younger brother named Allie who died as a child, a mother who experiences nervous spells, a prep school roommate named Stradlater, and a history teacher named Mr. Spencer.[15] In both works, the protagonist leaves his resident institution and takes mass transit to New York, where he nearly has sex but ultimately decides not to; finds himself drawn to Central Park; has a huge breakfast (which is unusual for him); stands on a hill next to a cannon watching a sporting event; makes reference to the film *The 39 Steps*; is

---

[11] 510 U.S. 569 (1994).

[12] 268 F.3d 1257, 60 USPQ2d 1225 (11th Cir. 2001).

[13] *Campbell*, 510 U.S. at 582.

[14] *Salinger*, 641 F. Supp. 2d at 260.

[15] *Id.* at 264.

disgusted by the thought of Mr. Spencer wearing a robe that exposes his hairy chest; refers to his own propensity to lose things; and notes the ease with which his sister Phoebe wakes up.[16] The court wasted no time in finding that Salinger had likely established a prima facie case of copyright infringement, both with respect to his novel and the fictional character of Holden Caulfield as depicted in the novel.

In light of the many similarities, the crux of the case for or against the issuance of an injunction was the defendants' claim that *60 Years* was a fair use of the Salinger novel. Interestingly, however, the court's fair use discussion does not immediately turn to the text of Section 107 of the Copyright Act, which sets forth the statutory factors to be considered. Rather, the court begins by remarking on the fundamental purposes of copyright and the relationship between copyright and the First Amendment. The court quoted the Eleventh Circuit's *SunTrust Bank* decision to observe that the constitutional copyright clause and the First Amendment were "'drafted to work together to prevent censorship.'"[17] In *SunTrust*, the court refused to enjoin a critical parody of Margaret Mitchell's *Gone With the Wind*, which retold the story from the slaves' point of view, on the ground that it was a socially valuable commentary on the original novel.

The *Salinger* defendants' hopes of a similar result could not have lasted long, however, once the court began its analysis under Section 107. As with many recent fair use decisions, much of the *Salinger* court's attention was devoted to the first factor, "the purpose and character of the use."[18] Here, the court's main question boiled down to whether *60 Years* was a parody of the Salinger work itself, or merely a comment about something else that happened to use *Catcher* as a convenient vehicle. Parodies have frequently, indeed virtually always, been recognized as transformative uses since *Campbell*, but satires have not, on the theory that satire does not *need* to copy from the plaintiff's work to the same extent as parody, which "sharpens its knives for the very work from which it borrows."[19] The court in *Salinger* concluded that unlike the *Gone With the Wind* parody in *Suntrust Bank*, which, *inter alia*, sought to expose the latent racism and homophobia of the original, *60 Years* "contains no reasonably discernible rejoinder or specific criticism of any character or theme of *Catcher*."[20] The court dismissed the defendants' claims to have targeted *Catcher* or Holden Caulfield as the subject of *60 Years*' critical commentary as "post-hoc rationalizations employed through vague generalizations about the alleged naïveté of the original, rather than reasonably perceivable parody."[21]

---

[16] *Id.*

[17] *Id.* at 255 (quoting *SunTrust Bank*, 268 F.3d at 1263).

[18] *See id.* at 256–63.

[19] *Id.* at 256.

[20] *Id.* at 258.

[21] *Id.*

The court's skepticism about the defendants' asserted critique of *Catcher* seems to derive largely from the court's conclusion that *Catcher* is not itself a naive, uncritical portrait of its young protagonist:

> Holden Caulfield as delineated by Salinger was already often "miserable" and "unconnected" as well as frequently "absurd[]" and "ridiculous," as Colting says of his elderly version of the character. In fact, it was these very characteristics that led Caulfield to leave or be expelled from three boarding schools, to wander the streets of New York City alone for several days, to lack any close friends other than his younger sister Phoebe, and ultimately to become a patient in a psychiatric hospital. Hence, to the extent Colting claims to augment the purported portrait of Caulfield as a "free-thinking, authentic and untainted youth," and "impeccable judge of the people around him," displayed in *Catcher* by "show[ing] the effects of Holden's uncompromising worldview," those effects were already thoroughly depicted and apparent in Salinger's own narrative about Caulfield.[22]

Moreover, the court drops a telling footnote in which it recites a number of examples from the record where Colting himself expressed admiration for *Catcher* and disavowed any intention to ridicule or critique it. For example, the original book jacket described *60 Years* as "a marvelous *sequel* to one of our most *beloved* classics," and Colting is quoted in a May 2009 press report as having said, "[i]t's a tribute [to] the way Holden would have said it. . . . But this is no spoof."[23] Summarizing its central finding under the first factor, the court concluded that "*60 Years*' plain purpose is not to expose Holden Caulfield's disconnectedness, absurdity, and ridiculousness, but rather to satisfy Holden's fans' passion for Holden Caulfield's disconnectedness, absurdity, and ridiculousness . . . . Accordingly, the court finds that *60 Years* contains no reasonably perceived parodic character as to *Catcher* and Holden Caulfield."[24]

The court did, however, recognize some transformative value in the Colting book's criticism and commentary about J.D. Salinger, a point that Salinger conceded. This commentary centered on Salinger's noted reclusiveness and refusal to allow sequels or adaptations of his work, but the court observed that such commentary was not targeted at Salinger's *work*, and was moreover not a large part of the Colting book, appearing in "only 40 of 277 pages."[25] Although transformative, this Salinger-targeted material was deemed slight in relation to the extensive borrowing from *Catcher*, and thus did not alter the court's conclusion that Section 107's first factor favored the plaintiff.

As an aside, the court drops another important footnote to distinguish the recent Southern District decision in *Bourne Co. v. Twentieth Century Fox Film Corp.*,[26] relied on by the defendants, in which an anti-Semitic parody of the song "When You Wish Upon a Star," entitled

---

[22] *Id.* (citations omitted).

[23] *Id.* at 260 n.3 (emphasis added by court).

[24] *Id.*

[25] *Id.* at 262.

[26] 602 F. Supp. 2d 499 (S.D.N.Y. 2009).

"I Need a Jew," was held to be a fair use, in part because it was said to target the alleged anti-Semitism of Walt Disney, with whom the original song has an "intimate association." The court in *Salinger* noted that a critique of an author's personality does not always necessarily equate to a critique of the work, and in the case of *60 Years* it did not.[27]

Thus the first factor was held to weigh in Salinger's favor, even as the court acknowledged *some* transformative value in the Colting work. In doing so, the *Salinger* opinion joins a fairly short list of post-*Campbell* decisions that decline to equate "transformativeness" with fair use. (If a work is highly transformative, it is almost certainly a fair use.)

As usual, the second statutory factor, "the nature of the copyrighted work,"[28] was not given much discussion, apart from a cursory quote from *Campbell* to make the point that *Catcher* is a creative work that " 'falls within the core of the copyright's protective purposes.' "[29] Thus, the second factor favored Salinger. The third factor, which looks to the amount and substantiality of the borrowing,[30] was also held to favor Salinger because the copying was found to be more extensive than necessary in light of the book's "alleged transformative purpose of criticizing Salinger and his attitudes and behavior."[31] The court recognized that frequent and extensive use of Holden Caulfield's character traits "might arguably have been necessary to supplement a work of parody directed at *Catcher* or the character of Caulfield," but "for the non-parodic purpose of commenting upon Salinger, rather than his work, it was unnecessary for Colting to use the same protagonist with repeated and extensive detail and allusion to the original work."[32]

The fourth factor, which looks to likely market harm,[33] seems to play a smaller role in *Salinger* than it often does, but given the court's conclusion that *60 Years* is more a sequel than a parody, there may not have been much to say. Sequels, adaptations, and other derivative works lie at the heart of the copyright owner's market, as the Supreme Court recognized in *Campbell*. But *Campbell* also carved out an exception for certain types of adaptations—such as parodies and critical commentaries—that creators of original works would not " 'in general develop, or license others to develop.' "[34] The *Salinger* court applied this standard to

---

[27] *Salinger*, 641 F. Supp. 2d at 261 n.4. "Salinger's reclusive nature, fierce protection of his rights and privacy, and decision not to publish additional works—as well as *60 Years* criticism of those traits through the character of Salinger—do not cast any critique on *Catcher* analogous to the way that Walt Disney's alleged anti-Semitism casts further critique on the naïveté of 'When You Wish Upon a Star' when parodied by the racist song, 'I Need a Jew'." *Id.* n.4.

[28] *See id.* at 263.

[29] *Id.* (quoting *Campbell*, 510 U.S. at 586).

[30] *See id.* at 263–67.

[31] *Id.* at 263.

[32] *Id.* at 264.

[33] *See id.* at 267–68.

[34] *Id.* at 267 (quoting *Campbell*, 510 U.S. at 592).

conclude, first, that "whether defendants term *60 Years* a sequel or not, the Court finds that as a novel that continues the story of *Catcher* and its protagonist . . . it is the kind of work that an author would 'in general' develop or license others to develop."[35] Second, the court observed that "although Salinger has not demonstrated any interest in publishing a sequel or other derivative work of *Catcher*, the Second Circuit has previously emphasized that it is the 'potential market' for the copyrighted work and its derivatives that must be examined, even if the 'author has disavowed any intention to publish them during his lifetime.'"[36]

The court concluded its discussion of the fourth factor by noting that for some writers, the ability to *refuse* the making of sequels and derivative works might be a more powerful creative incentive than the financial rewards available from the market:

> This might be the case if, for instance, an author's artistic vision includes leaving certain portions or aspects of his character's story to the varied imaginations of his readers, or if he hopes that his readers will engage in discussion and speculation as to what happened subsequently. Just as licensing of derivatives is an important economic incentive to the creation of originals, so too will the right *not* to license derivatives sometimes act as an incentive to the creation of originals.[37]

Accordingly, even though an author might "in general" wish to market sequels or other derivative works, the decision to refrain from doing so in the case of a particular work should not serve to penalize the author under the fourth factor. Thus the fourth factor, like the first three, was found to favor Salinger, "albeit only slightly."[38]

After concluding its fair use analysis, the court added a brief paragraph on the issue of irreparable harm,[39] which is necessarily implicated in the decision to award an injunction. Notwithstanding the recent Supreme Court decision in *eBay, Inc. v. MercExchange*,[40] which held that there is no presumption of irreparable harm when the plaintiff establishes a *prima facie* case of patent infringement, the court in *Salinger* applied pre-*eBay* copyright precedent from the Second Circuit to find the presumption still applicable here, limiting the Supreme Court's *eBay* decision to the patent law context.[41]

On April 30, 2010, the district court decision granting a preliminary injunction was reversed and remanded on the injunction issue (see discussion *infra* in Chapter 8), but the Second Circuit did not disturb the district court's finding as to fair use.[42]

----

[35] *Id.*

[36] *Id.* at 268 (quoting Salinger v. Random House, Inc., 811 F.2d 90, 99, 1 USPQ2d 1673 (2d Cir. 1987)).

[37] *Id.* (emphasis in original).

[38] *Id.*

[39] *See id.* at 268–69.

[40] 547 U.S. 388 (2006).

[41] *Salinger*, 641 F. Supp. 2d at 269 & n.6.

[42] Salinger v. Colting, No. 09-2878, 2010 U.S. App. LEXIS 8956 (2d Cir. Apr. 30, 2010).

An asserted parody defense was likewise rejected in *Lorimar Music A Corp. v. Black Iron Grill Co.*,[43] where the district court rejected the defendants' fair use defense where the defendants publically performed copyrighted musical compositions by way of karaoke performances at a bar and restaurant. The plaintiff recording companies were members of ASCAP, to which they granted the nonexclusive right to license nondramatic public performance of their copyrighted musical compositions, including the eight musical compositions at issue here. ASCAP then licensed the music to establishments that wished to publicly perform copyrighted songs. The defendant Black Iron Grill and Restaurant, an S corporation owned by the defendants Mr. and Mrs. DeBuhr, was given the opportunity to purchase an ASCAP license, and repeatedly refused. An ASCAP investigator subsequently visited the Black Iron Grill and observed the performance of eight songs by means of a disc jockey using karaoke equipment. The plaintiffs brought an infringement action based on these performances, and thereafter moved for summary judgment. The defendants argued that the performance of karaoke was parody, and constituted a fair use under the Copyright Act. The defendants claimed that the karaoke performance significantly changed the character of the songs because the lyrics and music of the song are no longer the focus; instead, the performance attempt becomes the focus. The court found that karaoke is not parody; a karaoke singer is merely performing the underlying copyrighted song, and does not create a new work that "develops the meaning or message" or "comments on or criticizes the copyrighted work." The court also noted that musical composition, as a creative work, is deserving of strict copyright protection; that the entire work is generally performed during karaoke; and that if karaoke were protected as fair use parody, it would erode the market for licensed use of copyrighted songs.

(2) Parody and Market Harm

[Add the following text at the end of the section.]

In *Bouchat v. Baltimore Ravens Ltd. P'ship*,[44] the Fourth Circuit reversed the district court's finding that depictions of a historical Baltimore Ravens logo in highlight films were fair use. The plaintiff owned copyright in a "Shield logo" he created in 1995 and proposed for use as the Ravens team logo. The Ravens used a strikingly similar "Flying B" logo design during the team's first three seasons. In prior proceedings the Fourth Circuit affirmed a jury verdict of infringement, and a jury award of zero damages for infringement. In the current action the plaintiff sought an injunction prohibiting all current uses of the Flying B logo and requiring destruction of all items exhibiting the Flying B logo. The uses included Ravens highlight films of the 1996, 1997, and 1998 seasons. The district

---

[43]No. 09-6067, 2010 U.S. Dist. LEXIS 76484 (W.D. Mo. July 29, 2010).

[44]346 F.3d 514 (4th Cir. 2003).

court issued a decision determining that all of the defendants' depictions of the Flying B logo constituted fair use.

On the first fair use factor, the Fourth Circuit found no transformative purpose behind the depiction of the Flying B logo in highlight films; the use of the logo in the films served the same purpose it did when the defendants first infringed the plaintiff's logo design, i.e., identifying the football player wearing it with the Baltimore Ravens. The simple act of filming a game in which the copyrighted work was displayed did not add something new to the logo, or alter it with new expression, meaning or message. The court disagreed with the district court's conclusion that the purpose behind the use of the Flying B logo in highlight films was "primarily historical." The use of the logo in the films simply fulfilled its purpose of identifying the team, and continued to fulfill that purpose whenever the highlight film was shown. Because the logo was still being used as a logo, the purpose behind the use was not transformative. Because the defendants' use of the logo was nontransformative, the commercial nature of the use weighed against fair use. Finally, because the defendants were responsible for the original copyright infringement, the defendants could not assert that it was fair use to profit from the very same infringement when the purpose of the use was not transformed. On the second factor, the court agreed with the district court that the creative nature of the work weighed against fair use. On the third factor, the court of appeals found the district court erred in weighing the factor in favor of fair use because "the Flying B logo, although depicted in its entirety, is not a major component of the entire work in which it is used," citing Learned Hand's maxim that "no plagiarist can excuse the wrong by showing how much of his work he did not pirate."

As to the fourth factor, the court stated that the jury finding that none of the defendants' profits derived from the Flying B logo had no bearing on the "potential market for or value of the copyrighted work." The market "does not fail to exist" for the logo simply because the football team's profits do not ultimately derive from the use of that logo. Licensing of NFL logos for use in the sale of official team merchandise, in exchange for royalties, was exactly the type of potential market that existed for the plaintiff's logo. The NFL sold on its website consumer products decorated with historic logos from NFL teams and marketed as "throwback" merchandise. In light of the market in licensing historic logos, the defendants' unrestricted use of the infringing Flying B logo would result in a substantially adverse impact on the potential market for the plaintiff's logo. Judge Niemeyer, dissenting, stated, "[t]he Ravens and the NFL cannot now change history, nor can they reasonably be requested to blot it out. They have not attempted to reinstate the Flying B Logo as the identifying symbol of Ravens' franchise, nor have they focused on the Logo in any way. Rather, they seek only to display memorabilia and historic images which of necessity still contain the Flying B Logo. This is surely transformative use, lying squarely in the 'heart of the fair use doctrine's guarantee of breathing space within the confines of copyright.'"

ii. Transformative Non-Parody Uses

(1) Transformative Authorship

[Add the following text at the end of the section.]

In *Gaylord v. United States*,[45] the Federal Circuit recently reversed a decision by the Court of Federal Claims regarding the unauthorized use of a memorial sculpture on a postage stamp. The plaintiff, a professional sculptor, created a sculpture consisting of the stainless steel figures of 19 soldiers as part of the Korean War Veterans Memorial in Washington, D.C. After the memorial was constructed, a "retired United States Marine Corps pilot and earnest amateur photographer" took a photograph of the memorial during a snowstorm. In 2002, the Postal Service decided to issue a stamp commemorating the fiftieth anniversary of the armistice of the Korean War. The Postal Service incorporated the photograph into the stamp image, and paid Alli $1,500 for the use of his photograph. The Postal Service did not seek, and the plaintiff did not give, permission to depict the underlying sculpture on the stamp, and neither the stamp nor related retail goods identified the plaintiff as the creator of the sculpture. The plaintiff sued, alleging copyright infringement. The defendant asserted fair use.

On the first factor, the Court of Federal Claims found that while both the stamp and the sculpture were intended to honor veterans of the Korean War, the stamp was transformative, "providing a different expressive character" than the sculpture.[46] The artistic expression of the sculpture could be summarized as a three-dimensional sculptural snapshot of a group of soldiers on an undefined mission during the Korean War, captured as a single moment in time, the court stated. The photographer transformed the expression and message of the sculpture with his photograph, creating a "surrealistic environment with snow and subdued lighting" so that the viewer "experiences a feeling of stepping into the photograph, being in Korea with the soldiers, under the freezing conditions that many veterans experienced."[47] The Postal Service further altered the sculptor's expression by making the color in the photo even grayer, creating a nearly monochromatic image. The first factor thus weighed heavily in favor of the defendant. The court found that the transformative nature of the stamp caused the creative nature of the original work, under the second factor, to carry little weight in the fair use analysis. On the third factor, the court noted that the stamp depicted 14 of the 19 soldier figures in the original sculpture; this substantial number of statues visible on the stamp weighed against fair use. However, the court found, the efforts of the photographer and the Postal Service changed the qualitative message of the sculpture and mitigated

---

[45]85 Fed. Cl. 59 (Fed. Cl. 2008), *aff'd in part, rev'd in part, remanded by* 595 F.3d 1364, 94 USPQ2d 1116 (Fed. Cir. 2010).

[46]85 Fed. Cl. at 68.

[47]*Id.* at 68–69.

the weight of the third factor. Finally, the court found that the stamp had little or no impact on the market for, or value of, the sculpture. First, since the stamp was deemed transformative, market harm could not be presumed. In fact, the plaintiff conceded that the defendant's use actually increased the value of the sculpture. As for the market for derivative works, the record showed that the plaintiff had made only limited attempts to commercialize the sculpture copyright; the plaintiff had never sold photographs, postcards, magnets, or keychains, the court noted. The stamp thus had not impacted the plaintiff's attempts to market derivative works. Furthermore, it was unlikely that a 1×1½-inch stamp would be an adequate commercial substitute for future products sold by the plaintiff. Thus, the stamp had no impact on the potential market for the sculpture and the fourth factor weighed in favor of fair use.

The Federal Circuit reversed,[48] largely because it found the use to lack sufficient transformative character. Among other errors, the Federal Circuit held that the Court of Claims was wrong to consider the effect of the snowy weather as a "transformative" element of the new work, noting in a memorable phrase that "[n]ature's decision to snow cannot deprive Mr. Gaylord of an otherwise valid right to exclude."[49] Moreover, the court held that the stamp and the original sculpture had the same purpose, i.e., to honor the veterans who served in the Korean conflict.

Even a transformative use is not necessarily always fair, however. In *Bridgeport Music, Inc. v. UMG Recordings, Inc.*,[50] the Sixth Circuit affirmed a jury verdict of no fair use in a case involving a nonsampling use of preexisting music in a hip-hop track. In 1998, the defendants released a song entitled "D.O.G. In Me" which incorporated elements of the George Clinton funk classic, "Atomic Dog." The defendants copied three elements from "Atomic Dog": use of the word "dog" as musical punctuation, rhythmic panting, and a "bow wow" refrain ("bow-wow-wow, yippee-yo-yippee-yay"). The jury returned a verdict denying, inter alia, the defendants' proffered fair use defense. On appeal, the defendants argued that their defense of fair use at trial—that the copied elements constituted an "homage or tribute" to the original work—was negated by an improper instruction to the jury on the law as to this point; the district court had instructed the jury that an homage or tribute is "not necessarily fair use."[51] The court of appeals held that the instruction was "an accurate statement of the law,"[52] and noted furthermore that the defendants introduced no evidence to explain how they were honoring "Atomic Dog" such as in the album's credits or liner notes. The court found that only the transformative use sub-factor weighed in favor of the

---

[48]595 F.3d 1364, 94 USPQ2d 1116 (Fed. Cir. 2010).

[49]*Id.* at 1374.

[50]585 F.3d 267 (6th Cir. 2009).

[51]*See id.* at 278.

[52]*Id.* ("*See* 17 U.S.C. § 107 (purpose and character of the use is only one factor); *Campbell*, 510 U.S. at 578–90 (weighing all factors in light of the purposes of copyright).")

defendants, but that the combined weight of the other factors favoring the plaintiff was greater. This is a comparatively rare case of a transformative use not qualifying as fair under at least some of the other factors.

Where the transformative value is less pronounced, the courts have even less trouble finding in plaintiff's favor, as in *HarperCollins Publishers L.L.C. v. Gawker Media LLC.* [53] In that case, the district court held that the pre-publication online posting of scanned pages from a book was not transformative, and not fair use. The plaintiff held exclusive publishing rights in *America By Heart*, by former vice-presidential candidate Sarah Palin, set for release on November 23, 2010. On November 17, 2010, the defendant online media company published images of 21 full pages from the book on the Gawker.com website, under the title "Sarah Palin's New Book: Leaked Excerpts." The plaintiff on the same day sent a letter to the defendant demanding that the material be taken down. The plaintiff received no response, and the material remained on Gawker. On November 19, 2010, the plaintiff filed suit for copyright infringement, and sought a temporary restraining order. At a November 20 TRO hearing, the defendant argued that the posting was fair use. The court noted that the defendant's use of copyrighted material was not for Section 107 preamble "purposes such as criticism, comment, news reporting, teaching..., scholarship, or research." Posts on Gawker consisted of very brief introductions followed by copied material. This, the court noted, was far less than reporting and commentary the Supreme Court found inadequate to establish fair use in *Harper & Row*. As to the first factor, the defendant had not used the copyrighted material to help create something new, but had merely copied material in order to attract viewers to Gawker. The defendant essentially engaged in no commentary or discussion. The use of the copyrighted material was commercial in two ways. First, the copyrighted material was placed alongside links to advertisements; the more clicks those links received, the more compensation the defendant could ask of advertisers. Second, the more visitors Gawker received because of the posting of copyrighted material, the more attractive it became to potential advertisers on its site and, again, the more compensation the defendant could ask of advertisers. On the second factor, the excerpts used by the defendant came from an unpublished work, substantially weakening the defendant's fair use claim. The third factor also weighed against fair use, as the defendant published what amounted to a substantial portion of the book. The fourth factor was a "matter of speculation," and neither helped nor harmed either side on the fair use issue. The court concluded that the plaintiff had a likelihood of success on the merits in connection with the claim of copyright infringement, as against the defense of fair use.

(2) Transformative Reproductions

[Add the following text at the end of the section.]

---

[53]721 F. Supp. 2d 303 (S.D.N.Y. 2010).

Warren Publishing Co. v. Spurlock[54] represents an extension, or arguably an over-extension, of the reasoning in *Bill Graham Archive*, finding fair use where the defendant made extensive and overtly "aesthetic" use of 1960s and 1970s magazine cover paintings in a coffee-table book about the artist who created them. The plaintiff published 191 issues of the magazine *Famous Monsters of Filmland* starting in 1958. The defendant approached the plaintiff about collaborating on a career retrospective of Basil Gogos, the artist whose work appeared most frequently on the cover of *Famous Monsters,* but the parties never reached agreement. The defendant made a deal with the artist himself to create a book called *Famous Monster Movie Art of Basil Gogos,* intended to "carefully and respectfully illustrate the vast output and evolution of the artist."[55] The book contained 24 images that first appeared in *Famous Monsters*: 10 of actual magazine covers, and 14 of Gogos cover art alone, without the text that originally appeared on the published covers. On summary judgment, the court held that the use was transformative under the first factor. While the plaintiff had used the cover art as a tool "to generate public interest" and "to convey information," the defendant's book used the images "as historical artifacts to document and represent the work product of an accomplished artist."[56] On the second factor, the defendant conceded that the covers fell within the "core" of the Copyright Act's protective purposes since they were creative expression. The court found, however, that the magazines' out-of-print status had "some bearing" on the second factor.[57] As to the third factor, the court held that "[t]he covers were not the qualitative 'heart' of the plaintiffs' magazines, but were instead used to catch the eye of potential readers at the newsstand and advertise the content of the magazine. The quality and importance of these covers as used in the original magazines are relatively minor."[58] On the fourth factor of market harm, the court found that "the disputed facts . . . which, when inferred in favor of Plaintiffs, slightly favors Plaintiffs,"[59] but noted also that the plaintiff's failure to exploit its old magazines for decades was a case "where the copyright owner has exhibited virtually no interest at all in utilizing his copyrights. It would defy logic for this Court to accept [the plaintiff's] argument that, where a copyright owner has failed to utilize his copyrights for several decades, a district court's prohibition of a defendant's productive and transformative use serves copyright's 'purpose, "[t]o promote the Progress of Science and useful Arts. . . ."' This alone places the fourth factor in favor of [the defendant]."[60]

---

[54] 645 F. Supp. 2d 402 (E.D. Pa. 2009).

[55] *Id.* at 406.

[56] *Id.* at 420 (internal quotations omitted).

[57] *Id.* at 422.

[58] *Id.* at 425.

[59] *Id.* at 428.

[60] *Id.* at 426 (quoting *Campbell,* 510 U.S. at 575 (quoting U.S. CONST. art. I, §8)).

Where a court finds the purpose to be transformative, even technical flaws in the defendant's presentation of the argument can be overlooked, as in *Sedgwick Claims Management Services, Inc. v. Delsman.*[61] There, the district court granted a pro se defendant's inartfully drafted motion for summary judgment, liberally construing it as a motion to dismiss. The plaintiff insurance claim service company sued the defendant, a former employee of one of the plaintiff's customers, for copyright infringement. The defendant created "WANTED"-style fugitive postcards featuring copyrighted photographs of the plaintiff's CEO and COO, with derogatory claims about the plaintiff's business practices. The defendant also morphed the photographs into images of Adolph Hitler and Heinrich Himmler, and sent them to employees of the plaintiff. The defendant argued that its use of the plaintiff's works (the copyrighted photos) was fair use. The court evaluated the merits of the defense, despite the plaintiff's argument that fair use is not to be decided on a motion to dismiss because no material facts were in dispute.[62] The district court found the first statutory fair use factor to weigh strongly in favor of the defendant because the defendant's uses of the plaintiff's work, even when unaltered, were transformative, in that they transformed the plaintiff's promotional photographs into vehicles for publicizing and criticizing the plaintiff's alleged business practices. The district court found the second factor to be neutral because neither party argued it and because when transformativeness is found this factor is not terribly significant. The court also found the third factor to be neutral because the use of entire images for "WANTED"-style fugitive postcards was reasonable given the purpose of the defendant's use. On the fourth factor, the court rejected the plaintiff's argument that the defendant's use of the plaintiff's images diminished their value of use for future marketing purposes; "the relevant question is not whether the work itself has lost value, but rather, whether the secondary use has usurped the commercial demand for the original. Here, there is no such demand, since there is no commercial market for them."[63] Furthermore, " 'when a lethal parody, like a scathing theater review, kills demand for the original, it does not produce a harm cognizable under the Copyright Act.' "[64] Finding that two factors weighed in favor of the defendant and that two factors were neutral, the court held the defendant's use to be fair and dismissed the plaintiff's copyright claim.

---

[61] No. 09-1468, 2009 U.S. Dist. LEXIS 61825 (N.D. Cal. July 16, 2009).

[62] "[T]he Ninth Circuit has held that a defendant's 'assertion of fair use may be considered on a motion to dismiss, which requires the court to consider all allegations to be true, in a manner substantially similar to consideration of the same issue on a motion for summary judgment, when no material facts are in dispute.' " *Id.* at *11 (quoting Leadsinger, Inc. v. BMG Music Publ'g, 512 F.3d 522, 530 (9th Cir. 2008)).

[63] *Id.* at *18 (citation omitted). "And even if there were, Defendant's use of the photographs is sufficiently transformative that it would not be a 'substitute' for the original." *Id.* at *19 (citation omitted).

[64] *Id.* (quoting *Campbell*, 510 U.S. at 591–92).

4.   *Fair Use—Specific Applications*

b.   *Photographs, Stills and Illustrations*

[Add the following text at the end of the section.]

In *Monge v. Maya Magazines, Inc.*,[65] the district court granted the defendant's motion for summary judgment that the defendant's publication of the plaintiffs' photographs constituted fair use. The plaintiffs were an "internationally renowned pop singer and model," and "one of the most recognized managers and music producers in the Latin music industry." They married secretly in Las Vegas, where multiple photographs of them were taken throughout the wedding night. The defendant, a weekly magazine focusing on newsworthy Latin American personalities, published five of 400 wedding photographs, purchased by the defendant from the wedding chapel staff. The plaintiffs sued for copyright infringement. The defendant moved for summary judgment, asserting an affirmative defense of fair use. The district court granted the defendant's motion. The court found that the first factor supported a finding of fair use because the photographs were used not in their original context, but rather as confirmation of the accompanying text challenging the plaintiffs' public denial of their marriage. Further, the transformative use of the photographs outweighed the commercial nature of the publication. The court found the second and third factors to be neutral due to the factual nature of the photographs documenting events on the plaintiffs' wedding night, and due to the defendant publishing the photographs only to the extent necessary to corroborate news of the plaintiffs' clandestine marriage. The fourth factor supported a finding of fair use because the publication of the wedding photographs did not usurp any market. No such market existed because the plaintiffs went to great lengths to conceal their marriage, including from the husband's mother.

e.   *News (Other Than Film Clips)*

[Add the following text at the end of the section.]

Some legitimate news uses fail to qualify as fair use even where the plaintiff's work is "factual." This is particularly the case when the court finds that the defendant's use, if it became widespread, would be injurious to the copyright owner's market. For example, in *Fitzgerald v. CBS Broadcasting, Inc.*[66] the court granted the plaintiff's motion for summary judgment, rejecting the fair use defense for the inclusion of photos in a broadcast. The plaintiff freelance photographer sued the defendant broadcasting corporation for broadcasting, without authorization, the plaintiff's works, two photographs of well-known mobster Stephen Flemmi in police custody shortly after his arrest in the 1990s. In 2004, after criminal sentencing of John Martorano, who was a cooperating

---

[65] 96 USPQ2d 1678 (C.D. Cal. 2010).

[66] 491 F. Supp. 2d 177, 83 USPQ2d 1460 (D. Mass. 2007).

witness in Flemmi's investigation and arrest, the defendant broadcast the plaintiff's works again without authorization on two affiliate television stations, and posted them on the website of one of the defendant's television stations. The plaintiff sued for infringement based on the 2004 uses, and the defendant asserted a fair use defense. The court held that the defendant's 2004 uses of the plaintiff's works were not fair use. The purpose and character of use weighed in favor of the defendant; the defendant's use fell within the enumerated category of news reporting because the Flemmi arrest was related to Martorano's sentencing which, in itself, was news. The defendant's use was non-transformative, however, because it merely cropped state troopers out of the plaintiff's works. Any transformation did not change the meaning or message of the photos, but was limited to a downgrading of Flemmi's arrest "from breaking news to a supplementary part of a larger story," and such a distinction "is so fine that it ceases to have meaning in the context of ordinary news practice."[67] The defendant's use was commercial because "newscasts without imagery draw fewer viewers, ratings fall, and revenue falls in turn."[68] Accordingly, the defendant stood to profit from the use of the plaintiff's works.

The nature of the plaintiff's works favored the defendant, because creativity for purposes of fair use is harder to establish than creativity for purposes of threshold copyrightability under *Feist*. For purpose of the fair use doctrine, the plaintiff's photographs were held to be factual works, due to the minimal authorial decisions (*e.g.*, framing, angle, timing) exercised by the plaintiff. The amount of the plaintiff's works used by the defendant favored the plaintiff because the defendant used the heart of the plaintiff's works, *i.e.*, a rare image of Flemmi. Perhaps most crucially, the court found that the effect of the use upon the potential market favored the plaintiff. Although the extent of market harm caused by this specific infringing incident favored the defendant, the impact on the plaintiff should the defendant's practice become widespread favored the plaintiff, as the defendant's use usurped the sole market for the plaintiff's works, namely, media licensing.

i.   File Sharing

[Add the following text at the end of the section]

More recently, in *Sony BMG Music Entertainment v. Tenenbaum*,[69] the District of Massachusetts granted summary judgment for the plaintiff record labels, rejecting the argument by individual file-sharing defendant Joel Tenenbaum that his P2P activities were fair use. Although "the Court was prepared to consider a more expansive fair use argument than other courts have credited,"[70] the defendant "mounted a

---

[67] *Id.* at 186.

[68] *Id.* at 187.

[69] 672 F. Supp. 2d 217 (D. Mass. 2009).

[70] *Id.* at 220.

broadside attack that would excuse all file sharing for private enjoyment. . . . In his view, a defendant just needs to show that he did not make money from the files he downloaded or distributed—i.e., that his use was 'non-commercial'—in order to put his fair use defense before a jury. And every non-commercial use, to him, is presumptively fair. Beyond that threshold, the matter belongs entirely to the jury, which is entitled to consider any and all factors touching on its innate sense of fairness—nothing more and nothing less. . . . Defendant's version of fair use is, all in all, completely elastic, utterly standardless, and wholly without support."[71] The court noted that the defendant's own counsel, and several experts named as possible testifying witnesses, had publicly rejected the argument that file sharing was fair use. The court considered whether fair use, as an equitable defense, was ever properly resolved by the jury, but "[s]ince two leading copyright historians suggest that the equitable label may be a misnomer, and since neither party pressed the point, the Court will assume that fair use is a jury question, and leaves the equitable origins of this defense for another court to answer."[72] The issue was moot, however, because the defense was inapplicable to the defendant—Tenenbaum "offered few disputed facts and little, if any, legal authority for his position" which would allow a jury to find in his favor.[73]

Applying the first statutory factor, the court declined to label Tenenbaum's use "commercial," but noted that "the label is not critical to the 'fair use' analysis. More important for this inquiry, and weighing against defendant, is the conclusion that this use was not accompanied by any public benefit or transformative purpose that would trigger the core concerns of the doctrine. . . . Nothing about Tenenbaum's use of these sound recordings was remotely transformative, or served other public ends."[74] The second factor was of little import to the question of fair use, as usual. Under the third factor, the defendant argued that "it is the albums in which the plaintiffs registered their copyrights, while the individual songs are 'works made for hire.' "[75] But the court rejected this argument as "the proverbial distinction without a difference. Individual songs are regularly treated as the relevant unit for evaluating the infringement or fair use of musical works."[76] The fourth factor also weighed against the defendant because the court "sees little difference between selling these works in the public marketplace and making them available for free to the universe of peer-to-peer users. If anything, the latter activity is likely to distribute even more copies—and therefore result in a bigger market impact—because there is no cost barrier at all. It is

---

[71] *Id.* at 221.

[72] *Id.* at 223–24 (citing 4 WILLIAM F. PATRY, PATRY ON COPYRIGHT §10:3 (2009); Pierre N. Leval, *Toward a Fair Use Standard*, 103 HARV. L. REV. 1105 (1990)).

[73] *Id.* at 221.

[74] *Id.* at 228–29.

[75] *Id.* at 229.

[76] *Id.* (citing cases).

difficult to compete with a product offered for free."[77] The defendant's argument "would simply eliminate the market for digital downloads among individual consumers by transforming all file sharing for private enjoyment into fair use. Who would continue to use the iTunes Store or its equivalents, under the circumstances? The Copyright Act grants the plaintiffs an exclusive right to distribute these works; file sharing effectively displaces that right, and the market it represents, by offering the same works for free."[78]

The court also considered various nonstatutory factors raised by the defendant such as assumption of risk and failure to protect, but found them insufficient to raise a genuine issue as to fair use. As to the defendant's argument that "plaintiffs allegedly assumed the risk that their hugely popular music would be dispersed over peer-to-peer networks like KaZaA," this action, without an intent to waive, did not result in a "waiver or abandonment of copyright."[79] Moreover, "[a]s for the plaintiffs' failure to encrypt [CD recordings], the Copyright Act makes plain that not even copyright registration, deposit, or notice is needed to legally protect artistic works. *See* 17 U.S.C. §§405(a), 407(a), 408(a). Requiring even more substantial affirmative steps by copyright holders, like encryption, would be inconsistent with these provisions. As a practical matter, it would be akin to the idea that the copyright holders of literary works must mount a campaign against the photocopier or scanner in order to preserve their legal rights. The ease of reproduction or transmission is simply not relevant to liability; copyright law is itself the source of protection."[80]

The court was more sympathetic to the defendant's argument that the plaintiffs did not offer consumers any viable licensed alternative to illegal downloads during the early years of the Internet, but "[w]hatever the availability of authorized digital alternatives when peer-to-peer networks first became widespread in 1999, it is clear that by August 2004—when Tenenbaum's file sharing was detected—a commercial market for digital music had fully materialized. . . . A different defendant, who was accused of file sharing prior to the iTunes Music Store's market-changing debut, might have a different case. In light of the chronology here, the unavailability of paid digital music is simply not relevant."[81] As to the alleged "injustice" of the plaintiffs' litigation overall, the court noted that the defendant's "sweeping referendum on 'fairness' . . . encompasses every possible inequity that might be found in the facts of this case," yet the court also noted that it was "very, very concerned that there is a deep potential for injustice in the Copyright Act as it is currently written. It urges—no implores—Congress to amend the statute to reflect the

---

[77] *Id.* at 231.

[78] *Id.* at 232.

[79] *Id.* at 232–33.

[80] *Id.* at 234–35.

[81] *Id.* at 236.

realities of file sharing."[82] The court also repeated that it could "envision a scenario in which a defendant sued for file sharing could assert a plausible fair use defense," such as where a defendant "shared files during a period before the law concerning file sharing was clear and paid outlets were readily available," or upon consideration of factors like "with whom he shared files—a few friends or the world—as well as how many copyrighted works he shared, and for how long."[83] Ultimately, however, the court concluded that "[w]hether the widespread, unlimited file sharing that the record suggests he engaged in benefits the public more than our current copyright protections is a balance to be struck by Congress, not this Court."[84]

iv. Trivia Books, Guides, and Plot Summaries

[Add the following text at the end of the section.]

In *Warner Brothers Entertainment, Inc. v. RDR Books,*[85] the Southern District of New York issued an unusually thoughtful decision regarding the fair use defense as applied to the Harry Potter Lexicon, an encyclopedic guide to the fictional universe created by J.K. Rowling in her highly successful series of Harry Potter novels. Although the court recognized that the Lexicon had at least some transformative value, the court ultimately concluded that the new work took too much expressive content from the Rowling books relative to the alleged transformative purpose. The court issued a permanent injunction and awarded $6,750.00 in statutory damages.

---

[82] *Id.* at 237.

[83] *Id.* at 237–38.

[84] *Id.* at 238.

[85] 575 F. Supp. 2d 513, 88 USPQ2d 1723 (S.D.N.Y. 2008).

7

Other Defenses

I. TYPES OF DEFENSES

[Add the following text at the end of the section.]

Even though the statute of limitations for copyright claims is three years, this does not mean that *facts* from more than three years prior to commencement of the action are not relevant or discoverable. For example, statutory damages can be computed based on four years of unlicensed use, not three, as shown in *Broadcast Music, Inc. v. H.S.I., Inc.*[1] There, the court granted the plaintiff's motion for summary judgment against the defendants, who owned and operated bars that featured the public performance of copyrighted music without licenses. The plaintiff, serving as an intermediary between copyright owners and those wishing to publicly perform copyrighted works, sent the defendants over 33 letters that both offered licenses to perform copyrighted songs and demanded that the defendants cease copyright infringement. The defendants never responded, and continued their unlicensed performances of copyrighted works. As to damages, the plaintiff urged the court to base the amount of damages on the number of copyrighted songs the defendants admitted to performing publicly. The court held that unpaid license fees actually provide a superior measurement of the appropriate statutory damages. The court also found willful infringement, since the defendants ignored 33 letters, between 2002 and 2006, demanding they obtain a license to play the plaintiff's copyrighted works. The court accordingly awarded statutory damages consisting of three times the unpaid fees over the 2002–2006 period. The court made no mention of the three-year limitations period, presumably because the total award was within the statutory range. Thus, at least in this circumstance, the defendants' conduct outside the limitations period served as part of the calculation for a permissible award, but not as an independent basis for an award on that conduct per se.

Similarly, discovery can reach back into facts and documents existent more than three years prior to the commencement of suit. Thus, in *Frank Betz Associates, Inc., v. J.O. Clark Construction, L.L.C.,*[2] the district court denied the defendants' motion for a protective order to limit the scope of the plaintiff's written discovery to the three years prior to filing. The defendants argued that the "injury rule," i.e., commencing when the infringement occurred, should apply to the three-year statute of limitations under the Copyright Act to determine when a copyright-infringement claim accrues. The court refused to take this position, and held that the "discovery rule," i.e., commencing when the plaintiff knew or had reason to know of the injury, should apply because permitting a wider scope for discovery is more appropriate so as not to prejudge dispositive issues.

A. Statute of Limitations, Laches, Estoppel, and Delay

1. *Statute of Limitations*

a. *Rolling Infringement*

[Add the following text at the end of the section.]

In *MDM Group Associates, Inc. v. ResortQuest International, Inc.,*[3] a Colorado district court held that the plaintiff's claims alleging infringing acts

---

[1] No. C2-06-482, 2007 U.S. Dist. LEXIS 86642 (S.D. Ohio Nov. 26, 2007).

[2] No. 3-08-159, 2009 U.S. Dist. LEXIS 850 (M.D. Tenn. Jan. 7, 2009).

[3] No. 06-1518, 2009 U.S. Dist. LEXIS 82318 (D. Colo. Sept. 9, 2009).

occurring more than three years prior to the filing of the complaint were time-barred. The plaintiff designed a rental unit damage waiver brochure for use by the defendant in the rental of vacation properties to clients. The parties terminated their agreement, but the defendant continued to use the brochure. The plaintiff demanded that the defendant cease the use, but later found that the defendant had used the brochure on at least one subsequent occasion. The defendant argued that all claims were barred, since the first related infringement was outside the three-year window. The plaintiff contended that certain claims were timely, on the theory that each infringement act was separate and distinct, and that the claims outside the three-year window were not time-barred due to the defendant's fraud. The court agreed that each claim was separate and distinct; accordingly, claims within the three-year window were timely. As to claims for earlier infringement, however, the court declined to toll the statute of limitations based on the defendant's alleged fraudulent concealment. The plaintiff did not produce evidence that the defendant knowingly and intentionally concealed its infringing use of the brochure after termination of the parties' agreement. The court further rejected the plaintiff's tolling argument based on the "continuing wrong" doctrine, which the Tenth Circuit had not considered, but had been rejected by district courts in the Tenth Circuit.

b.   *Rolling Infringement and Ownership Claims*

[Add the following text at the end of the section.]

In *Kwan v. Schlein,*[4] the Second Circuit affirmed the district court's dismissal of the plaintiff's copyright infringement claim on grounds that the core issue was a dispute over the copyright ownership, and the plaintiff's ownership claim was time-barred. The plaintiff was a freelance editor hired to assist with a book for which the defendants were the primary author and publisher. The plaintiff worked on the book in 1998 and 1999, and requested credit as the co-author at that time. The first edition of the book was published in January 1999 and listed the plaintiff as editor, not co-author. The plaintiff received a share of royalties for the first and second editions of the book. In 2002, the defendants published a third edition, and notified the plaintiff that she would not receive royalties for that edition, which "had been completely re-written." In 2005, the plaintiff brought an infringement suit and applied to register copyright in the book in her own name. The court noted that ownership claims under the Copyright Act must be brought within three years after accrual, even though infringement claims may be brought within three years of any infringing act. The court found that the plaintiff's claim accrued at least as early as January 1999, when the first edition of the book was published. The court held that infringement claims where "ownership forms the backbone of the 'infringement' claim" are

---

[4]634 F.3d 224 (2d Cir. 2011).

time-barred when the underlying ownership claim is time-barred, and dismissed the plaintiff's claim.

2.   *The Role of Plaintiff's Knowledge—The "Discovery Rule"*

[Add the following text at the end of the section.]

The plaintiff has a "reasonable man" duty of diligence in order to qualify for the benefit of the discovery rule. In *Williams v. Curington*,[5] for example, plaintiff Esther Williams filed a complaint against defendant Robert Curington and several others, claiming copyright infringement pursuant to the 1909 Act, as well as various common law claims for breach of contract, false light, and violation of right of publicity. All other defendant parties had either settled with Williams or were dismissed. Curington filed a motion for summary judgment, arguing that Williams' copyright infringement claim was time-barred because it arose from a recording agreement she signed in 1975. Williams argued that "the Copyright Act does not prohibit copyright owners from pursuing copyright claims occurring more than three years before filing suit if the owner did not discover, and reasonably should not have discovered the infringement before the commencement of the three-year period."[6] She also argued that "each individual sale of product containing unauthorized samples of [her] copyrighted sound recording constitutes a separate and distinct act of infringement."[7] The court held that "the release date of each allegedly infringing song is an appropriate date on which to begin running the statute of limitations."[8] Regarding a sampling of her song "Last Night Changed It All" by rap artist Tupac Shakur in his recording "Late Night" which was released by Curington's licensee four and one-half years before Williams filed her complaint, the court noted that "[c]ourts have been careful not to make the statute of limitations for copyright infringement too harsh—such as by barring a claim when a plaintiff 'through no fault of its own, discovers an act of infringement more than three years after the infringement occurred,'" as Williams here asserted.[9] However, a copyright plaintiff has a "'duty of diligence: it is not enough that he did not discover he had a cause of action, if a reasonable man could have.'"[10] The court noted that "as a self-proclaimed music industry insider with an interest in 'Last Night Changed It All,' it is reasonable to conclude that Williams should have discovered the sampling in 'Late Night' within three years of its release."[11] "Therefore, Williams's copyright infringement claims arising out of sales of 'Late

---

[5] 662 F. Supp. 2d 33 (D.D.C. 2009).

[6] *Id.* at 38.

[7] *Id.* (internal quotation marks omitted).

[8] *Id.*

[9] *Id.* at 39 (quoting Polar Bear Prods., Inc. v. Timex Corp., 384 F.3d 700, 706 (9th Cir. 2004)).

[10] *Id.* (quoting *Polar Bear Prods.*, 384 F.3d at 707).

[11] *Id.*

Night' that occurred more than three years before her complaint was filed are time-barred."[12]

3. The Discovery Rule and Ownership Claims

a. What Is Notice?

i. Notice Found

[Add the following text at the end of the section.]

An interesting example of repudiation is described in the First Circuit's *Cambridge Literary Properties, Ltd. v. W. Goebel Porzellanfabrik G.m.b.H. & Co.*,[13] where the plaintiff filed suit seeking a share of profits reaped by the defendants from use of images taken from the 1934 German book, *Das Hummel-Buch.* The book contained 40 drawings by Berta Hummel, a German nun who had talent for drawing images of children in folk dress. Viennese poet Margarete Seemann was contracted by the publisher to write 50 poems for the book. The book listed the publisher as the copyright owner, and Hummel and Seemann as authors or translators. Franz Goebel, then head of the defendant companies, separately obtained the exclusive right to manufacture and market figurines based on Hummel's drawings, and Goebel companies still produce well-known Hummel figurines to this day.

In 1971, Goebel purchased all of the book publisher's copyrights in the Hummel works, including the copyright for *Das Hummel-Buch.* The plaintiff company was formed by an attorney specifically to seek an assignment of copyright interest from Seemann's heirs in order to exploit any remaining Seemann interest in *Das Hummel-Buch.* In 1995, the plaintiff contacted the two remaining heirs and took an assignment from one, and in 1999 took an assignment from the other. The plaintiff then filed an action seeking an accounting from Goebel of profits from the use of the book, including the sale of two- and three-dimensional works derived therefrom, as well as restitution and a decree imposing a constructive trust on Goebel's intellectual property derived from the book. The plaintiff alleged that the book was a joint work between Hummel and Seemann, and copyright in the book therefore granted Seemann rights in the full content of the book, including the illustrations. Accordingly, the plaintiff alleged, it was owed half of the proceeds of the sale of figurines and other Hummel imagery in the United States. Rather than seek adjudication of its ownership rights, the plaintiff simply asserted in the complaint that it was a co-owner, and brought Massachusetts state law claims for accounting and the imposition of an equitable trust.

The court held, however, that the plaintiff had to first establish ownership under the Copyright Act; the plaintiff's failure to seek declaratory judgment of ownership did not remove the issue from the case. Since the ownership question was governed by the Copyright Act,

---

[12] *Id.*

[13] 510 F.3d 77, 85 USPQ2d 1321 (1st Cir. 2007).

the statute-of-limitations issue was governed by the Act as well. The court granted, and the First Circuit affirmed, summary judgment on statute-of-limitations grounds. Since the plaintiff did not file suit within three years of acquiring rights from the first heir, the claim was barred. Herrmann, the plaintiff's sole shareholder, knew that Goebel claimed all rights in the book, and that the heir was not receiving royalties. The best evidence of claim accrual, the court found, was the plaintiff's motive in seeking the assignment, namely, to purchase a cause of action against Goebel. With respect to rights acquired from the second heir, that heir should reasonably have known about the basis for his claim of co-ownership prior to granting the assignment of rights. When the plaintiff contacted the heir about assignment, the heir had a motive to ascertain his potential rights in the book, which investigation would have revealed numerous repudiations of the rights that the plaintiff sought to acquire. Publicly available documents in the Copyright Office and in prior litigation cast doubt on the heirs' rights in the book, and Goebel engaged in widespread exploitation of those rights. This constituted plain and express repudiation of the heir's purported co-ownership rights, sufficient to trigger the statute of limitations.

ii.   No Notice Found

[Add the following text at the end of the section.]

Applying a reasonable-diligence standard, the First Circuit in *Warren Freedenfeld Associates, Inc. v. McTigue*[14] found that inquiry notice was not triggered because there was no triggering event. In that case, the defendant hired the plaintiff architecture firm to design a hospital pursuant to a design agreement. After the parties' relationship soured, the plaintiff sent the defendant a letter warning that the plans and drawings produced by the plaintiff were proprietary, and that neither the defendant nor its successors could make use of them to complete the project. The defendant replied to the letter, pronouncing the plans and drawings "useless," stating that they had been "discarded," and that he would have to pay another architect to finish the project, which the defendant did. Four years after the hospital opened for business, the plaintiff read an article in a trade publication featuring a drawing of the floor plan and reporting that the design had won a merit award. The plaintiff obtained a copy of the building plan and, believing that its copyright had been infringed, filed suit. The defendant asserted a statute-of-limitations defense. The district court found that a "reasonably diligent person" in the plaintiff's position "would have learned of the supposed infringement no later than the date when the hospital opened."[15] Since the plaintiff's action was instituted more than five years after the hospital opening, the district court concluded that the three-year statute of limitations barred the plaintiff's claim.

---

[14]531 F.3d 38, 87 USPQ2d 1301 (1st Cir. 2008).

[15]*Id.* at 43.

The First Circuit vacated the district court's order of dismissal. The court noted that under the "discovery rule," "a claim accrues only when a plaintiff knows or has sufficient reason to know of the conduct upon which the claim is grounded."[16] Moreover, the court noted that "a plaintiff can be charged with inquiry notice, sufficient to start the limitations clock, once he possesses information fairly suggesting some reason to investigate whether he may have suffered an injury at the hands of a putative infringer."[17] The court determined that the plaintiff could not be charged with inquiry notice because there was no "triggering event" that would have brought the potential infringement to the plaintiff's attention. The court reasoned that the plaintiff's letter warned the defendant that the plans and drawings could not be used to complete the project and therefore the plaintiff had no reason to believe the defendant would ignore its warning. Further, the defendant's reply, that the plans and drawings were "useless" and had been "discarded," would have made a reasonable person in the plaintiff's position believe that infringement was not likely. The defendant argued that the availability of the plans and the opening of the hospital put the plaintiff on inquiry notice. The court disagreed, finding nothing in the record suggesting that the plaintiff reviewed the plans or toured the building, or had any duty to do so, prior to discovering the article in the trade publication.

6.   *Estoppel; Laches and Delay*

a.   *Estoppel*

i.   Defendant's Reliance

[Add the following text at the end of the section.]

In *Sierra-Pascual v. Pina Records, Inc.*,[18] the district court in Puerto Rico denied the defendant's motion for summary judgment based on equitable estoppel, finding material issues of fact relating to the extent of the parties' knowledge of facts relating to a claimed implied, nonexclusive license agreement between the parties. The plaintiff alleged that the defendant published and distributed the song "Noche Triste" without the plaintiff's consent. The parties collaborated on the initial recording of the song, which was released on the Internet. When the song became popular, the parties together recorded a second version of the song and the plaintiff agreed to appear in the related music video. The plaintiff alleged that the defendant subsequently released "Noche Triste" for sale in its album called *Masterpiece* without the plaintiff's consent. The plaintiff brought a copyright infringement action. The defendant filed a motion for summary judgment, asserting among other defenses the affirmative defense of equitable estoppel. The defendant claimed that the plaintiff granted an implied nonexclusive license to the defendant

---

[16] *Id.* at 44.

[17] *Id.*

[18] 660 F. Supp. 2d 196 (D.P.R. 2009).

and was therefore barred by his own actions from bringing the claim. The court noted that equitable estoppel requires the following: "'(1) the party to be estopped must know the facts; (2) the party must intend that his conduct be acted upon (or must act in a way that leads the party asserting the estoppel to believe it is so intended); (3) the latter must be ignorant of the true facts; and (4) he must rely on the estopping conduct to his detriment.'"[19] Here, the court found material issues of fact relating to the extent of both parties' knowledge and intent.

b.   Laches and Delay

   iv.   Reliance and Expectation Prejudice

[Add the following text at the end of the section.]
   The district court in *Jedson Engineering, Inc. v. Spirit Construction Services*,[20] rejected the defendants' argument that the plaintiff's claims of copyright infringement were barred by laches because the plaintiff had waited nine months to raise its claims. In connection with three projects involving the design and construction of tissue manufacturing plants, the plaintiff created designs and drawings for the defendant Spirit Construction Services. For the third project, Spirit ultimately worked instead with the defendant Baisch Engineering, and agreed to provide Baisch with access to the plaintiff's drawings from the prior two projects and the plaintiff's preliminary drawings for the third project. The plaintiff brought the action for copyright infringement based on this distribution of its drawings by Spirit and the use of its drawings by Baisch. Because the plaintiff waited nine months to bring its claims, Baisch's work on the third project was 90 percent complete when the plaintiff brought its claims. Citing Sixth Circuit precedent, the court noted that "[a] party asserting laches must show: (1) lack of diligence by the party against whom the defense is asserted, and (2) prejudice to the party asserting it." Concluding that the defendants had not presented evidence sufficient to lead to a finding of undue prejudice, the court denied the defendants' motion for summary judgment to the extent it relied upon the doctrine of laches.

B.   Misuse

2.   Misuse and Antitrust

[Add the following text at the end of the section.]
   A copyright-misuse defense was rejected in *UMG Recordings, Inc. v. Lindor*,[21] where the plaintiffs, a group of record companies, brought a copyright-infringement action against the defendant based on the

---

[19]*Id.* at 205 (quoting Plumley v. Southern Container, 303 F.3d 364, 374 (1st Cir. 2002)).

[20]720 F. Supp. 2d 904 (S.D. Ohio 2010).

[21]531 F. Supp. 2d 453, 85 USPQ2d 1297 (E.D.N.Y. 2007).

defendant's alleged use of KaZaA, a peer-to-peer online media distribution system. The defendant raised the affirmative defense of copyright misuse. The plaintiffs moved to strike. The court first acknowledged that a motion to strike is strongly disfavored, and " 'will be granted only if: (1) there is no question of fact that might allow the defense to succeed; (2) there is no substantial question of law, the resolution of which would allow the defense to succeed; and (3) plaintiff shows prejudice if the defense is allowed to stand.' "[22] Despite this high standard, the court struck the misuse defense. The court stated that copyright owners "commit copyright misuse when they attempt to extend the scope of their copyrights and use them anticompetively [*sic*] in violation of antitrust laws."[23] The court gave as examples tying arrangements, anticompetitive contracts or licensing agreements, and refusal to license to competitors. The court analyzed the unifying characteristic of these as situations in which "the copyright owner has used its copyright to gain an impermissible competitive advantage."[24] The court reasoned that collectively bringing infringement suits was not such anticompetitive behavior.

Turning to the third factor, the court reasoned that allowing discovery to proceed on the antitrust claim would be prejudicial to the plaintiffs because of the onerous nature of antitrust discovery. Accordingly, the court struck the affirmative defense of copyright misuse.

F.   First Sale

4.   *Ownership of Lawfully Made Copy*

[Add the following text at the end of the section.]

The Ninth Circuit in *Universal Music Group v. Augusto*[25] affirmed a finding that distribution of promotional CDs by a record label was a sufficient "sale" to allow redistribution by the recipient under Section 109(a). Relying on "Promotional Use Only—Not For Resale" and similar language on discs, the labels contended that the CDs were merely licensed to recipients and that title never passed. The district court disagreed under the authority of *United States v. Wise*,[26] and held that the recipient's right to perpetual possession of discs precluded a finding that recipient was a mere licensee, not an "owner." On appeal, the Ninth Circuit affirmed, but applied the more nuanced reasoning of *Vernor v. Autodesk Inc.*[27] *Vernor* recognized that "the mere labeling of an arrangement as a license rather than a sale, although it was a factor to be considered, was not by itself dispositive of the issue.... Our conclusion that the recipients

---

[22]*Id.* at 458 (quoting Microsoft Corp. v. PTI (USA), Inc., No. 01-2018, 2003 U.S. Dist. LEXIS 5767 (E.D.N.Y. Mar. 14, 2003)).

[23]*Id.* at 458.

[24]*Id.*

[25]628 F.3d 1175 (9th Cir. 2011).

[26]550 F.2d 1180 (9th Cir. 1977).

[27]621 F.3d 1102 (9th Cir. 2010).

acquired ownership of the CDs is based largely on the nature of UMG's distribution. First, the promotional CDs are dispatched to the recipients without any prior arrangement as to those particular copies. The CDs are not numbered, and no attempt is made to keep track of where particular copies are or what use is made of them.... [A]lthough UMG places written restrictions in the labels of the CDs, it has not established that the restrictions on the CDs create a license agreement." The court also held that "because the CDs were unordered merchandise, the recipients were free to dispose of them as they saw fit under the Unordered Merchandise Statute, 39 U.S.C. §3009," which provides that "(a) [e]xcept for ... free samples clearly and conspicuously marked as such, ... the mailing of unordered merchandise ... constitutes an unfair method of competition and an unfair trade practice...; (b) Any merchandise mailed in violation of subsection (a) of this section ... may be treated as a gift by the recipient, *who shall have the right to retain, use, discard, or dispose of it in any manner he sees fit without any obligation whatsoever to the sender*" (court's emphasis). The purported license language on the CDs was also insufficient to create a license because the recipients never communicated assent to the labels' terms: "Because the record here is devoid of any indication that the recipients agreed to a license, there is no evidence to support a conclusion that licenses were established under the terms of the promotional statement. Accordingly, we conclude that UMG's transfer of possession to the recipients, without meaningful control or even knowledge of the status of the CDs after shipment, accomplished a transfer of title."

5. First Sale and Importation

[Add the following text at the end of the section.]

Most recently, in *Omega S.A. v. Costco Wholesale Corp.*,[28] the Ninth Circuit reversed the district court's grant of summary judgment to defendant Costco, an unauthorized retailer of "grey market" watches bearing the plaintiff's registered design that were manufactured by the plaintiff in Switzerland but not authorized for sale in United States. The Court of Appeals held that the first sale doctrine under Section 109(a) was not a defense to infringement that involves "(1) foreign-made, nonpiratical copies of a U.S.-copyrighted work, (2) unless those same copies have already been sold in the United States with the copyright owner's authority."[29] The court further held that its interpretation of the first sale doctrine was not "clearly irreconcilable" with the Supreme Court's decision in *Quality King Distributors, Inc. v. L'anza Research International, Inc.*,[30] which held that the first sale doctrine applied to "round trip" importation where "a product with a U.S.-copyrighted label was manufactured inside

---

[28]541 F.3d 982, 88 USPQ2d 1102 (9th Cir. 2008), *cert. granted*, 176 L. Ed. 2d 720, No. 08-1423, 2010 U.S. LEXIS 3424 (Apr. 19, 2010).

[29]*Id.* at 983.

[30]523 U.S. 135 (1998).

the United States, exported to an authorized foreign distributor, sold to unidentified third parties overseas, shipped back into the United States without the copyright owner's permission, and then sold in California by unauthorized retailers."[31] Here, no authorized copies were made within the United States. The Supreme Court granted certiorari on the case for the 2010–2011 term and affirmed it by an equally divided vote of 4–4.[32]

On facts very similar to those in *Costco*, the Southern District of New York held *dubitante* in *Pearson Education, Inc. v. Liu*[33] that it was compelled by the unanimous dicta in *Quality King* to hold the first sale doctrine inapplicable to foreign-made copies.[34] The plaintiffs were book publishers that held U.S. copyrights or exclusive rights to reproduce and distribute textbooks in the United States. The defendants purchased foreign editions of the plaintiffs' books, which were lawfully manufactured abroad and were of lower quality than domestic editions, then imported them into the United States and resold them to domestic purchasers. The plaintiffs sought preliminary and permanent injunctions prohibiting the defendants from selling these foreign editions in the United States. In denying the defendants' motion to dismiss, the court held "*dubitante*, that the first-sale doctrine does not apply to copies of a copyrighted work manufactured abroad."[35] The court reasoned that because the foreign editions were manufactured abroad, the defendants did not acquire ownership of copies "lawfully made under" Title 17, as required by Section 109(a). In February 2010, the question was certified to the Second Circuit for interlocutory appeal,[36] and it has not been decided as of this writing. Because the *Costco* ruling from the Ninth Circuit was affirmed 4–4 by an equally divided Supreme Court, the Second Circuit is not bound by precedent to reach the same conclusion.

---

[31] *Omega*, 541 F.3d at 987.

[32] 131 S. Ct. 565, 178 L. Ed. 2d 470, 2010 U.S. LEXIS 9597 (Dec. 13, 2010).

[33] 656 F. Supp. 2d 407 (S.D.N.Y. 2009).

[34] *Id.* at 408 ("[T]he Supreme Court has said, in unanimous *dicta*, that the doctrine does not apply to copies of a copyrighted work manufactured abroad. Because the case for a contrary interpretation is not so strong as to justify disregarding the Supreme Court's considered views, defendants' motion to dismiss will be denied.").

[35] *Id.* at 416.

[36] No. 1:08-cv-06152, 2010 U.S. Dist. LEXIS 15740 (S.D.N.Y. Feb. 22, 2010).

8

Remedies

I. DAMAGES AND PROFITS

A. Actual Damages and Lost Profits

1. *Calculating Defendant's Profits*

b. *Direct Profits—Defendant's Deductions*

i. Overhead

[Add the following text at the end of the section.]

In *Thomas M. Gilbert Architects, P.C. v. Accent Builders & Developers, LLC,*[1] the Fourth Circuit affirmed a district court's grant of summary judgment holding that the defendants infringed the plaintiff's architectural plans for townhouses, and rejected the defendants' argument that the district court improperly refused to subtract the defendants' operating expenses in awarding damages for profits. The Fourth Circuit agreed with the district court that the defendants "simply failed to carry their burden of allocating that portion of their operating expenses attributable to the two units that were sold."[2] The court rejected the defendants' argument that the district court should have assumed the burden of allocation. The court noted that the defendants' claim that their accountant followed GAAP rules in deducting the entirety of the defendants' operating expenses was not relevant for assessing damages for copyright infringement, as some of the defendants' operating expenses had no relation to their infringing acts. Accordingly, the court affirmed the award of infringing profits without deducting operating expenses from gross revenues.

ii. Apportionment

[Add the following text at the end of the section.]

It has been held that a jury should be entitled to decide whether an architect's license fee is already included within an award of profits. In *Semerdjian v. McDougal Littell,*[3] the district court denied in part the defendant textbook company's motion for summary judgment on this basis. The plaintiff, heir of a professional painter, entered into a licensing agreement with the defendant to include reproductions of the painter's works in textbooks. The license permitted the reproduction of the paintings in 40,000 copies of a textbook; the defendant, however, reproduced over 1.3 million copies. The plaintiff sued for infringement and sought disgorgement of the defendant's profits pursuant to Section 504(b). The defendant argued that the plaintiff must show evidence not only of gross revenues from the infringing products, but also which portion of the revenues related to the infringement. The court disagreed, holding

---

[1]No. 08-2103, 2010 U.S. App. LEXIS 9299 (4th Cir. May 6, 2010).

[2]*Id.* at **17–18.

[3]641 F. Supp. 2d 233 (S.D.N.Y. 2009).

that the plaintiff's burden, at this stage, was merely to show the relationship between infringement and revenues and the price and number of copies sold, which the plaintiff did. The defendant argued further that even if proceeds were attributable to the infringement, profits are necessarily included in a reasonable license fee; thus, under Section 504(b), profits would already be included in actual damages, and any further recovery would be prohibited. The court disagreed, holding that the issue was one of material fact that centered on whether images operate in a competitive input market. If so, then profits would be duplicative of a reasonable license fee and unrecoverable; if not, then profits would not be duplicative and thus could be disgorged. Regardless, any such determination was not appropriate at the summary judgment stage.

2. *Actual Damages*

[Add the following text at the end of the section.]

A plaintiff need not always elect between receiving contract damages and copyright-infringement damages; sometimes both are available, though not for the same conduct, as illustrated by the decision in *J.S. Nicol, Inc. v. Peking Handicraft, Inc.*[4] There, the court denied the defendant's renewed motion for judgment as a matter of law, finding that the plaintiff's suit for breach of contract "does not preclude the plaintiff's right to seek copyright damages for infringing behavior beyond and outside the contract period."[5] The plaintiff, a design company and licensor, sued the defendant, its manufacturer and licensee, for breach of contract and copyright infringement after the defendant breached the parties' renewable three-year license agreement one year before the contract period ended. The defendant also continued to use certain of the plaintiff's copyrighted fabric designs following the defendant's termination of the license agreement and beyond the three-year contract term. The defendant moved for judgment as a matter of law, arguing that the plaintiff's election to pursue a breach-of-contract claim precluded the copyright infringement claim. The court denied the defendant's motion, permitting the plaintiff to recover contract damages for unauthorized use of the plaintiff's works by the defendant during the three-year contract period and to also recover copyright damages for unauthorized use by the defendant that occurred subsequent to said period.

Courts have also held that the plaintiff's cost of producing its own authorized work can be relevant in determining actual damages, as in *Imig, Inc. v. Electrolux Home Care Products, Ltd.*[6] There, plaintiff Imig, a company that sells commercial vacuum cleaners, sued defendant Electrolux for interference with business relations. Electrolux counterclaimed, asserting, *inter alia*, that Imig copied protected contents of its user manuals. Electrolux prevailed on the counterclaim and sought

---

[4]No. 03-1548, 2008 U.S. Dist. LEXIS 32608 (S.D.N.Y. Apr. 18, 2008).

[5]*Id.* at *13.

[6]No. 05-529, 2008 U.S. Dist. LEXIS 25478 (E.D.N.Y. Mar. 31, 2008).

damages based on Imig's profits from the sale of vacuums. The court, however, concluded that a more proper assessment was the amount of Imig's profit *attributable* to the copyrighted work, *i.e.*, user manuals, and not the profit Imig realized by selling vacuums. The court stated that employing the latter methodology "plainly overcompensates Electrolux," as "the profits it seeks to recover are not those associated with the sale of its copyrighted Owner's Guide."[7] The court explained that the cost to Electrolux of producing the Owner's Guide "provide[d] a comparatively reliable measure of what Imig would have had to spend to develop it's [*sic*] own manual for the . . . vacuums it sold if it had not misappropriated Electrolux's copyright-protected work."[8]

B.   Statutory Damages

1.   *How Many Statutory Awards?*

[Add the following text at the end of the section.]

In the context of television programs, it has been held that each episode of a series is a separate work, even where a number of episodes are packaged together into a single DVD. For example, in *U2 Home Entertainment, Inc. v. Hong Wei International Trading, Inc.*,[9] the plaintiff was the exclusive distributor in the United States of Chinese-language films, soap operas and programs on DVD and VCD. The defendant operated a video store in New York City that sold and rented video material to its customers. In a prior action, the plaintiff sued the defendant for copyright infringement for duplicating and selling copies of a soap opera series. The case settled, and led to a permanent injunction and sublicense agreement. The defendant immediately violated both, leading to a contempt order and a new infringement action. The plaintiff moved for summary judgment, seeking a statutory damages award for each episode infringed. The court considered whether each DVD, containing multiple episodes of the series, or each episode on each DVD, constituted a separate "work" for purposes of statutory damages computation. The court held that each episode was a separate work for which a separate award of statutory damages could be made, since each episode was produced separately and could stand on its own. The court found the minimum of $750 per infringed episode appropriate, in light of a clear need for deterrence and the defendant's "blatant defiance of the court-ordered Permanent Injunction." The court awarded statutory damages based on 52 series sold, containing 894 episodes for a total of $670,500 in statutory damages.

The Second Circuit recently cast doubt on the reasoning of *U2 Home Entertainment*, however, and held that such a focus on the potential independent economic value of the individual parts of a compilation is

---

[7] *Id.* at *66.

[8] *Id.* at *67.

[9] No. 04-6189, 2008 U.S. Dist. LEXIS 64297 (S.D.N.Y. Aug. 21, 2008).

improper. In *Bryant v. Media Right Productions, Inc.*,[10] defendants copied and made unauthorized sales of the plaintiffs' music albums *Songs for Dogs* and *Songs for Cats* and of tracks from those albums (each of which contained ten tracks). The district court held that the defendants were liable for only one award of statutory damages per album, rather than one award per song, even assuming that the plaintiffs separately registered at least some of the individual songs.

The Second Circuit affirmed. The court stated that under Section 504(c)(1), the Act allows only one award of statutory damages for any "work" infringed, and specifically states that "all the parts of a compilation . . . constitute one work" for purposes of determining statutory damages. Because the plaintiffs' albums were compilations, the fact that each song was separately registered was irrelevant to the statutory damages analysis.[11]

The court distinguished its own previous decisions in *Twin Peaks Productions, Inc. v. Publications International, Ltd.*,[12] and in *WB Music Corp. v. RTV Communication Group, Inc.*[13] In *Twin Peaks*, the Second Circuit held that the plaintiff could receive a separate award of statutory damages for each of eight teleplays because the plaintiff had issued the works separately, as independent episodes, each at a different time. In *WB Music*, the circuit held that the plaintiff could receive a separate award of statutory damages for each song because the plaintiff had separately issued each song, and it was the defendant who had issued the songs in album form.

Here, by contrast, the court emphasized that it was the plaintiffs themselves "who issued their works as 'compilations'; they chose to issue Albums. In this situation, the plain language of the Copyright Act limits the copyright holders' statutory damage award to one for each Album."[14] The court expressly declined to adopt the independent economic value test, which was articulated by the First Circuit in *Gamma Audio & Video, Inc. v. Ean-Chea*,[15] which held that "a work that is part of a multi-part product can constitute a separate work for the purposes of statutory damages if it has 'independent economic value and . . . is viable.' "[16] The court noted that the economic value test has been applied by a number of other circuits as well.[17] But for the Second Circuit in

---

[10]603 F.3d 135 (2nd Cir. 2010).

[11]*See id.* at 141 ("Based on a plain reading of the statute, therefore, infringement of an album should result in only one statutory damage award. The fact that each song may have received a separate copyright is irrelevant to this analysis.").

[12]996 F.2d 1366 (2nd Cir. 1993).

[13]445 F.3d 538 (2nd Cir. 2006).

[14]*Bryant*, 603 F.3d at 141.

[15]11 F.3d 1106 (1st Cir. 1993).

[16]*Bryant*, 603 F.3d at 141 (quoting *Gamma*, 11 F.3d at 1116–17).

[17]*See id.* at 142, *citing* "MCA Television Ltd. v. Feltner, 89 F.3d 766, 769 (11th Cir. 1996) (holding that each episode of a television show can be the subject of a separate statutory damage award because each episode has independent economic value); Columbia Pictures Television v. Krypton Broad. of Birmingham, Inc., 106 F.3d 284, 295

Bryant, the language of the Copyright Act did not allow an exception for separate parts of a compilation that have independent economic value. The court simply found that "all parts of a compilation" constituted one work for purposes of statutory damages.

The courts have consistently declined to grant separate statutory awards for a defendant's different infringing acts involving the same work. In *Hamlin v. Trans-Dapt of California, Inc.,*[18] for example, the court granted the defendant's motion for summary judgment on its request to grant only one award of statutory damages. The plaintiff author created his work as a guide/manual to assist readers in the installation of engines in Chevrolet pickup trucks. The defendant company's employees bought a copy of the plaintiff's work on eBay, and conceded copying pictures and some text from the manual for purposes of an Instruction Sheet they created to go along with the sale of car parts. Upon learning of the infringement, the plaintiff sent a cease-and-desist letter, but when the defendant did not completely cease infringement, the plaintiff filed suit for infringement, including a claim for statutory damages for each infringement of the work. The defendant argued that since only one work was infringed, only one statutory award should be given. The court agreed, "and finds that [the plaintiff's] argument for damages based on the number of infringements is premised on a prior version of the Copyright Act, which was amended in 1976."[19] The plaintiff attempted to cite cases that permitted damages based on each separate infringement of the same work, but the court held that the number of statutory damages awards depends " 'on the number of works that are infringed and the number of individually liable infringers, regardless of the number of infringements of those works.' "[20]

2. *How Much to Award?*

[Add the following text at the end of the section.]

Even though the statutory maximum for willful infringement is $150,000 per work, awards seldom reach that amount, even on default judgment. In *Scholz Design, Inc. v. Campbell Signature Homes, LLC,*[21] for example, plaintiff Scholz Design filed a complaint against defendant Campbell Signature Homes, alleging two counts of copyright infringement on certain architectural drawings. The defendant failed to answer the complaint, and the plaintiff filed a motion for entry of a default

---

(9th Cir. 1997) (same) (reversed on other grounds, 523 U.S. 340, 118 S. Ct. 1279, 140 L. Ed. 2d 438 (1998)); Walt Disney Co. v. Powell, 897 F.2d 565, 569, 283 U.S. App. D.C. 111 (D.C. Cir. 1990) (holding that plaintiff could not receive a separate statutory damage award for each, separate picture of Mickey Mouse and Minnie Mouse in different poses, because each picture did not have independent economic value)."

[18]584 F. Supp. 2d 1050 (M.D. Tenn. 2008).

[19]*Id.* at 1053–54.

[20]*Id.* at 1055 (quoting WB Music Corp. v. RTV Comm'n Group, Inc., 445 F.3d 538, 540, 78 USPQ2d 1637 (2d Cir. 2006)).

[21]No. 08-1087, 2009 U.S. Dist. LEXIS 10562 (C.D. Ill. Feb. 12, 2009).

judgment, noting that "had [the defendant] answered the complaint and had discovery been performed, [the plaintiff] would have been able to ascertain the scope of [the defendant's] business and whether there were additional acts of infringement."[22] The plaintiff requested that the court enter default judgment finding that the defendant had willfully infringed the plaintiff's copyrights, and that the plaintiff was entitled to statutory damages in the amount of $150,000 per act of infringement. The court issued an order explaining that it was unable to ascertain, based on the plaintiff's submissions, whether the plaintiff was entitled to maximum statutory damages, noting that in setting statutory damages, the court "considers the expenses saved and profits reaped by a defendant in connection with the infringements, the revenues lost by a plaintiff as a result of a defendant's conduct, and the infringer's state of mind whether willful, knowing, or merely innocent."[23] The court directed the plaintiff to file supplemental arguments as to why the court should impose the statutory maximum. The plaintiff failed to file supplemental arguments. The court found that the defendant's infringement "was knowing, willful and intentional, because [the plaintiff] made this allegation in its Complaint."[24] The court nonetheless awarded only $20,000 per work infringed, reasoning that the statutory maximum was "not justified" because the plaintiff had "fail[ed] to provide legal authority justifying the imposition of the statutory maximum."[25] The court stated that "even when a default judgment is warranted based on a party's failure to defend, the allegations in the complaint with respect to the amount of the damages are not deemed true." Instead, the district court must "conduct an inquiry in order to ascertain the amount of damages with reasonable certainty."[26]

In the context of file sharing, at least one court has taken the unusual step of remitting a jury's statutory damage award to a much lower figure in the belief that even an award within the statutory range was too high. In *Capitol Records v. Thomas-Rasset*,[27] the jury in the defendant's first trial awarded statutory damages of $222,000 for willful infringement of 24 works ($9,250 per recording). Defendant Thomas moved for a new trial on various grounds, but the court requested further briefing on an additional ground which it raised sua sponte: whether the court itself erred in the jury instruction it gave regarding the definition of "distribution." In September 2008, the court concluded that the jury instruction was in fact erroneous and therefore that a new trial was required.[28] In ordering

---

[22]*Id.* at *2.

[23]*Id.* at *3.

[24]*Id.* at *4.

[25]*Id.* at *5.

[26]*Id.* at *4. *But see Prince v. Williams*, No. 03-5324 (E.D.N.Y. May 25, 2004) (slip op.) ($150,000 statutory damage award on default).

[27]680 F. Supp. 2d 1045 (D. Minn. 2010).

[28]579 F. Supp. 2d 1210 (D. Minn. 2008).

a new trial, the court also opined that the first jury's verdict—$9,250 per track—was an "unprecedented and oppressive"[29] award. (The court had noted that the defendant was not a business but was a "single mother" who "sought no profit from her acts."[30]) In the second trial, the jury completed its deliberations quickly and returned a verdict of $1.92 million ($80,000 for each song) for willful infringement, nearly nine times larger than the first jury's verdict.

Thomas moved again for a new trial, asserting that the statutory damages provision of the Copyright Act violates the Due Process Clause of the U.S. Constitution by, inter alia, permitting the unfettered exercise of discretion for the court to make oppressive awards without proper guidelines or notice. In making this argument, Thomas relied upon Supreme Court cases on punitive damages which impose due process requirements on such awards. In their briefs in opposition, the plaintiffs and the U.S. Department of Justice, as *amicus* supporting the constitutionality of the statute, argued that the due process concerns articulated in punitive damages cases do not apply to statutory damages awards, and that Section 504(c) provides adequate notice of potential damages awards. Moreover, they argued, sufficient guidelines may be found in Section 504(c)'s tripartite classification of infringing activity as non-willful, willful or innocent, as well as in its legislative history. Finally, they argued that in view of the carefully chosen statutory scheme, Section 504(c) is entitled to highly deferential review when challenged on due process grounds. In January 2010, the court sidestepped the due process challenge and instead vacated and remitted the statutory damage figure to a lesser amount under its traditional common-law power of remittitur. The court lowered damages to $2,250 per song (a total of $54,000)—three times the statutory minimum of $750 per title that Thomas had urged, but far below the $80,000 per song that the second jury had awarded. Defending the remittitur, the court explained: "The need for deterrence cannot justify a $2 million verdict for stealing and illegally distributing 24 songs for the sole purpose of obtaining free music."[31] The court offered the following rationale for the lower award:

> [A]lthough Plaintiffs were not required to prove their actual damages, statutory damages must still bear *some* relation to actual damages.
>
> The Court has labored to fashion a reasonable limit on statutory damages awards against noncommercial individuals who illegally download and upload music such that the award of statutory damages does not veer into the realm of gross injustice. Finding a precise dollar amount that delineates the border between the jury's wide discretion to calculate its own number to address Thomas-Rasset's willful violations, Plaintiffs' far-reaching, but nebulous damages, and the need to deter online piracy in general and the outrageousness of a $2 million verdict is a considerable task. The Court concludes that setting the limit at three times the minimum statutory damages amount in this case is the most reasoned solution.

---

[29] *Id.* at 1228.

[30] *Id.* at 1227.

[31] *Thomas-Rasset*, 680 F. Supp. 2d at 1053.

This award constitutes the maximum amount a jury could reasonably award to both compensate Plaintiffs and address the deterrence aspect of the Copyright Act. *This reduced award is significant and harsh.* It is a higher award than the Court might have chosen to impose in its sole discretion, but the decision was not entrusted to this Court. It was the jury's province to determine the award of statutory damages and this Court has merely reduced that award to the maximum amount that is no longer monstrous and shocking. Plaintiffs have seven days from the date of this Order to decide whether to accept the remittitur or request a new trial on the issue of damages.[32]

After the reported decision, the plaintiffs declined to accept remittitur and requested a new trial. In their notice advising the court of this decision, Document 371 in the court's PACER docket, the plaintiffs faulted the court for creating an apparent cap of three times the statutory minimum damage award for any "noncommercial individuals who illegally download and upload music" and for ignoring the many jurors who awarded much larger sums after hearing the evidence of willful infringement adduced at trial. A third trial was held in October and November 2010, and the jury returned a verdict of $1.5 million. That award is presently being challenged in post-trial motion practice on the due process issue, and will likely go up on appeal regardless of the outcome.

Under very similar circumstances, the District of Massachusetts reached quite a different result. In the only other music file-sharing case to reach a jury, *Sony BMG Music Entertainment v. Tenenbaum,*[33] the defendant challenged the jury award of $675,000, which had been assessed against him (at $22,500 per song) in connection with his unauthorized distribution of thirty songs. Though the facts were similar to *Thomas-Rasset,* the court in *Tenenbaum* explicitly rejected the approach of the *Thomas-Rasset* court and concluded that common-law remittitur was not an appropriate way to address the size of the jury award. Instead, the court issued a lengthy decision vacating the award as a violation of due process under the standards set forth in *BMW of North America, Inc. v. Gore.*[34]

Although the court recognized that remittitur "in theory provides an avenue for me to avoid Tenenbaum's constitutional challenge while still reducing the jury's award,"[35] the court also noted that the plaintiffs would likely opt for a new trial as they did in *Thomas-Rasset* rather than accept the reduced award, and that the constitutional issue would necessarily be part of the retrial. Therefore, "Tenenbaum's constitutional challenge appear[ed] unavoidable."[36]

The court applied the *Gore* standard, rather than the more directly on-point reasoning of *St. Louis Iron Mountain & Southern Railway Co. v.*

---

[32] *Id.* at 1048–49 (emphasis in original).

[33] 721 F. Supp. 2d 85 (D. Mass. 2010).

[34] 517 U.S. 559 (1996).

[35] *Tenenbaum,* 721 F. Supp. 2d at 93.

[36] *Id.* at 94.

Williams,[37] but took the position that the award would fail "under either test."[38]

Interestingly, after choosing to engage in this lengthy constitutional analysis and finding the jury award to be a due process violation, the court ultimately remitted the award to the same figure—$2,250 per song—that the *Thomas-Rasset* court arrived at by the common-law remittitur process, finding that number to be "the outer limit of what a jury could reasonably (and Constitutionally) impose in this case."[39] That amount, again, is three times the statutory minimum of $750 per work. The *Tenenbaum* court explains that this arguably arbitrary amount "at least has the virtue of finding some basis in the long history of courts and legislators sanctioning treble damages to deter willful misconduct."[40] It might be noted, however, that the legislators who drafted the Copyright Act chose not to provide for treble damages, but instead established a precise statutory range, to be applied by a jury.[41] As this Supplement goes to press, a notice of appeal has been filed.

3. Awarded Against Whom?

b. "Joint Action"

[Add the following text at the end of the section.]

Where there is both a primary and a secondary infringer involved in a given infringement, one statutory damage award is imposed upon both of them, and they are liable jointly and severally. Thus, in *Smith v. NBC Universal,*[42] the court held that the plaintiff was entitled to only one award of statutory damages where a single work was infringed by multiple defendants. The plaintiff brought an action based upon unauthorized use of video footage of an orca attacking the plaintiff. The footage was incorporated into an episode of a television series. Defendant MG Perin authorized defendant Universal Television Networks to broadcast the episode at issue. The court found that because MG Perin contributed to Universal's infringement, as opposed to independently infringing the plaintiff's work, the defendants were jointly and severally liable. The

---

[37]251 U.S. 63 (1919).

[38]*Tenenbaum,* 721 F. Supp. 2d at 101.

[39]*Id.* at 117.

[40]*Id.* at 118.

[41]The court cites *Thomas-Rasset* where Chief Judge Davis noted that "the Digital Millennium Copyright Act, 17 U.S.C. §1203(c)(4), and the Telephone Consumer Protection Act of 1991, 47 U.S.C. §227(b)(3), (c)(5) . . . explicitly 'allow for an increase in statutory damages, up to triple statutory damages, when the statutory violation is willful or demonstrates a particular need for deterrence,'" *id.* at 117 (quoting *Thomas-Rasset,* 680 F. Supp. 2d at 1056). But District Judge Gertner in *Tenenbaum* noted that "17 U.S.C. §504(c) does not, by its own terms, limit the statutory damages available in cases such as Tenenbaum's to three times the statutory minimum." *Id.*

[42]No. 06-5350, 2008 U.S. Dist. LEXIS 15714 (S.D.N.Y. Feb. 28, 2008). See the facts of this case in its earlier proceedings at 2008 U.S. Dist. LEXIS 13280, 86 USPQ2d 1579 (S.D.N.Y. Feb. 22, 2008), and 524 F. Supp. 2d 315 (S.D.N.Y. 2007).

court also noted that because the plaintiff's claims against MG Perin and Universal were "related in time, space, origin, and motivation, [were] convenient to try together, and business understanding suggest[ed] that they [were] a single claim,"[43] the plaintiff would be unable to recover from each of the defendants if he filed actions against them separately. Because there was only one work at issue and the defendants were joint tortfeasors, the plaintiff was entitled to only a single award of statutory damages.

4. *Willful Infringement*

a. *Proving Willfulness*

[Add the following text at the end of the section.]

Willfulness was clearly established in *Yurman Studio, Inc. v. Castaneda,*[44] where the district court granted statutory damages for willful infringement over a five-day period. After an August 19, 2008 opinion and order of the district court holding that the defendants had infringed the plaintiffs' copyrights, the defendants continued marketing infringing jewelry items. On August 28, 2008, the defendants' attorney notified the defendants which items were found to be infringing, at which point the defendants simply moved the infringing items to a section of the defendants' web page marked "final sale." The infringing items remained on the defendants' "final sale" page until September 2, 2008, when, at a court status conference, the plaintiffs brought the defendants' continued sale of infringing items to the court's attention. The plaintiffs sought statutory damages for willful infringement. The court found that the defendants' continued sale of infringing items between August 28, 2008 and September 2, 2008 was without excuse and willful. The placement of infringing goods on the "final sale" site was definitive proof of willfulness.

Where no statutory damages are available, because the plaintiff failed to timely register copyright in the work at issue, the court may not even permit evidence of willfulness to be introduced. In *Faulkner v. National Geographic Society,*[45] the court granted the defendants' motion *in limine* to limit the plaintiff to potential actual damages, and precluded the plaintiff from introducing evidence of willful infringement. The plaintiff asserted that pursuant to agreements with defendant National Geographic Society ("NGS") regarding NGS's use of the plaintiff's photographs in its print magazine, NGS could not use, without authorization, the plaintiff's five print photographs in a CD-ROM version of NGS's magazine. Because the plaintiff did not have copyright registrations for his works before the infringement commenced, however, he could recover only actual damages, not statutory damages. Additionally, before trial on the plaintiff's claim, the defendants argued that the plaintiff's claim for punitive

---

[43] *Smith,* 2008 U.S. Dist. LEXIS 15714, at *8.

[44] Nos. 07-1241, 07-7862, 2008 U.S. Dist. LEXIS 99849 (S.D.N.Y. Dec. 1, 2008).

[45] 576 F. Supp. 2d 609, 88 USPQ2d 1830 (S.D.N.Y. 2008).

damages should be stricken and the plaintiff should be precluded from offering any evidence of willful infringement. The court agreed with the defendants, reaffirming that punitive damages are not available in statutory copyright-infringement actions and, because the plaintiff need not prove wrongful intent or culpability in order to determine actual damages, evidence of willful conduct would serve only to unfairly prejudice the defendants before the jury.

5. Non-Willful Infringement

[Add the following text at the end of the section.]

The Fifth Circuit has recently held that the presence of a proper copyright notice on tangible copies of a plaintiff's works is sufficient to defeat the "innocent infringer" defense, even when the defendant copied the works from digital files bearing no notice. In *Maverick Recording Co. v. Harper*,[46] the court reversed a finding that the defendant was entitled to an innocent infringer defense. The plaintiff record company sued the individual defendant for copyright infringement based on the defendant's downloading and sharing of the plaintiff's copyrighted music on a peer-to-peer network. The lower court denied the plaintiff's request for statutory damages of $750 per infringed work. The defendant claimed she was an innocent infringer under Section 504(c)(2), which provides for a reduction of statutory damages. If she could prove that she "was not aware and had no reason to believe that . . . her acts constituted an infringement of copyright, the court in its discretion may reduce the award of statutory damages to a sum of not less than $200."[47] The lower court awarded the plaintiff $200 per infringing work. But the court of appeals noted that Section 402 limits the innocent infringer defense "when a proper copyright notice 'appears on the published . . . phonorecords to which a defendant . . . had access,'" and if so, "'then no weight shall be given to such a defendant's interposition of a defense based on innocent infringement in mitigation of actual or statutory damages.'"[48] In other words, the notice precludes any claim by a young or unsophisticated defendant that she did not understand what she was doing. The court of appeals found the plaintiff entitled to $750 per work infringed as a matter of law. The plaintiff's copyright notice on each published phonorecord was sufficient to overcome the innocent infringer defense, and render the defendant's claims of ignorance irrelevant for purposes of statutory damages. On petition for certiorari,[49] which was denied, Justice Alito took the unusual step of issuing a separate dissent from the denial. Justice Alito questioned the relevance of copyright notice in the digital context, and opined that the sole issue should be the defendant's awareness as

---

[46] 598 F.3d 193 (5th Cir. 2010).

[47] 17 U.S.C. §504(c)(2).

[48] *Maverick Recording*, 598 F.3d at 198 (quoting 17 U.S.C. §402(d)).

[49] 131 S. Ct. 590, 178 L. Ed. 2d 511, 2010 U.S. LEXIS 9042 (Nov. 29, 2010).

well as other "objective characteristics" of the infringer "such as age,"[50] regardless of the presence or absence of notice.

6.   Attorney's Fees

[Add the following text at the end of the section.]

If a claim is dismissed on motion for lack of subject matter jurisdiction, the prevailing defendant may not be awarded attorney's fees. In *Giddings v. Vision House Production, Inc.*,[51] the court denied the defendant's motion for attorney's fees after the plaintiff's complaint for copyright infringement was dismissed for lack of subject matter jurisdiction. The defendant filed a motion for costs and attorney's fees. The court held that, in the Ninth Circuit, if a district court lacks subject matter jurisdiction with regard to the underlying claim, then it also lacks subject matter jurisdiction over a claim for costs and attorney's fees with respect to the underlying claim. Further, "the fee-shifting provision of the substantive statute under which the suit was brought cannot confer subject matter jurisdiction that is otherwise absent."[52]

a.   Registration and "Commencement"

[Add the following text at the end of the section.]

It is not possible for a plaintiff to plead its way out of the registration requirement for statutory damages and attorney's fees simply by limiting its pleadings to acts occurring after registration. For example, in *Cassetica Software, Inc. v. Computer Sciences Corp.*,[53] the Northern District of Illinois dismissed the plaintiff's copyright claim for statutory damages and attorney's fees, finding that the alleged infringement began before registration of the plaintiff's copyright. The plaintiff computer software developer had granted the defendant a nonexclusive, nontransferable license to download its program called NotesMedic which addressed problems experienced when the application LotusNotes crashed. The license expired in 2003, but the defendant allegedly continued to download the plaintiff's program through at least February 2009. The plaintiff obtained copyright registration for its program in January 2007 and brought the action in January 2009. The plaintiff's allegations revealed that the alleged infringement began before registration of its copyright. Although the plaintiff alleged that the defendant continued to download the plaintiff's program after registration of its copyright, the court held that "[a] plaintiff may not recover statutory damages or attorney's fees when the alleged infringement *commenced* before the effective date of the copyright registration."[54] This was so even where the plaintiff

---

[50] *Id.*, 131 S. Ct. at 591, 178 L. Ed. 2d at 512, 2010 U.S. Lexis 9042, at *4.

[51] No. 05-2963, 2009 U.S. Dist. LEXIS 54931 (D. Ariz. June 11, 2009).

[52] *Id.* at *3.

[53] No. 09-0003, 2009 U.S. Dist. LEXIS 51589 (N.D. Ill. June 18, 2009).

[54] *Id.* at *4 (citing 17 U.S.C. §412) (emphasis added).

attempted "to limit its claim of infringement to events that occurred after registration."[55] Because the allegations revealed that the alleged infringement commenced before the plaintiff registered its copyright, the court dismissed the claim for statutory damages and attorney's fees.

b.   Prevailing Party

[Add the following text at the end of the section.]

The Ninth Circuit, in *Cadkin v. Loose*,[56] reversed an award of attorney's fees to the defendants when the plaintiff voluntarily dismissed without prejudice a lawsuit that included copyright claims. The plaintiff filed a complaint including copyright infringement, false designation of origin, and California state law claims. The plaintiff alleged that the defendant removed the plaintiff's name as author and publisher of music cues composed by the plaintiff, incorporated those cues into the defendant's library with the defendant as sole author, and registered the cues with the Copyright Office, allowing the defendant to obtain the full royalty from the cues. The plaintiff amended its complaint twice, and the defendant moved to dismiss, arguing that "(1) . . . state law claims were preempted by the Copyright Act, (2) the factual allegations lacked specificity and (3) any federal copyright or trademark claims were waived because they were not included in the amended pleading."[57] The plaintiff opposed the motion to dismiss and filed a notice of voluntary dismissal. The defendants sought attorney's fees and costs, which the district court granted in view of *Corcoran v. Columbia Broadcasting System, Inc.*,[58] which held that when a plaintiff "voluntarily dismisses without amending his pleading, the party sued is the prevailing party within the spirit and intent of [17 U.S.C. §40 of the 1909 Copyright Act] even though he may, at the whim of the plaintiff, again be sued on the same cause of action."[59]

The Ninth Circuit, however, held that the "material alteration" test articulated in *Buckhannon Board & Care Home, Inc. v. West Virginia Department of Health & Human Resources*[60] "governs the prevailing party inquiry under §505 of the Copyright Act" and "overrule[d] *Corcoran* to the extent it is inconsistent with *Buckhannon*."[61] The plaintiffs' voluntary dismissal "'does not alter the legal relationship of the parties because [the defendants] remain[ ] subject to the risk of re-filing' following a dismissal without prejudice."[62] The defendants were not prevailing parties and therefore were not entitled to attorney's fees.

---

[55]*Id.* at **4–5.

[56]569 F.3d 1142 (9th Cir. 2009).

[57]*Id.* at 1146.

[58]121 F.2d 575 (9th Cir. 1941).

[59]*Id.* at 576.

[60]532 U.S. 598 (2001).

[61]*Cadkin*, 569 F.3d at 1149.

[62]*Id.* (quoting Oscar v. Alaska Dep't of Educ. & Early Dev., 541 F.3d 978, 981 (9th Cir. 2008).

Outside the context of dismissal, it is clear that a plaintiff need not win all of its copyright claims to be the prevailing party. In *Brighton Collectibles, Inc. v. Coldwater Creek, Inc.,*[63] for example, the district court granted the plaintiff's motion for attorney's fees, and denied the defendant's, on this basis. The court found that the plaintiff obtained a high degree of success on one of its copyright-infringement claims, insofar as the jury found willful infringement by the defendant and awarded substantial damages. The court denied the defendant's claim for attorney's fees with respect to the plaintiff's other copyright claim, which was dismissed on summary judgment, noting that dismissal of one of the plaintiff's copyright claims did not prevent it from being deemed the overall prevailing party.

c.   *Merits—The Fogerty Standard*

   i.   Reasonableness

   (2) Claims of Non-Prevailing Party Found Unreasonable

   [Add the following text at the end of the section.]

   The factor of objective unreasonableness is so significant in the *Fogerty* analysis that some courts recognize it as dispositive. In *Hudson v. Universal Studios, Inc.,*[64] for example, the court granted the defendants' motion for attorney's fees when it prevailed over a pro se plaintiff who "has been suing defendants and others since 2002, in the Eastern District of New York and in this court, contending that defendants' motion picture *Life* was plagiarized from his plays, *Bronx House* and *No Harm, No Foul.*"[65] The Eastern District of New York dismissed the claims, finding that " 'no reasonable jury could find a substantial similarity between the protected elements of *No Harm, No Foul* and *Life,*' " and that the claim of similarity between *Bronx House* and *Life* was similarly " 'meritless.' "[66] The plaintiff then sued in the Southern District of New York,[67] which initially dismissed the claims on grounds of res judicata. The Second Circuit affirmed dismissal of the claims related to *No Harm, No Foul,* but vacated and remanded the claims related to *Bronx House* for further proceedings, finding "some confusion" in the Southern District's record as to whether the *Bronx House* claims were properly before the court then.[68] Further proceedings resulted in a finding on the merits that the *Bronx House* claims were without merit.[69]

---

[63]No. 06-1848, 2009 U.S. Dist. LEXIS 4005 (S.D. Cal. Jan 20, 2009).

[64]No. 04-6997, 2009 U.S. Dist. LEXIS 18729, 90 USPQ2d 1664 (S.D.N.Y. Mar. 4, 2009).

[65]*Id.* at *1.

[66]*Id.* (quoting Hudson v. Universal Pictures Corp., No. 03-1008, 2004 U.S. Dist. LEXIS 11508, at *10, 12, 70 USPQ2d 1727 (E.D.N.Y. Apr. 29, 2004)).

[67]*See* No. 04-6997, 2006 U.S. Dist. LEXIS 25090 (S.D.N.Y. Apr. 28, 2006).

[68]*See* 235 Fed. Appx. 788, 790, 2007 U.S. App. LEXIS 12519 (2d Cir. 2007).

[69]*See* No. 04-6997, 2008 U.S. Dist. LEXIS 86146, 89 USPQ2d 1132 (S.D.N.Y. Oct. 23, 2008).

On the fee issue, objective reasonableness is a factor that should be given substantial weight; indeed, the court noted, the courts in the Second Circuit " 'have awarded attorneys' fees to prevailing defendants solely upon a showing that the plaintiff's position was objectively unreasonable, without regard to any other equitable factor.' "[70] It was clear that the plaintiff's claims with respect to *Bronx House* were objectively unreasonable; the court found that "no reasonable person could have believed that the minor similarities, intrinsic to any drama of unjustified incarceration, warranted a conclusion that the two works were similar."[71] "Whether or not Hudson's claims were subjectively in bad faith, his obsessive pursuit of claims already rejected, coupled with the objective unreasonableness of the claims advanced here, warrant the conclusion that the defendants deserve compensation, and that an award of fees here could deter others from bringing frivolous claims, without fear of deterring plaintiffs whose claims have potential merit."[72] The court noted that the plaintiff's lack of resources was "not relevant to *whether* an award of fees is appropriate, but that 'financial disparities may be a factor considered in determining the magnitude of an award once it has been resolved that such an award is appropriate.' "[73] However, the court held that "[f]urther discussion of this issue . . . is best deferred until defendants have submitted documentation of their expenses, and plaintiff has had an opportunity to submit a sworn statement of his income and net worth."[74]

iii. Standards for Plaintiff Versus Standards for Defendant

[Add the following text at the end of the section.]

Courts have also stated that a fee award may be appropriate to ensure that a plaintiff does not lose money enforcing its valid copyright against a flagrant infringer. In *Dunn & Fenley, LLC v. Allen,*[75] for example, the losing defendant asserted that the plaintiff's attorney's fees request should be denied in its entirety, or alternatively, that any award should not exceed $100,000. In exercising its discretion, the court concluded first that the plaintiff was very successful in establishing that the defendant had infringed, and second that the defendant acted frivolously in refusing to settle, in light of the overwhelming similarity of the works in question (ads for "lasik" eye surgery). The court next concluded that the defendant's motivation for not settling was to run up the plaintiff's attorney's fees, which concurred with the jury's finding that the infringement was willful.

---

[70] 2009 U.S. Dist. LEXIS 18729, at *5 (quoting Baker v. Urban Outfitters, Inc., 431 F. Supp. 2d 351, 357 (S.D.N.Y. 2006)).

[71] *Id.* at *7.

[72] *Id.* at *9.

[73] *Id.* at *10 (quoting Penguin Books U.S.A., Inc. v. New Christian Church of Full Endeavor, Ltd., No. 96 Civ. 4126, 2004 U.S. Dist. LEXIS 5648; 70 USPQ2d 1393 (S.D.N.Y. Apr. 6, 2004)) (emphasis in original).

[74] *Id.* at *11.

[75] No. 02-1750, 2007 U.S. Dist. LEXIS 75292 (D. Or. Oct. 9, 2007).

Finally, the court noted that if the plaintiff were not compensated for its attorney's fees, it would have expended more protecting its copyright from obvious and willful infringement than it would recover in damages.

It has also been held that fees can be awarded to a prevailing defendant under Section 505 even where the plaintiff had no standing to bring a legitimate claim under the Copyright Act. Evidently, the fact that the plaintiff asserts the claim under the Copyright Act is sufficient to bring the Act's fee-shifting provision into play, even if the claim is dismissed on "jurisdictional" grounds. Thus, in *Hyperquest, Inc. v. N'Site Solutions, Inc.*,[76] the court found that the defendants were entitled to an award of attorney's fees following dismissal of the plaintiff's copyright action for lack of standing. The plaintiff was a licensee of certain works which it claimed the defendants infringed. Under a separate opinion, the court dismissed the plaintiff's action because the plaintiff was not an exclusive licensee, or "a legal or beneficial owner of an exclusive right under a copyright," as is required by the Copyright Act in order to bring an action for copyright infringement. Following dismissal, the defendants moved for attorney's fees as the "prevailing party" pursuant to Section 505. In opposition to the defendants' motion, the plaintiff argued that dismissal of the action for lack of standing was equivalent to dismissal for lack of subject matter jurisdiction, and therefore the court did not have power to award attorney's fees. The plaintiff's opposition papers were partially premised upon the fact that, in its decision dismissing the plaintiff's action, the court itself stated that the action was dismissed "for lack of subject matter." In rejecting the plaintiff's argument, the court conceded that its use of this language was not appropriate, and distinguished between dismissal for lack of standing and dismissal for lack of subject matter jurisdiction. The court reasoned that dismissal for lack of subject matter jurisdiction is based upon a determination that the court does not have the power to decide the issues presented, whereas dismissal for lack of standing is a "'material alteration of the legal relationship of the parties'"[77] resulting in a dismissal "with prejudice" which thereby renders the defendants "prevailing parties" entitled to attorney's fees.[78]

d.   *Types of Claims*

[Add the following text at the end of the section.]

Courts have also granted fees under Section 505 in connection with common-law claims, as in *Pearson Education, Inc. v. Tjiptowidjojo*.[79] In that case, the court observed that "rarely has the court encountered such a compelling case for granting such an award."[80] The defendant, the court

---

[76]559 F. Supp. 2d 918 (N.D. Ill. 2008).

[77]*Id.* at 921 (quoting Buckhannon Bd. & Care Home, Inc. v. West Va. Dep't of Health & Human Res., 532 U.S. 598, 604 (2001)).

[78]*Id.*

[79]84 USPQ2d 1697 (S.D.N.Y. 2007).

[80]*Id.* at 1698.

found, knowingly distributed copyrighted materials, and continued to do so after repeated warnings by the plaintiff to stop; moreover, the defendant's legal defenses and counterclaims were objectively unreasonable. The defendant argued that a portion of the plaintiff's fees was not recoverable under Section 505 because the defendant's counterclaims arose under common law, not the Copyright Act. The court held that all of the defendant's counterclaims were "inextricably intertwined, both legally and factually, with defendant's willful copyright infringement."[81] Accordingly, the court concluded, fees for legal services relating to the plaintiff's defense against common-law claims may properly be included in a motion brought under Section 505.

The District of Oregon has gone further to hold that a prevailing copyright litigant can recover fees on non-copyright claims, even if they are *not* inextricably intertwined with the copyright claims. In *Atlantic Recording Corp. v. Andersen*,[82] the court, overruling both the plaintiffs' and the defendant's objections, confirmed the Magistrate Judge's Findings and Recommendation awarding attorney's fees to the defendant. The plaintiffs, citing *Gracie v. Gracie*,[83] contended that fees for non-copyright claims are compensable under the Copyright Act only where they are "so intertwined" with the copyright claims "that it is impossible to differentiate between work done on the claims."[84]

The court disagreed; the "inextricably intertwined" standard articulated in *Gracie* addressed the calculation of fees under the Lanham Act, under which attorney's fees are recoverable only in exceptional cases and only for work performed in connection with claims filed under the Lanham Act. In contrast, the court remarked (perhaps inaccurately after *Fogerty*) that an award of attorney's fees to the prevailing party is " 'the rule rather than exception' under the Copyright Act, and 'should be awarded routinely.' "[85] Therefore, contrary to the plaintiffs' argument, the "efforts expended on unsuccessful related non-copyright claims may be compensable."[86]

e.   Determining the Amount of the Fee

[Add the following text at the end of the section.]

As to the reasonableness of the fee award sought by the prevailing party, it has been held that the amount of fees expended by the non-prevailing party can be relevant. In *Hyperquest, Inc. v. N'Site Solutions, Inc.*[87] the court awarded attorney's fees to the prevailing defendants.

---

[81]*Id.*

[82]No. 05-933, 2008 U.S. Dist. LEXIS 48357 (D. Or. June 24, 2008).

[83]217 F.3d 1060, 55 USPQ2d 1256 (9th Cir. 2000).

[84]*Id.* at 1070.

[85]*Andersen*, 2008 U.S. Dist. LEXIS 48357, at *5 (quoting Virgin Records Am., Inc. v. Thompson, 512 F.3d 724, 726, 85 USPQ2d 1379 (5th Cir. 2008)).

[86]*Id.* at *6.

[87]No. 08-483, 2008 U.S. Dist. LEXIS 88752 (N.D. Ill. Nov. 3, 2008).

The plaintiff corporation alleged copyright infringement against the defendant companies; the defendants prevailed on the plaintiff's lack of standing to sue. The defendants then moved for attorney's fees. The court refused to award the amount of fees requested by the defendants, holding that "[t]his Court's review of [defendant] Unitrin's materials has left it with the strong and abiding sense . . . that the amount that has been requested reflects major overkill in terms of the time and resources devoted to the task."[88] The court stated that:

> a few basic considerations point the way toward a reasonable determination:
>
> 1. . . . From the very nature of the dispute, defendants had to expend more time and effort in defending against HQ's claim than HQ had to spend to pursue it.
>
> 2. With more than one defendant involved, an efficient handling of the defense (the hallmark of reasonableness) ought not to involve a doubling of the efforts of plaintiff's counsel, any more than it should simply involve one-to-one matching efforts.
>
> 3. There is a great deal of force in the individual challenges posed to the amount of time expended by defendants on various phases of the litigation . . . .
>
> For those and other reasons, what remains for this Court is an abiding conviction that the amount requested is not only excessive but grossly excessive as a proposed measure for fee-shifting under Section 505.

The court devised its own award of $131,000.

f.   Federal Rules of Civil Procedure—Rule 68

[Add the following text at the end of the section.]

In *Bryant v. Media Right Productions, Inc.*,[89] the Second Circuit affirmed the district court's denial of attorney's fees to the plaintiffs, who had prevailed on their copyright infringement claim but were entitled to only minimal statutory damages. The defendants, seeking reasonable resolution of the matter without a trial, had "made an Offer of Judgment in the amount of $3000, which Appellants rejected, in favor of continuing to demand over $1 million in damages, notwithstanding the evidence that Appellees had received less than $600 in revenues from infringing sales."[90]

Even when the plaintiff accepts an offer of judgment, the issue of costs can be complicated if the parties are not clear as to the exact nature of the offer. In *Harrell v. Van Der Plas*,[91] the defendants in a copyright action served the plaintiff with a written offer of judgment pursuant to Federal Rules of Civil Procedure Rule 68, in the amount of $7,500. The offer of judgment was silent as to the issue of costs, however. The plaintiff served the defendants with written acceptance of the offer of

---

[88] *Id.* at **2–3.

[89] 603 F.3d 135 (2d Cir. 2010).

[90] *Id.* at 144.

[91] No. 08-8252, 2009 U.S. Dist. LEXIS 52572 (S.D.N.Y. June 19, 2009).

judgment. The acceptance requested the clerk of the court to enter judgment against the defendants for $7,500 "*with costs*, including reasonable attorneys' fees, to be set by the Court upon application of plaintiff."[92] The defendants served the plaintiff with an amended offer to clarify the original offer to recite that the defendants' offer of judgment included all costs. Because the original offer of judgment for $7,500 was silent as to costs and was accepted as such by the plaintiff, the court enforced the first offer, and allowed the plaintiff to make a separate application for costs, including attorney's fees. The court, however, did not award such costs in its order, noting first that the defendants contended that this case could be a simple breach of contract case, in which case no attorney's fees could be awarded; and second, that reasonable attorney's fees are discretionary under the Copyright Act, and it was not clear whether such a discretionary award would be appropriate. The court, therefore, directed the plaintiff "to file a properly supported application setting forth the basis for an award and documenting the fees sought" by the deadline set by the court.[93]

II. Injunction/Impoundment

A. Standard for Imposing an Injunction

[Add the following text at the end of the section.]

On April 30, 2010, the Second Circuit issued an important decision in *Salinger v. Colting*,[94] which will very likely alter the landscape for all copyright plaintiffs seeking injunctive relief. Although a lengthy discussion of *Salinger* is not possible here (see discussion of the district court decision *supra* in Chapter 6), the decision makes a significant break with past practice by eliminating the presumption of irreparable harm which had long been applied in copyright-infringement cases. Instead, following the Supreme Court patent ruling in *eBay, Inc. v. MercExchange*,[95] the court held that it was not sufficient for a copyright plaintiff merely to demonstrate a likelihood of success on the merits in order to establish irreparable harm, either for a preliminary or a permanent injunction. Not faulting the district court, but instead recognizing an inconsistency between circuit precedent and the recent Supreme Court ruling, the Second Circuit articulated its holding as follows: "We hold that, although the District Court applied our Circuit's longstanding standard for preliminary injunctions in copyright cases, our Circuit's standard is inconsistent with the 'test historically employed by courts of equity' and has, therefore, been abrogated by *eBay, Inc. v. MercExchange, LLC*."[96]

---

[92] *Id.* at *2 (internal quotations omitted) (emphasis added).

[93] *Id.* at *9.

[94] 607 F.3d 68 (2d Cir. 2010).

[95] 547 U.S. 388 (2006).

[96] *Salinger*, 607 F.3d at 74–75.

1.   Likelihood of Irreparable Harm to Plaintiff

[Add the following text at the end of the section.]

As the Second Circuit announced in *Salinger v. Colting*,[97] the venerable presumption of irreparable harm no longer applies in copyright injunctions simply upon a showing of likely success on the merits. In a case involving an alleged parody of J.D. Salinger's *The Catcher In the Rye*, the Second Circuit reversed that long-standing practice and instead applied the four-factor test from the Supreme Court's 2006 patent decision, *eBay, Inc. v. MercExchange, LLC*.[98] The court stated that the *eBay* test would apply "with equal force to preliminary injunctions issued on the basis of alleged copyright infringement."[99] In applying *eBay* to the copyright context, the court was guided by Justice Thomas' reliance, in his *eBay* majority opinion, on Supreme Court copyright cases, including *New York Times Co. v. Tasini* and *Campbell v. Acuff-Rose Music*, for the conclusion that injunctions should not automatically issue upon proof of likelihood of success in patent cases. In *eBay*, Justice Thomas stated: "[A]s in our decision today, this Court has consistently rejected invitations to replace traditional equitable considerations with a rule that an injunction automatically follows a determination that a copyright has been infringed."[100] Accordingly, the Second Circuit in *Salinger* observed that "it seems clear that the Supreme Court did not view patent and copyright injunctions as different in kind, or as requiring different standards."[101] Under the *eBay* analysis, the plaintiff must make an independent showing on each of four traditional equitable factors: "(1) that it has suffered an irreparable injury; (2) that remedies available at law, such as monetary damages, are inadequate to compensate for that injury; (3) that, considering the balance of hardships between the plaintiff and defendant, a remedy in equity is warranted; and (4) that the public interest would not be disserved by a permanent injunction."[102] The Second Circuit also cited the post-*eBay* Supreme Court opinion in *Winter v. Natural Resources Defense Counsel*[103] for the proposition that a district court, in the exercise of its discretion, must conduct an inquiry into and make specific findings with respect to each of the four *eBay* factors, regardless of the nature of the underlying cause of action. Thus the Second Circuit reversed and remanded the grant of an injunction by the district court, which had presumed irreparable harm without making any actual findings on that issue.

Even after *eBay*, however, courts have still granted copyright injunctions with regularity. For example, in *Momento, Inc. v. Seccion Amarilla USA*,[104] the plaintiff sought to enjoin the defendant from copying

---

[97]607 F.3d 68 (2d Cir. 2010).

[98]547 U.S. 388 (2006).

[99]*Salinger*, 607 F.3d at 70.

[100]*eBay*, 547 U.S. at 392–93.

[101]*Salinger*, 607 F.3d at 78.

[102]*Id.* at 77 (quoting *eBay*, 547 U.S. at 391).

[103]555 U.S. 7 (2008).

[104]No. 09-1223, 2009 U.S. Dist. LEXIS 62664 (N.D. Cal. July 6, 2009).

the plaintiff's Spanish Yellow Pages advertisements for use in its own Spanish-language directories. The court found that the plaintiff established a likelihood of success on the merits. The court agreed with the defendant that in view of the Supreme Court's decision in *eBay*, irreparable harm should not be automatically presumed. However, the court, applying the traditional four-factor test, found that the plaintiff established the possibility of irreparable harm in the absence of an injunction. The court stated that it was reasonable for the court to consider protecting the competitive position of the plaintiff, a family-owned publisher of Spanish Yellow Pages in Northern California, where the plaintiff demonstrated that the defendant, the largest publisher of Spanish Yellow Pages in the world, "has built [its] business around plaintiff's works."[105] Accordingly, the court granted the plaintiff relief, ordering the defendant to retrieve directories stored in distribution points, but not directories already picked up by consumers, and enjoined the distribution of directories in a neighboring area. The court so ordered notwithstanding its recognition that the injunction created hardship on the defendant, since the defendant proceeded with production of infringing materials despite the plaintiff's cease-and-desist letter. The court enjoined the defendant from copying any of the plaintiff's copyrighted works, including derivative works. It also ordered that the defendant "not destroy or conceal or in any way dispose of any reproduction, copy, facsimile, excerpt, scanned version, or derivative of any copyrighted work of Momento, including those stored on computers or computer files."[106]

a. Delay

[Add the following text at the end of the section.]

In *Institute for Motivational Living, Inc. v. Sylvan Learning Center*,[107] a delay of three months was not fatal to the plaintiff's application for a preliminary injunction and temporary restraining order. The plaintiff was a training and publishing company, asserting claims against a tutoring service provider for copyright infringement of the plaintiff's customized testing materials for students and training materials for instructors ("Assessments"). The parties entered into a licensing agreement for the Assessments, whereby the defendant agreed to pay royalties for the use of the plaintiff's copyrighted works. The defendant terminated the license in January 2007 but did not instruct its franchisees to discontinue using the Assessments. The court found that the plaintiff established a prima facie case of copyright infringement—the defendant's franchisees could have accessed, printed and distributed the Assessments without accounting after the termination of license—giving rise to a presumption of irreparable injury. The court rejected the defendant's argument that the plaintiff's delay in seeking injunctive relief negated the harm element because the plaintiff was entitled to a reasonable time—here,

---

[105]*Id.* at *10.

[106]*Id.* at *14.

[107]No. 06-828, 2008 U.S. Dist. LEXIS 9631 (W.D. Pa. Feb. 7, 2008).

three months—to investigate the scope of alleged infringement. As with all cases applying a presumption of irreparable injury in copyright infringement, this ruling must be questioned in light of the Second Circuit's 2010 decision in *Salinger.*

D. Scope of Injunctions

3. *Third-Party Infringers*

[Add the following text at the end of the section.]

Even when the court grants a preliminary injunction, however, a recall of infringing products is not automatic. For example, in *City Merchandise, Inc. v. Broadway Gifts, Inc.*,[108] the Southern District of New York granted the plaintiff's motion for a preliminary injunction, but declined to issue a recall. The defendants' "Broadway Souvenir Line" allegedly infringed the plaintiff's "NYC Skyline Collection." For purposes of the plaintiff's motion, the defendants conceded that the plaintiff owned valid copyrights and that the defendants had access to the plaintiff's works. Since the works at issue contained both protectable and unprotectable elements, the court applied the "more discerning ordinary observer" test to determine whether there was substantial similarity, comparing the "total concept and feel" of the protected work and the allegedly infringing work.[109] Both works possessed the same "non-geometrical whimsical style of drawing, similar scales, similar methods of arrangement, and similar color schemes."[110] The court found that because the parties' works shared substantially similar look, feel, and overall aesthetic appeal, there was a significant likelihood that a jury would find the plaintiff's copyrighted works and the defendants' allegedly infringing works to be "substantially similar" under the "more discerning ordinary observer" test, and therefore granted the preliminary injunction. However, after considering the "likely burden and expense of a recall" to the defendants, and balancing that burden against the "benefit that would accrue" to the plaintiff, the court held that the plaintiff had failed to demonstrate the need for recall.[111]

III. SANCTIONS

B. Discovery and Evidence

[Add the following text at the end of the section.]

In copyright matters, as in all federal litigation, a litigant has a duty to preserve evidence after a cease-and-desist letter is received, or at least once a discovery request is served, and failure to do so can readily result

---

[108]No. 08-9075, 2009 U.S. Dist. LEXIS 5629 (S.D.N.Y. Jan. 27, 2009).

[109]*Id.* at *5, *6.

[110]*Id.* at *6.

[111]*Id.* at **7–8.

in sanctions. In *Arista Records LLC v. Usenet.com, Inc.,*[112] the Southern District of New York granted the plaintiff record companies' motion for sanctions based upon the defendants' spoliation of evidence, allowing the adverse inference that the destroyed evidence would have been unfavorable to the defendants. The plaintiffs alleged that the defendants provided customers with access to online bulletin boards that allowed users to upload and download the plaintiffs' sound recordings. The plaintiffs alleged that the defendants stored recordings on their servers and made them available to users. The plaintiffs served discovery requests and subsequently moved for sanctions based on alleged spoliation of usage data evidence (records reflecting requests by the defendants' subscribers to download/upload sound recordings), digital music files (digital copies of copyrighted sound recordings), and promotional materials previously available on the defendants' website.

In the Second Circuit, a party bringing a spoliation motion must show that: (1) the adversary had control of the evidence and a duty to preserve it; (2) the adversary had a "culpable state of mind" when the evidence was lost or destroyed; and (3) the lost or destroyed evidence was "relevant" to the moving party's claims.[113] The court held that, in a copyright matter, a cease-and-desist letter triggers a duty to preserve evidence even prior to the filing of a litigation. At the very latest, the duty to retain evidence was effective once the data was the subject of discovery requests. The court rejected the defendants' contention that they had no obligation to preserve electronic data that was transient in nature, finding that a duty to preserve relevant data, even if transient, is imposed once that data is specifically requested. The court also found that the defendants took affirmative steps to disable preservation of evidence, and therefore acted with a "culpable state of mind." The destroyed evidence was relevant to the "volume and proportion of infringement," and therefore relevant to the plaintiffs' claims.[114]

The plaintiffs asked that the court deem relevant facts to be established, but the court instead imposed the lesser sanction of allowing the adverse inference that the spoliated evidence would have been unfavorable to the defendants.

2. *False Evidence*

[Add the following text at the end of the section.]

In *Arista Records, LLC v. Usenet.com, Inc.,*[115] the court imposed harsh sanctions for spoliation of computer files and for other misconduct in an on-line music infringement case, but declined to order the "ultimate sanction" of a default judgment against the defendants. The plaintiff produced evidence which showed that the defendants "wiped" seven

---

[112]608 F. Supp. 2d 409 (S.D.N.Y. 2009).

[113]*Id.* at 430.

[114]*Id.* at 441.

[115]633 F. Supp. 2d 124 (S.D.N.Y. 2009).

computer hard drives, removed computers used by other employees, failed to produce extensive email files, engineered witness unavailability for depositions ("by causing them to travel to Europe on an expense-paid vacation" and by attempting "to persuade the employees to remain out of the jurisdiction"[116]), and "knowingly served false responses to interrogatories."[117] The court determined that the "appropriate sanction" was not an entry of default but was the preclusion of the defendants' assertion of "their affirmative defense of protection under the DMCA's safe harbor provision," which was a central element of their defense.[118]

IV. PUNITIVE DAMAGES

[Add the following text at the end of the section.]

In *Football Association Premier League Ltd. v. YouTube, Inc.*,[119] the court rejected the plaintiffs' demand for punitive damages in a putative class action against YouTube, dismissing it under Federal Rules of Civil Procedure Rule 12(c), judgment on the pleadings. Judge Stanton, who had allowed a claim for punitive damages to go forward in one earlier case before rejecting it in another, stated flatly that "[t]here is no circumstance in which punitive damages are available under the Copyright Act of 1976."[120] The court rejected the plaintiffs' argument that treaty obligations require such damages to be available under the Copyright Act for foreign works, but also noted that "any ruling on whether plaintiffs may seek punitive damages for pre-1972 sound recordings under state law, or infringements for whicn [*sic*] foreign law determines the remedies, is deferred."[121]

---

[116] *Id.* at 137.

[117] *Id.*

[118] *Id.* at 142.

[119] 633 F. Supp. 2d 159 (S.D.N.Y. 2009).

[120] *Id.* at 167.

[121] *Id.* at 168.

9

Preemption

II. THE SUBJECT MATTER REQUIREMENT OF SECTION 301(A)

A. In General

[Insert the following text at the end of the section]

In *Robinson v. HSBC Bank USA*,[1] the district court denied a motion to dismiss on preemption grounds under a general-scope analysis. The defendant placed a mortgage advertisement, which included multiple photographs of the plaintiffs' home, in a local newspaper. The plaintiffs alleged that the home was free and clear of any mortgage, that they had had no contact with the defendant, and that they did not give the defendant permission to use the pictures in the advertisement. The plaintiffs alleged further that the implication of the advertisement was

---

[1] 732 F. Supp. 2d 976 (N.D. Cal. 2010).

that the plaintiffs' home was subject to a mortgage and/or that the plaintiffs were looking to sell the property. The plaintiffs alleged violation of their right of publicity, trade libel, unjust enrichment, false and misleading advertisement, and violations of the California Consumers Legal Remedies Act and Unfair Competition Law. The defendant filed a Section 12(b)(6) motion to dismiss, alleging that plaintiffs' state-law claims were preempted. The court held under the subject matter prong that since photographs of buildings taken from a public place were exempted from the scope of the Architectural Works Copyright Protection Act, the plaintiffs could not assert a copyright infringement claim with respect to photographs of their property taken from a public place. Accordingly, the interests they sought to protect did not fall within the subject matter of the Copyright Act.

E.   Merger Doctrine

[Add the following text at the end of the section.]

State claims will not be held preempted where they pertain solely to unfixed works, because such works are not within the general subject matter of copyright. For example, in *220 Laboratories, Inc. v. Babaii*,[2] the Central District of California, after removal from state court, granted the plaintiff's motion to remand back to state court where the plaintiff sued nondiverse defendants on 14 state-law causes of action. The plaintiff had entered into an oral contract with the defendants to develop and manufacture a line of hair care products. The plaintiff provided the defendants with the plaintiff's work, namely, a marketing idea "to incorporate volcanic ash from an island in the Vanuatu Island chain in the South Pacific" into its beauty products. The plaintiff did not allege that the work was fixed in a tangible medium of expression. In the complaint, the plaintiff alleged that the plaintiff's work was "provided" to the defendants. The defendants had removed the case to federal district court, claiming that the plaintiff's causes of action were preempted by the Copyright Act. However, the court rejected the defendants' argument that the plaintiff's use of the word "provided" was an admission of fixation because intangibles can be "provided," just as tangibles can. Similarly, although the complaint contained a cause of action for conversion, and conversion generally applies to tangible property, the courts have found conversion of intangible property under appropriate circumstances. Accordingly, the plaintiff's claim of conversion was also not an admission of fixation. The court further found that the work was not within the subject matter of copyright because it was not fixed in a tangible medium of expression. Therefore, the causes of action were not preempted.

---

[2]No. 08-6125, 2008 U.S. Dist. LEXIS 102443 (C.D. Cal. Dec. 8, 2008).

III. EQUIVALENT STATE RIGHTS

A. Contract Claims

1. *Extra Elements*

b. *Software Contracts*

[Add the following text at the end of the section]

In *Banxcorp v. Costco Wholesale Corp.*,[3] the district court granted in part and denied in part a motion to dismiss the plaintiff's various state-law claims as preempted. The plaintiff company published database compilations and market indices for use by the finance industry, described as systematic compilations to be used as industry benchmarks. The plaintiff and the defendant Costco entered into a license agreement allowing Costco to use the indices. The plaintiff, upon learning Costco had permitted the co-defendant Capital One to access the indices, filed various state-law claims, namely hot news misappropriation, breach of contract, unfair competition, and unjust enrichment. The defendants filed a motion to dismiss the claims as preempted. Under the hot news misappropriation claim, one of the key additional elements needed to survive preemption is the "time-sensitive value of information." The court held that the plaintiff legitimately showed that the defendant reproduced the plaintiff's indices on a daily basis; thus, the court could infer that some information reproduced was "hot," negating preemption. As to the breach of contract claim, a key additional element to survive preemption was the promise not to distribute under the license agreement. The court denied the defendants' motion to dismiss the breach of contract claim, holding that, as a general matter, breach of contract actions are not preempted by the Copyright Act, in part because the parties enter into license agreements to avoid the cost of litigating copyright validity. The court granted the defendants' motion to dismiss the unfair competition claim as preempted, holding that no fiduciary relationship existed, which is the key additional element of many unfair competition claims. Because it was simply a business relationship whereby one party acted in bad faith (but without any additional fiduciary duty), the unfair competition claim was preempted by the Copyright Act. Finally, the court granted the defendants' motion to dismiss the unjust enrichment claim, holding that unjust enrichment claims are by nature preempted because, under the Copyright Act, the plaintiff seeks to protect its works from illegal distribution and publication, and unjust enrichment claims do not contain any additional elements that would not otherwise be subsumed under a copyright infringement claim.

d. *Contract Termination*

[Add the following text at the end of the section.]

---

[3]723 F. Supp. 2d 596 (S.D.N.Y. 2010).

In *Latin American Music Co. v. ASCAP*,[4] the First Circuit affirmed a jury instruction and finding on the issue of which law, state or federal, governed the termination of an exclusive license. The defendant's predecessor-in-interest granted the plaintiffs' predecessor-in-interest an exclusive license in the popular folk song "Caballo Viejo." The contract granting the exclusive license was silent as to termination. At trial, the defendant presented videotaped deposition evidence that its president orally terminated the exclusive license in a conversation with the plaintiffs' CEO. The district court instructed the jury that state law applied to termination of the contract. On appeal the plaintiffs urged that the Copyright Act, requiring transfers of copyright ownership to be in writing and signed by the transferor, preempted state law, which, the defendants contended, did not require written termination but only "reasonable notice." The court of appeals found no support for the argument that the Section 204(a) writing requirement for transfers of copyright ownership should be extended to the termination of exclusive licenses. The court reasoned that to extend the law as proposed by appellants "would lead to untenable results." For example, "[a] transferee of a copyright interest could effectively veto a lawful termination of that interest by refusing to reconvey that interest to the terminating party" by refusing to sign an instrument of conveyance.[5] Accordingly, the court affirmed the jury instruction and the finding that the Copyright Act does not preempt state law regarding termination of contracts granting exclusive licenses.

B. Right of Publicity Claims—Equivalent or Not?

1. *Derivative Works*

[Add the following text at the end of the section]
In *Jules Jordan Video, Inc. v. 144942 Canada Inc.*,[6] the plaintiff, Gasper, an adult movie star who performs under the pseudonym "Jules Jordan," was the president/sole shareholder of plaintiff, Jules Jordan Video (JJV) and the creator of videos in which he appears. The plaintiffs sued the defendants (numerous video companies), alleging that the defendants copied and sold 13 copyrighted adult DVDs owned by JJV or Gasper that featured Gasper's performances. The district court rejected the defendants' claim that Gasper's right of publicity claim under California Civil Code §3344 was preempted by the Copyright Act. The defendants appealed the decision, and the Ninth Circuit reviewed de novo. The Ninth Circuit reversed the district court's decision and vacated Gasper's judgment against the defendants for violation of Gasper's right of privacy under California law. In so finding, the Ninth Circuit noted that "[w]hether a claim is preempted under Section 301 does not turn on what rights the alleged infringer possesses, but on whether the rights

---

[4]593 F.3d 95 (1st Cir. 2010).

[5]*Id.* at 100–01.

[6]617 F.3d 1146 (9th Cir. 2010).

asserted by the plaintiff are equivalent to any of the exclusive rights within the general scope of the copyright. The question is whether the rights are works of authorship fixed in a tangible medium of expression and come within the subject matter of the Copyright Act. If a the plaintiff asserts a claim that is the equivalent of a claim for infringement of a copyrightable work, that claim is preempted, regardless of what legal rights the defendant might have acquired." In the instant case, the Ninth Circuit concluded that Gasper's right of publicity claim fell within the subject matter of the Copyright Act because the "essence" of Gasper's claim was that the defendants reproduced and distributed the DVDs without authorization.

2. Voice Imitations

[Add the following text at the end of the section]

In *Aronson v. Dog Eat Dog Films, Inc.*,[7] the Western District of Washington granted a motion to dismiss state-law right-of-publicity claims where the defendant used a video and song by the plaintiff in the defendant's documentary film *Sicko*. The plaintiff argued against preemption because the subject matter of the state-law claims was a depiction of likeness and voice, which are not "works of authorship" within the meaning of the Copyright Act. The court held that the plaintiff's state-law claims arose solely from the use of the home video in the documentary; and as such, the plaintiff's state-law claims were within the subject matter of copyright. As to the second element, the rights asserted under state law were held to be equivalent to rights protected under the Copyright Act. The court held that the essence of the plaintiff's state-law claims was the defendant's unauthorized distribution of the plaintiff's home video, which had no extra elements vis-à-vis the Copyright Act.

C. Unjust Enrichment

1. Derivative Works and Adaptations

The district court in *Bachner + Co. v. White Rose Food, Inc.*,[8] granted the defendant's motion to dismiss an unjust enrichment count, finding it preempted by the Copyright Act. The plaintiff, a well-known and respected brand strategist, was in the process of negotiating with the defendant, a large independent food wholesaler and distributor, over a contract to redesign the defendant's logos and packaging. The plaintiff provided the defendant with initial logos and labeling designs for some of the defendant's products, which the defendant, after entering a confidentiality agreement with the plaintiff, applied to its products for evaluation purposes. The defendant, however, selected a different company to redesign its product, which essentially duplicated proprietary

---

[7]738 F. Supp. 2d 1104 (W.D. Wash. 2010).

[8]No. 09-2640, 2010 U.S. Dist. LEXIS 82096 (D.N.J. Aug. 11, 2010).

designs provided by the plaintiff. The plaintiff filed a complaint alleging grounds including copyright infringement and unjust enrichment. The defendant moved to dismiss, arguing in part that the unjust enrichment claim was preempted by the Copyright Act. The court found that the plaintiff's alleged proprietary work, i.e., logos and labeling designs, fell within the type of work protected by copyright law, and that the rights asserted were equivalent to the bundle of rights already protected by copyright law, and thus the unjust enrichment claim was preempted. The court also noted that the plaintiff's initial complaint itself asserted copyright infringement claims, which it voluntarily dismissed. Accordingly, the court dismissed the unjust enrichment claim.

E. Misrepresentation/Fraud

[Add the following text at the end of the section.]

In *Shuptrine v. McDougal Littell*,[9] the court in the Eastern District of Tennessee held that the plaintiff's fraud claim was not preempted, in a case alleging the unlicensed use of a painting in a textbook. The painter licensed the use of the work for a print run of 40,000, but the publisher eventually printed over 1.2 million copies. The painter's widow brought an infringement claim and also alleged fraud under Tennessee common law, asserting that the publisher intentionally understated the size of the print run to induce the painter to grant a lower royalty rate. The defendant publisher asserted that the fraud claim was preempted under Section 301, but the court refused to dismiss the claim under Rule 12(c) of the Federal Rules of Civil Procedure. Noting that "there is no uniform rule as to whether fraud claims are preempted by the Copyright Act,"[10] the court surveyed Sixth Circuit law and concluded that the "[d]efendant entered into a relationship with Shuptrine allegedly under false pretenses designed to lower the cost of obtaining Shuptrine's paintings. Plaintiff's fraud allegation is a qualitatively different offense than merely exceeding the licensing agreement."[11] The court was not persuaded by the contrary result in a parallel New York action on the same facts, *Semerdjian v. McDougal Littell*,[12] rejecting the conclusion of that court that a fraud claim was preempted because the "damage" element of fraud could exist only if there were copyright infringement. The Tennessee court held that "although damages are an essential element of both claims, the test is not whether an element overlaps but whether there is an extra element that changes the nature of the action so it is qualitatively different."[13] Damages are not actually an element of a copyright-infringement claim, but the court's error in saying so is immaterial; the court's position on

---

[9]535 F. Supp. 2d 892 (E.D. Tenn. 2008).

[10]*Id.* at 895.

[11]*Id.* at 897.

[12]No. 07 Civ. 7496, 2008 U.S. Dist. LEXIS 662 (S.D.N.Y. Jan. 2, 2008).

[13]*Shuptrine*, 535 F. Supp. 2d at 897.

preemption would, if anything, be even more compelling if the court had properly identified the elements of a copyright-infringement action.

In another fraud claim, *Business Audio Plus, L.L.C. v. Commerce Bank, NA*,[14] the plaintiff asserted causes of action consisting of federal copyright infringement claims and state-law claims for breach of implied covenant of good faith and fair dealing, unjust enrichment and fraud by concealment. The defendant moved to dismiss the state-law claims as preempted. The court found that the state-law claims were not equivalent to a copyright claim, because the alleged restriction on the defendant's use of the material "creates a right not existing under copyright law," and "constitutes an extra element that makes these causes of action qualitatively different from one for copyright." As such, the court found that breach of an implied covenant of good faith and fair dealing, unjust enrichment and fraud by concealment claims were not statutorily preempted by the Copyright Act.

F. Misappropriation

[Add the following text at the end of the section.]

In *Scranton Times, L.P. v. Wilkes-Barre Publishing Co.*,[15] plaintiffs Scranton Times and Times Partner LLC sued defendant Wilkes-Barre Publishing Company for publishing obituaries that the plaintiffs alleged were copied from their newspapers or websites, thus violating the plaintiffs' copyrights, or, in the alternative, constituting misappropriation of hot news. The defendant asserted various affirmative defenses including preemption of the plaintiffs' hot-news misappropriation claim. The court found the plaintiffs' misappropriation claim was preempted under the *National Basketball Ass'n v. Motorola*[16] standard. However, the plaintiffs' other state claims, including conversion and breach of contract, were not preempted.

In *Agora Financial, LLC v. Samler*,[17] however, the court declined to follow *NBA v. Motorola* and reached a different result as the magistrate judge recommended denial of the plaintiffs' motion for default judgment after the defendant failed to respond to the plaintiffs' claim of "hot news" misappropriation based on the defendant's posting of the plaintiffs' writers' investment recommendations on his website, as the judge determined that the plaintiffs' materials were nonfactual, and therefore the plaintiffs' claims were preempted by the Copyright Act. The plaintiffs, publishers of financial investment newsletters, brought unfair competition claims grounded in *International News Service v. Associated Press* (*INS v. AP*)[18] and Section 43(a) of the Lanham Act. After review

---

[14]No. 10-2064, 2011 U.S. Dist. LEXIS 7299 (E.D. Mo. Jan. 26, 2011).

[15]92 USPQ2d 1269 (M.D. Pa. 2009).

[16]105 F.3d 841, 41 USPQ2d 1585 (2d Cir. 1997).

[17]725 F. Supp. 2d 491 (D. Md. 2010).

[18]248 U.S. 215 (1918).

and discussion of *INS v. AP, Feist, National Basketball Ass'n v. Motorola* (*NBA v. Motorola*),[19] and the legislative history related to Section 301 of the Copyright Act, the magistrate judge noted that the Fourth Circuit has never applied or discussed the *NBA v. Motorola* five-element test for when "hot news" claims survive preemption by the Copyright Act; and in 2003, a Maryland district court declined to follow *NBA v. Motorola.* The magistrate judge concluded that the plaintiffs' claims would be preempted even under the logic of *NBA v. Motorola* because the plaintiffs failed to prove that the materials at issue constituted factual information rather than original works of authorship. The court summed up when "hot news" claims might survive preemption: "[t]he distinction ... between the rights protected under a copyright infringement claim and a 'hot news' misappropriation claim is that copyright law protects a copyright holder's exclusive right to reproduce, distribute, perform, or display 'original' material while the 'hot news' misappropriation theory protects an individual's exclusive right to profit or otherwise benefit from the labor expended in discovering, gathering, and generating certain 'non-original' material, such as factual information."

G. Conversion

[Add the following text at the end of the section.]

A conversion claim was categorically held preempted in *Architects Collective v. Gardner Tanenbaum Group, L.L.C.*,[20] where the court granted defendant's motion to dismiss. The plaintiff held copyright in drawings and related written materials relating to the design and development of a multifamily housing project. The plaintiff brought copyright infringement and conversion claims against the defendant for providing, without the plaintiff's authorization, copies of copyrighted materials, and for modifying copyrighted materials for the preparation of other plans. The plaintiff argued that the conversion claim was not preempted because it sought the return of tangible property, namely copyrighted material. The court held the first element was satisfied, since the drawings and written materials were registered and protected under the Copyright Act. As to the second element, the court held that, although the plaintiff sought the return of copies of copyrighted matter allegedly made by the defendant, the plaintiff also sought damages resulting from the defendant's unauthorized use and copying of the material. The court stated that where a conversion claim is based on the defendant's unauthorized possession of copyrighted works and their subsequent copying and use, the claim is equivalent to a Copyright Act claim, and is preempted. Where a conversion claim seeks recovery of damages flowing from reproduction and distribution of copyrighted work, the plaintiff's rights are also equivalent to the Copyright Act and are preempted.

---

[19]105 F.3d 841 (2d Cir. 1997).

[20]No. 08-1354, 2010 U.S. Dist. LEXIS 66942 (W.D. Okla. July 6, 2010).

I.   Misappropriation of Trade Secrets/Breach of Confidential Relationship

[Add the following text at the end of the section.]

The district court in *Warren Sign Co. v. Piros Signs, Inc.,* [21] granted the defendants' motions to dismiss state-law claims for misappropriation of trade secrets and civil conspiracy as preempted by the Copyright Act. The plaintiff sign designing and fabricating company had submitted to the defendant, its client, a design for a sign, along with a proposal to construct and install the sign. The client rejected the proposal, but immediately submitted an application for a sign permit that attached a drawing allegedly identical to the plaintiff's, but for the date on the drawing having been altered and the plaintiff's logo removed. The permit was granted; the co-defendant, a competitor sign company, fabricated and installed the sign; and the plaintiff commenced the action, pleading state-law claims and a claim under the Copyright Act. With respect to the claim of misappropriation of trade secrets, where the alleged misappropriation was based solely upon copying, the court found that there is no qualitative difference between such a claim and a claim under the Act.

The trade secret claim in *White House/Black Market, Inc. v. Cache Inc.*[22] fared better, because it included allegations beyond mere copying. The plaintiff and the defendant were direct competitors in the business of selling fashionable clothing and accessory items to women 25 years and older with moderate-to-high income. Two former employees of the plaintiff, who were intimately involved in the development of the plaintiff's clothing lines, became employed by the defendant. Soon thereafter, the defendant issued a clothing line that the plaintiff alleged was nearly identical to the plaintiff's line. The plaintiff brought multiple claims against the defendant in state court, including misappropriation of trade secrets. The plaintiff did not allege copyright infringement. The defendant removed the action to federal court. The plaintiff moved by order to show cause to remand the action back to state court. The defendant contended that the plaintiff's claim for misappropriation of trade secrets was preempted by the Copyright Act because it was based in part on the defendant's alleged misappropriation of clothing and fabric designs. The plaintiff disagreed, arguing that the claim for misappropriation of trade secrets requires proof of the extra element of breach of fiduciary duty that makes a misappropriation claim qualitatively different from a copyright infringement claim. The plaintiff argued further that its complaint alleged facts in support of this element, i.e., that the plaintiff's former employees, who were current employees of the defendant, disclosed the plaintiff's confidential information to the defendant in violation of a written confidentiality agreement signed while employed by the plaintiff. The district court agreed with the plaintiff, and granted the motion to remand.

---

[21] 2010 WL 3034637 (E.D. Md. 2010).

[22] No. 10-5266, 2010 U.S. Dist. LEXIS 75123 (S.D.N.Y. July 26, 2010).

S. Artist's Rights

[Add the following text to the end of the section.]

In *Alvarez-Rivon v. Cengage Learning, Inc.*,[23] the district court denied the defendant's motion to dismiss moral rights claims under the law of Puerto Rico against the defendant, who without permission reproduced several of the plaintiff's cartoon characters in a textbook. The Puerto Rico moral rights claims were not preempted by the Copyright Act because they sought to protect the artist's reputation and the physical integrity of the work.

[Add the following new sections.]

V. Intentional Infliction of Emotional Distress [New Topic]

In *Giddings v. Vision House Production, Inc.*,[24] the District of Arizona found that a claim for intentional infliction of emotional distress was preempted where the claim arose from a dispute over a contract giving the defendants limited permission to reproduce and distribute the plaintiff's copyrighted artwork. The plaintiff claimed that the defendants reproduced and distributed the art in violation of the contract. The defendants contended that the plaintiff's common-law claims, including the emotional-distress claim, were preempted. The court agreed, and granted the defendants' motion for judgment on the pleadings. With regard to the basic breach-of-contract claim, the court explained that the claim was preempted because the plaintiff's contract with the defendants promised only to protect the rights to reproduce and distribute the plaintiff's copyrighted artwork, which were "exactly the same rights that are covered by federal copyright law."[25] The court explained that the intentional infliction of emotional distress claim was preempted because the allegedly "extreme and outrageous" behavior that the plaintiff relied upon to establish the claim was simply the defendants' unlawful reproduction, sales, distribution, and forgery of the plaintiff's art, which "also serves as the core of Plaintiff's copyright infringement claim."[26] The plaintiff's fraud claim was preempted because it was "rooted in Defendants' alleged misrepresentation of the artist's signature and of limited-edition prints" and "[t]hese two allegations are derived from Defendants' unauthorized reproduction and distribution of Plaintiff's artwork."[27]

W. Record Piracy Statutes [New Topic]

With state record piracy statutes, which continue to apply in many cases despite the 1972 recognition of sound recordings as a form of

---

[23] No. 09-1605, 2010 U.S. Dist. LEXIS 71798 (D.P.R. July 16, 2010).

[24] No. 05-2963, 2007 U.S. Dist. LEXIS 58438 (D. Ariz. Aug. 3, 2007).

[25] *Id.* at *5.

[26] *Id.* at *7.

[27] *Id.* at *8.

federally protected copyrightable authorship, the precise text of the statute is important to determine whether the state claim involves a true "extra element." In an Illinois case, *People v. Williams*,[28] one section of the state criminal code involving sound recording piracy was deemed preempted while the adjacent statutory section was not. The case was a criminal prosecution: It was after midnight on March 10, 2004, when Valerie Herrera, working at Bubble Land Laundromat in Chicago, noticed Paul Williams. Mr. Williams, carrying his usual black suitcase, was also working. Walking around inside and outside of Bubble Land, Mr. Williams was trying to make sales—$5 per CD, $10 per DVD, presumably cash-and-carry. Ms. Herrera, showing grace under pressure, hit her laundromat's panic button, summoning officers with due haste. When Officer Hoover and her partner arrived, they questioned Mr. Williams about his permit to sell his wares, determined that he had none, and sent him to jail.

The next morning, J. Martin Walsh, former postal inspector, now Recording Industry Association of America investigative supervisor, made a determination that Mr. Williams' CDs, burned on CDRs, poorly labeled, with photocopies of album covers, were counterfeit. At trial, over the protests of defense counsel, Mr. Williams was convicted of violating Sections 16-7 and 16-8 of the Illinois Criminal Code. Section 16-7 provides, inter alia, that "(a) A person commits unlawful use of recorded sounds or images when he: (1) Intentionally … transfers … without the consent of the owner, … any sound or audio visual recording … [or] (2) Intentionally … sells … any such article described in subsection 16-7(a) (1) without consent of the owner." Section 16-8, entitled "Unlawful use of unidentified sound or audio visual recordings," provides, in relevant part, that "[a] person commits unlawful use of unidentified sound or audio visual recordings when he intentionally … sells … unidentified sound or audio visual recordings…."[29]

Williams appealed, contending, among other things, that Sections 16-7 and 16-8 were preempted by the Copyright Act. The state appellate court reasoned that the state laws "unquestionably" covered the same subject matter. The court first disposed of arguments that merely being a criminal statute obviated any possible preemption, noting that the weight of authority indicated that federal copyright law could preempt state criminal law. The question can only be answered by a close reading of the statutes at issue. With regard to Section 16-7, the court found that the statute was designed to "criminalize record piracy—that is, to prohibit the unauthorized reproduction or distribution of sound or audio visual recordings."[30] The court therefore concluded that it was preempted. With regard to Section 16-8, however, the court reasoned that the statute

---

[28] 376 Ill. App. 3d 875, 876 N.E.2d 235, 315 Ill. Dec. 235, 84 USPQ2d 1626 (Ill. App. Ct. 2007).

[29] *Id.*, 84 USPQ2d at 1629–30.

[30] *Id.* at 1635.

required the sound recording to be "unidentified," either through the absence of the name and address of the manufacturer, or by the listing of an incorrect manufacturer.[31] The court therefore concluded that this mislabeling aspect of the law provided an "extra element," which made the state statute not equivalent to the Copyright Act and therefore not preempted.

IV. CONSTITUTIONAL PREEMPTION

B. Before and After *Dastar*

[Add the following text to the end of the section.]

Lanham Act claims were explicitly held preempted in *Cyber Websmith, Inc., v. American Dental Associates*,[32] where the district court granted the defendant's motion to dismiss Lanham Act and Illinois Deceptive Trade Practices Act claims. The plaintiff sought damages for alleged willful infringement of registered copyrights in website templates. The defendant operated an Internet website comprised of HTML website pages, text, graphics, and photographs directly copied from the plaintiff's website templates. The defendant distributed copies of the copyrighted templates, and marketed and sold website design and marketing services based on the copied templates. The plaintiff also alleged that the defendant acted in direct competition with the plaintiff's business of providing website design and marketing services to dental practices, and caused consumer confusion, mistake, and deception by creating an association between services and works offered by the defendant and the American Dental Association (ADA), and deceptively conferred an air of legitimacy among the public by selling design and marketing services incorporating ADA trademarks. The defendant filed a motion to dismiss the Lanham Act and deceptive practices claims, arguing the claims were preempted. The plaintiff argued that consumer confusion and deception were additional elements that qualitatively changed the nature of the claims, and thus the Lanham Act and deceptive practices claims were not duplicative of a copyright claim. The court reasoned that such elements alone do not bar preemption; that the plaintiff did not allege that the defendant made representations that it was affiliated with the plaintiff; and that in each of its claims the plaintiff argued that the harm it suffered resulted from the defendant's alleged misappropriation of the plaintiff's copyrighted works. Accordingly, the Lanham Act and deceptive practices claims were preempted. The court dismissed the claims without prejudice, giving the plaintiff an opportunity to amend its complaint.

A contrary result was reached in *Berklee College of Music, Inc. v. Music Industry Educators, Inc.*,[33] where the district court denied a motion

---

[31] *Id.* at 1635–36.

[32] No. 09-6198, 2010 U.S. Dist. LEXIS 80206 (N.D. Ill Aug. 4, 2010).

[33] 733 F. Supp. 2d 204 (D. Mass. 2010).

to dismiss the plaintiff's claims for deceptive trade practices as pre-empted, where the claim was based in both copyright and trademark law. The plaintiff Berklee operated websites at www.berklee.edu and www.berkleemusic.com, which offered online music courses and provided information, including copyright-protected course descriptions, to current and potential students. The defendant Music Industry Educators, Inc. (MIE) operated several websites offering online music courses. Berklee brought a copyright infringement action alleging, inter alia, that sections of Berklee's copyrighted course descriptions appeared on MIE's websites in connection with courses offered by MIE. The defendants moved to dismiss the plaintiff's state-law deceptive trade practices claim as preempted, because it was grounded in allegations of copyright infringement, an area of exclusive federal regulation. The plaintiff argued that the deceptive trade practices claim was not preempted because it was based on both trademark *and* copyright infringement. Adopting the plaintiff's argument, the court held that the plaintiff's underlying trademark claims added an "extra element, something more than, and indeed different from, copyright infringement." Since the plaintiff's deceptive trade practices claim was based in part on trademark infringement under the Lanham Act, and the Lanham Act did not preclude state unfair competition claims, the deceptive trade practices claim was not preempted.

10

The Digital Millennium Copyright Act

III. ANTI-CIRCUMVENTION

C. Broadcast Systems (Satellite/Streaming Media Online)

[Add the following text at the end of the section.]

In *EchoStar Satellite, LLC v. Viewtech, Inc.*,[1] the Southern District of California made clear that a distributor of copyrighted works has standing to assert a claim under Section 1201. The plaintiff satellite company brought an action against a software company, alleging claims based on the DMCA that the defendants "unlawfully designed, developed, and distributed devices and other technology intended to facilitate the illegal and unauthorized reception and decryption of EchoStar's subscription and pay-per-view television programming."[2] The defendants moved to dismiss the complaint, arguing that the plaintiff, as a distributor, was not the copyright owner of the programming and thus lacked standing to bring a claim under the DMCA. The court rejected the defendants' argument, quoting Section 1203(a), which explicitly states: "Any person injured by a violation of section 1201 or 1202 may bring a civil action in an appropriate United States district court for such a violation."[3] Though the defendants conceded that courts have granted standing under the DMCA to parties other than copyright owners—to those who have "'control of the technological measure that protects the copyrighted work,'"[4] they argued that EchoStar did not allege such authority. The court disagreed. As a distributor, the plaintiff controlled such measures and could be injured as a result of the defendants' activities, and thus had standing to bring its claim under the DMCA.

F. Copyright Notice

[Add the following text at the end of the section.]

It is clear from the statute that copyright-management information under the DMCA is not limited to electronic information, as the court noted in *Associated Press v. All Headline News Corp.*,[5] where plaintiff Associated Press brought an action against an online venture that disseminated news reports to customer websites. The plaintiff alleged that the defendants violated the DMCA by "removing and/or altering copyright-management information from Associated Press news reports."[6] The DMCA defines "'copyright management information' as including '[t]he name of, and other identifying information about, the copyright owner of the work, including the information set forth in a notice of copyright.'"[7] The defendants argued that the DMCA should be construed only "'to protect copyright management performed by the technological measures of automated systems.'"[8] The court denied the defendants' motion to

---

[1]543 F. Supp. 2d 1201 (S.D. Cal. 2008).

[2]*Id.* at 1203.

[3]17 U.S.C. §1203(a).

[4]*EchoStar Satellite*, 543 F. Supp. 2d at 1205–06 (quoting defendants' Reply 1:27-2:1).

[5]608 F. Supp. 2d 454, 89 USPQ2d 2020 (S.D.N.Y. 2009).

[6]*Id.* at 461.

[7]*Id.* (quoting 17 U.S.C. §1202(c)(3)).

[8]*Id.* (quoting IQ Group, Ltd. v. Wiesner Publ'g LLC, 409 F. Supp. 2d 587, 597, 78 USPQ2d 1755 (D.N.J. 2006)).

dismiss the plaintiff's DMCA claim, noting that "[t]he defendants have cited no textual support for limiting the DMCA's application to 'the technological measures of automated systems'—a phrase that appears nowhere in the statute."[9]

Similarly, in *Fox v. Hildebrand*,[10] the court denied the defendants' motion under Federal Rules of Civil Procedure Rule 12(b)(6) in a case involving unauthorized use of architectural plans. The plaintiff alleged that the defendants posted copies of the plaintiff's plans on a website, "erroneously designating [d]efendant Hildebrand as the owner of the copyrighted work."[11] The court rejected the defendants' motion to dismiss under a claim of implied license. The court turned to the text of Section 1202 to rebut the defendants' argument that the plaintiff's handwritten copyright notice was insufficient under the DMCA. The defendants argued that "this DMCA provision [Section 1202(a) and (b)] applies only to copyright notices that are digitally placed on a copyrighted work." The court pointed out that under Section 1202(c), the definition of "copyright management information," includes notice in digital form. The court held that "[t]he use of 'including in digital form' removes any doubt that notices in digital form are covered, but in no way limits the definition to notices made in digital form"[12] despite two contrary decisions cited by the defendant (including one in the same jurisdiction). Although the statutory language was clear, the court also noted that its reading was supported by the legislative history of Section 1202, *i.e.*, "'CMI [copyright management information] need not be in digital form, but CMI in digital form is expressly included.'"[13]

G. Sovereign Immunity

[Add the following text at the end of the section.]

Government waiver of sovereign immunity under the DMCA is a virtually impossible argument to make because the statue does not expressly waive the defense, as the Federal Circuit held in *Blueport Co., LLC v. United States*.[14] In that case, the plaintiff company was an assignee of rights from the assignor, an Air Force programmer, who created an updated software program for use by the entire U.S. Air Force. The programmer-assignor refused to turn over the source code, and defendant Air Force (U.S. Government) eventually hired a company to help it extend the use of the program, without having to compensate the programmer-assignor. The plaintiff sued the government for copyright infringement and violation of the DMCA. The Court of Federal Claims

---

[9]*Id.* at 462.

[10]No. 09-2085, 2009 U.S. Dist. LEXIS 60886 (C.D. Cal. July 1, 2009).

[11]*Id.* at *2.

[12]*Id.* at *7 (quoting 17 U.S.C. §1202(c)).

[13]*Id.* at *8 n.3 (quoting S. REP. NO. 105-190 at **16–17 (1998) (defining CMI broadly)).

[14]533 F.3d 1374, 87 USPQ2d 1512 (Fed. Cir. 2008).

("CFC") dismissed the plaintiff's claims for lack of jurisdiction. The plaintiff appealed, claiming that the defendant had waived sovereign immunity for copyright infringement and DMCA claims under 28 U.S.C. §1498(b). The plaintiff's argument centered on the contention that the Section 1498(b) provisos were affirmative defenses, not jurisdictional limitations, and needed to be proven by the defendant, or alternatively, that the plaintiff's claim did not fall within any of the provisos that give the defendant sovereign immunity.

The Federal Circuit disagreed with the plaintiff's arguments in total. The court held that the provisos of Section 1498(b) are exceptions to waiving sovereign immunity, and the scope of waiver of sovereign immunity should be broad and read in the light most favorable to the sovereign; therefore, the burden of showing that the claim was not barred jurisdictionally by the Section 1498(b) provisos fell to the plaintiff. Additionally, the court held that the facts at bar fell within the second exception under Section 1498(b), relating to a Government employee's ability to "order, influence, or induce" the use of copyrighted work by the Government. The court held that the programmer-assignor distributed the work to officials and shared copies of the work to such an extent that he could influence the Air Force's use of the program. The Federal Circuit summarized that "the CFC correctly determined that [the plaintiff's] copyright infringement claim falls within the 'order, influence or induce' proviso of Section 1498(b). Accordingly, [the plaintiff's] claim is outside the scope of the Government's waiver of sovereign immunity for copyright infringement claims, and the CFC was correct to dismiss the claim for lack of jurisdiction."[15] With regard to the plaintiff's DMCA claim, the Federal Circuit again ruled against the plaintiff, holding that it had been established that waivers to sovereign immunity must be express, and "[t]he DMCA itself contains no express waiver of sovereign immunity" since it cites only "persons," not the "Government."[16]

Moreover, the DMCA grants jurisdiction only to federal district courts, not to the Court of Federal Claims. Hence, the Federal Circuit affirmed the CFC's holding on all claims.

[Add the following new section.]

IV. SECTION 114 AND INTERACTIVITY [NEW TOPIC]

In the only significant case so far on the issue of interactivity under the Section 114 compulsory sound recording license, the Second Circuit in *Arista Records, LLC v. Launch Media, Inc.,*[17] affirmed a jury finding that the defendant webcasting service was not an interactive service as a matter of law. The plaintiffs had sued, alleging that the defendant willfully infringed the plaintiffs' sound recording copyrights and violated Section

---

[15] *Id.* at 1382.

[16] *Id.* at 1383.

[17] 578 F.3d 148 (2d Cir. 2009).

114 of the DMCA. The defendant's LAUNCHcast webcasting service enabled a user to create "stations" that played songs within a particular genre or similar to a particular artist or songs the user selected. Under the statute, "[a]n interactive service is defined as a service 'that enables a member of the public to receive a transmission of a program specially created for the recipient, or on request, a transmission of a particular sound recording..., which is selected by or on behalf of the recipient.' "[18] If a service is interactive, it must pay individual licensing fees to copyright holders of the sound recordings played for users. If a service is not interactive, the webcaster need only pay a compulsory or statutory licensing fee set by the Copyright Royalty Board. The Second Circuit held that interactivity presented an issue of law. The court rejected the plaintiffs' contention that "any service that reflects user input is specially created for and by the user and therefore qualifies as an interactive service."[19] Noting that federal judges' "familiarity with the ever-changing terms and technology of the digital age is, to say the least, varied," the court "attempted to portray the processes and procedures of LAUNCHcast in lay terms, understandable to ourselves and the public."[20] The court found that with LAUNCHcast, "the only thing the user can control—is that by rating a song at zero the user will not hear that song on that station again."[21] The court noted further that LAUNCHcast listeners "do not even enjoy the limited predictability that once graced the AM airwaves on weekends in America when 'special requests' represented love-struck adolescents' attempts to communicate their feelings to 'that special friend.' Therefore, we cannot say LAUNCHcast falls within the scope of the DMCA's definition of an interactive service created for individual users."[22]

---

[18]*Id.* at 150 (quoting 17 U.S.C. §114(j)(7)).

[19]*Id.* at 152.

[20]*Id.* at 157 n.8.

[21]*Id.* at 164.

[22]*Id.*

11
International Issues

There have been no significant legal decisions or developments in this area since the publication of the Main Volume.

12

Tax, Insurance, Antitrust, and Bankruptcy Issues

II. INSURANCE ISSUES

B. Advertising Policies

2. *What Is Advertising?*

[Add the following text at the end of the section.]

In *Toffler Associates, Inc. v. Hartford Fire Insurance Co.*,[1] the Eastern District of Pennsylvania granted in part and denied in part the parties' cross-motions for summary judgment, regarding the duty of the plaintiff insurer ("Hartford") to the plaintiff ("Toffler," defendant in the underlying action) under an advertising injury provision. The plaintiff was sued for copyright infringement by another party, Inside Washington Publishers ("IWP"), for reproducing and distributing IWP's articles in its *Toffler Associates Morning Brew* publication, which Toffler emailed to employees "and about 300 people in the defense industry, the intelligence community, and corporate America." Hartford denied Toffler's claim for defense and indemnification coverage against IWP's copyright action. Hartford's representative concluded that the plaintiff's publication and distribution did not constitute "'widespread public distribution'" and that it "'was principally a medium to convey information and was not advertisement'"[2] within the meaning of the insurance policy. The court found that the defendant "had a duty to defend Toffler under the advertising injury provision of the Policy"[3] and noted that "a reasonable person in Toffler's position would have understood and expected that the Publication would fall within the Policy's description of 'information or images that has the purpose of inducing the sale of goods, products or services'"[4] which was the purpose of the Toffler's publication. However, the court found that the plaintiff's email distribution of its publication "was not widespread and public, as required for coverage under the Policy, and thus Hartford has no duty to indemnify."[5]

---

[1] 651 F. Supp. 2d 332 (E.D. Pa. 2009).

[2] *Id.* at 338 (quoting the representative's Letter II at 5).

[3] *Id.* at 342.

[4] *Id.* at 343.

[5] *Id.* at 344.

Table of Cases

*References are to supplement chapter and footnote number (e.g., **1:** 5, 68 refers to footnotes 5 and 68 in Supplement Chapter 1).*

About the Author

ROBERT W. CLARIDA, a partner at the New York firm of Reitler Kailas & Rosenblatt LLC, is widely recognized for his intellectual property expertise, having received professional peer recognition for the field of intellectual property in Chambers USA (2010), "New York Superlawyers" (2006, 2007, 2008, 2009, 2010, 2011, 2012), American Lawyer's "Best Lawyers in the U.S." (2006, 2007, 2008, 2009, 2010, 2011, 2012) and for the field of copyright in Legal 500 (2007). He advises clients in a wide range of industries including software, film, music, photography and new media. He has also litigated a number of high-profile copyright matters and argued significant federal appeals in several Circuits. He is admitted to the New York bar, and to the federal bars of the Southern, Eastern, Northern and Western Districts of New York, the Eastern District of Michigan, and to the U.S. Courts of Appeals for the First, Second, Seventh and Ninth Circuits.

Bob speaks and writes frequently on copyright issues, and is the principal author of the annual review of copyright decisions published each year by the Journal of the Copyright Society of the USA. He co-authors the regular copyright law column in the New York Law Journal, teaches a seminar on emerging intellectual property issues at Columbia Law School, is a past member of the AIPLA Board of Directors, the past chair of the Copyright and Literary Property Law Committee of the Association of the Bar of the City of New York, a past Trustee of the Copyright Society of the USA, and has served as an expert reviewer for the Multistate Bar Exam in the intellectual property area.

He earned his J.D. in 1993 from Columbia University, where he was a Harlan Fiske Stone scholar, after earning a Ph.D. in music composition from SUNY Stony Brook in 1987, and receiving a Fulbright fellowship to the Musicology Institute of Gothenburg University, Sweden.

PLEASE READ BEFORE USING THIS CD-ROM

This is a legal agreement between you, the individual or entity using this software ("You"), and The Bureau of National Affairs, Inc. d/b/a Bloomberg BNA (BBNA). Use of the software files and content included within this CD-ROM (collectively, "Software") is governed by the terms of the following license agreement ("Agreement"). Your use of this CD-ROM will constitute Your acceptance of each of the terms, conditions, and covenants set forth herein. If you do not agree to each of the terms of this Agreement, promptly return the CD-ROM package and the accompanying items (including associated book and packaging) to BBNA for a full refund or cancellation of all charges.

BBNA LICENSE AGREEMENT

(1) Grant of License. BBNA grants You a nonexclusive limited license to use the Software on a single-user computer.

(2) Transfer of License. You may not rent, loan, or lease the Software, but you may transfer the Software and the accompanying written materials in their entirety on a permanent basis provided you retain no copies, and the recipient agrees in writing to comply with each of the terms set forth in this Agreement. If the Software is an update, any transfer must include the update and all prior versions.

(3) Other Restrictions. You may not: reproduce, publish, distribute, sell, or otherwise use any material retrieved from or contained in the CD-ROM in any manner whatsoever that may infringe any copyright or proprietary interest of BBNA; distribute, rent, sublicense, lease, transfer (except as explicitly set forth herein), or assign the product or the License Agreement; decompile, disassemble, or otherwise reverse engineer the CD-ROM. Nothing herein, however, shall prevent you from using the material (electronic or written) in the normal course of business for which the material is intended.

(4) Copyright. The Software is owned by BBNA or its successors, assigns, or suppliers and is protected by United States copyright laws and international treaty provisions.

Notwithstanding any restrictions provided under applicable copyright law or this Agreement to the contrary, You may either (a) make one copy of the Software solely for backup or archival purposes, or (b) transfer the Software to a single hard disk provided you keep the original solely for backup or archival purposes.

DISCLAIMER

This publication is designed to provide accurate and authoritative information in regard to the subject matter covered. In publishing this book, neither the authors and editors, nor the publisher is engaged in rendering legal, accounting, or other professional service. If legal advice or other expert assistance is required, the services of a competent professional should be sought. Appendix documents may provide links to or refer to material on the Internet. While BBNA and the author(s) aim to provide the most current information available by referencing such external sources, users are cautioned that websites and documents on the Internet are subject to change without notice and their use may be subject to further restrictions; users should consult specific websites identified in this publication for updates and for further information on topics of interest.

LIMITED WARRANTY

BBNA warrants the physical media (i.e., CD-ROM) on which the Software is furnished to be free from defects in materials and workmanship under normal use for a period of one year from the date of delivery to you. This limited warranty gives you specific legal rights. You may have others, which vary from state to state. Some states do not allow the limitation or exclusion of some warranties, so the above limitation may not apply to you.

BBNA does not warrant that the functions contained in the program will meet your requirements. You assume responsibility for the installation, use, and results obtained from the program.

THE ENCLOSED SOFTWARE IS PROVIDED "AS IS" WITHOUT WARRANTY OF ANY KIND, EITHER EXPRESS OR IMPLIED, INCLUDING BUT NOT LIMITED TO IMPLIED WARRANTIES OF MERCHANTABILITY AND FITNESS FOR A PARTICULAR PURPOSE, WITH RESPECT TO THE SOFTWARE AND ANY OTHER ACCOMPANYING MATERIALS.

LIMITATION OF REMEDIES

If for any reason the limited warranty provided by this Agreement should be determined to be invalid or inapplicable to any claim related to the Software or this Agreement, the aggregate liability of BBNA, its affiliates agents shall be limited to the amount paid by you to BBNA for the original version of the Software.

IN NO EVENT WILL BBNA, ITS AFFILIATES, THEIR RESPECTIVE SUPPLIERS OR THIRD-PARTY AGENTS BE LIABLE TO YOU OR ANY OTHER PARTY FOR ANY DAMAGES, INCLUDING ANY LOST PROFITS, BUSINESS INTERRUPTION, LOST SAVINGS, LOSS OF BUSINESS INFORMATION, OR OTHER INCIDENTAL OR CONSEQUENTIAL DAMAGES RELATING TO THIS AGREEMENT OR ARISING OUT OF THE USE OR INABILITY TO USE SUCH SOFTWARE EVEN IF BBNA OR AN AUTHORIZED BBNA DEALER HAS BEEN ADVISED OF THE POSSIBILITY OF SUCH DAMAGES.

SOME STATES DO NOT ALLOW THE LIMITATION OR EXCLUSION OF LIABILITY FOR INCIDENTAL OR CONSEQUENTIAL DAMAGES, SO THE ABOVE LIMITATION OR EXCLUSION MAY NOT APPLY TO YOU.

This Agreement is governed by the laws of the Commonwealth of Virginia. If any provision of this Agreement shall be determined to be invalid or otherwise unenforceable, the enforceability of the remaining provisions shall not be impaired thereby. The failure of BBNA to exercise any right provided for herein shall not be deemed a waiver of any right hereunder. This Agreement sets forth the entire understanding of BBNA and You with respect to the issues addressed herein and may not be modified except by a writing executed by both parties.

The CD-ROM contains files in HTML and Adobe® Portable Document Format (PDF).

*Adobe® and Acrobat Reader® are registered trademarks or trademarks of Adobe Systems Incorporated.